R. Blackwell

The Confederation of
British Industry

The Confederation of British Industry

Wyn Grant and David Marsh

HODDER AND STOUGHTON
LONDON SYDNEY AUCKLAND TORONTO

ISBN 0 340 17613 X (Boards)
ISBN 0 340 21472 4 (Paperback)

First published 1977

Printed and bound in Great Britain for Hodder and Stoughton Educational,
a division of Hodder and Stoughton Ltd, Mill Road, Dunton Green, Sevenoaks, Kent,
by Morrison and Gibb Limited, London and Edinburgh.

W. G.   To my parents

D. M.   To my parents and Suzie

Acknowledgments

WE SHOULD LIKE TO THANK THE NUFFIELD FOUNDATION FOR A GRANT
which enabled us to interview a large number of CBI members and
officials. The material we collected from these interviews is used throughout, but is dealt with at length in Chapter 3.

Many people have read and commented on sections of this book. We
should particularly like to thank Professor Jack Hayward of the University
of Hull, Professor Malcolm Anderson of the University of Warwick, and
K. I. Vijay of the Polytechnic of Central London.

In addition we should like to thank the CBI members and officials for
their cooperation. In particular, we should like to mention Mr Eadie and
Mr Curtis of the Bristol Office of the CBI and Mr Gough, the ex-
Secretary of the organisation. They encouraged us when we needed their
aid. We would also like to thank the civil servants, Members of Parliament, party officials, trade unionists and directors of trade associations
who allowed us to interview them. Despite all this, the views expressed
here are ours and we accept responsibility for them.

The book is principally concerned with the CBI from its formation in
1965 up to the general election of February 1974. We have updated the
manuscript to take account of significant developments between 1974 and
the spring of 1976. We do not think that any of these developments
requires any change in the basic analysis of the role of the CBI presented
in this book.

London NW6   Wyn Grant
May 1976   David Marsh

Contents

Introduction

THIS BOOK ATTEMPTS TO ANALYSE THE PART PLAYED BY ONE OF Britain's most prominent interest groups, the Confederation of British Industry, in the British political system. There has been no general account of the work of the group, a fact which surprised us when we became interested in this field. The absence of such a study was obviously a major drawback in discussions of the operation of the British political system. However, the lack of such a study should not be so surprising. Indeed, there has been relatively little work in recent years on interest groups generally and on economic interest groups particularly. Why is this so?

One of the major developments in the study of politics in the 1950s and 1960s was the growth of research into political attitudes and voting behaviour. During the same period there was relatively less interest in the study of interest groups. Indeed, it is only recently that political scientists have become critical of this preoccupation with political attitudes. If researchers are interested in attempting to explain the operation of the political system, then they must be aware that the political attitudes, and more specifically the political behaviour, of a few people who have political influence have a larger role in shaping the development of that political system than have the attitudes and behaviour of the majority.[1] When this point is more widely accepted it seems likely that there will be a resurgence in the study of interest groups as more researchers and resources are directed towards this field.

It seems to us that the study of political influentials is more valuable than the study of political attitudes for those interested in the way a political system operates. However, when political scientists have looked at individuals who are politically active or influential in Britain they have tended to concentrate on parliamentarians rather than administrators or interest group leaders. Of course it is easier to study Parliament. Nevertheless, this preoccupation with Parliament seems surprising when all the available evidence would seem to suggest that its role in the political system, although perhaps greater than some writers have suggested, is of restricted significance. As the report of the Commission on Industrial Representation (the Devlin Report) commented: 'All executive policy and most legislation is conceived, drafted and all but enacted in Whitehall.'[2]

The study of interest groups is more time-consuming and perhaps subject to more methodological problems than the study of political attitudes or of Parliament, but this is not the only reason why they have received little attention. There seems to have been a general feeling that such studies have rather lost direction.[3] There are good reasons for such a view. Although there have been recent contributions by writers such as Coates,[4] the theoretical framework employed by students of British interest groups has tended to be that developed by Samuel Beer (first formulated in an article in 1956) and by Eckstein in *Pressure Group Politics* (first published in 1960). Articles appear from time to time drawing attention to the limitations of Eckstein's analytical framework[5] or calling for an intellectual dredging operation in one of the channels of access identified by Beer,[6] but major theoretical innovations have been noticeably lacking. Indeed, the only major contribution of recent origin seems to be in the work of Mancur Olson Jnr.[7] He has developed a by-product theory of interest groups with which we shall deal at length later in this book. Olson's work focuses on the problem of why people join, and remain members of, interest groups. Although the problems of how groups come to be formed and remain in being has a bearing on the distribution of power within the political system, Olson's work does not provide a comprehensive theoretical framework for the study of interest groups.

It seems fair to say then that for a number of reasons the study of interest groups has not flourished in Britain. However, it is also very significant that the majority of such studies which have been undertaken have dealt with groups like the British Medical Association,[8] the National Farmers Union[9] or the teachers' unions,[10] whose activity is restricted in scope and who deal mainly, if not exclusively, with one government department. Surprisingly little attention has been paid to industrial representation although it has grown in importance throughout this century, especially since 1945. There are of course exceptions. The study of the TUC by Allen[11] is a notable one, but he is largely concerned with the pre-1945 period and his work is mainly descriptive. In addition, the recent study by Dorfman represents an important contribution to our understanding of the role of the TUC in British politics, as is that by May.[12] As far as the TUC's counterpart on the employers' side is concerned, the major work is Blank's carefully documented study of the CBI's predecessor, the Federation of British Industries.[13] In addition there is a growing literature on government–industry relations, much of which is written by practitioners and has a strong polemical element. In particular, a great deal of work has been done on contractual relations between government and industry.[14] However, the problems posed by the increasing importance of government contracts for private industry are not a central concern of this book. Before the literature on government–industry relations can become more useful to the student of interest groups, students of such relations will need to develop a coherent and distinctive body of theory of their own. Probably such a development will not take place until students of government–industry relations have solved their identity problem in relation to public administration.[15]

In sum, there is little work on the interaction between government and industry and the effect that this interaction has upon the evolution and the administration of legislation. This is an important area of interest group activity which remains relatively under-researched.

The importance of this area is not difficult to demonstrate. One does not need to be a very acute observer of British politics to realise that problems associated with the management of the economy have increasingly dominated the work of post-war governments. The relationship between government and industry has become an increasingly close one. Apart from the importance of the nationalised industries in the economy and the growth in significance of government contracts, it has been estimated that government provided £1,248 million assistance to private industry in 1970–71.[16] In addition government legislation, in fields such as taxation, pollution, industrial standards or industrial safety, influences all aspects of industrial life. These developments mean that contacts between government and industry are both more frequent and more extensive than in the past. One consequence of these close contacts is that the form and nature of industrial representation become an important issue to both sides. Industry is anxious to ensure that its representative bodies are organised in such a way as to exert the maximum possible influence on government. On the other hand, government has become increasingly conscious of the need for strong and effective industrial representation to ensure that economic policy is evolved and implemented efficiently. Government displayed a close interest in the formation of the CBI and more recently actively encouraged the work of the Devlin Commission on Industrial Representation. It has even gone so far as to offer Crown premises to an industrial pressure group at a concessionary rate.[17] These developments inevitably mean that the CBI, as the peak organisation representing manufacturing industry, has since its establishment in 1965 become increasingly involved in consultations at all levels, including the very highest, about a great variety of areas of economic and industrial policy.

In the light of the rapid growth of industrial representation and of the increasing dominance exercised by industrial and economic policy in the life of governments, a study of the peak organisations which represent manufacturing industry seems long overdue. Blank's book, while not without considerable merits, deals almost exclusively with the old Federation of British Industries. The CBI has grown in stature since its formation and has become increasingly regarded by government as a spokesman for wide sections of industry. Yet we have no study of its effectiveness and of its success in influencing government policy. This is the main problem with which this book is concerned. It is intended to be more than a simple description of the internal structure and external relationships of the CBI. Our primary concern is to study the CBI, its history, organisation, policy and relations with government, in order to assess how influential a role it plays in contemporary British politics. In particular, we are interested in relating our findings about the CBI to the various schools of thought about the way in which power is distributed in modern Britain.

As long as people have studied political and social systems they have been concerned to describe the nature, distribution and use of power within societies and to suggest alternative distributions. Such problems have always been a key concern of political and social theorists and provide the main focus of political sociology.[18] There have been two models of the distribution of power within the British political system which have been dominant in the analyses of political scientists. There are obviously many variations on these two models, but in essence most political scientists are working with an implicit pluralist conception of how the political system works,[19] while a much smaller number is working with a Marxist conceptualisation. One of the major aims of this study is to examine the utility of the Marxist and pluralist models. However, before we can do this we need to set out our understanding of the two models.

The pluralist model contains a number of assumptions about the nature of pluralist democratic societies and the distribution of power within them. At the same time it implies that if such a distribution and use of power exists it is a healthy, proper and democratic one. Of course as the model represents in many senses an ideal type no society is likely to be a perfectly pluralistic one. However, most pluralists see American and, to a lesser extent, British society as approximating their model. There are, of course, many different pluralists with different conceptualisations. Our summary of the pluralist model is based mainly on the work of Truman and Dahl.[20]

1 The group is the key unit in society.[21] Society is made up of various actual, or potential, interest groups which mediate between the individual and the society.

2 In Britain and America, and other successful pluralist democracies, these groups influence and operate within the bounds of a consensus as to the basic nature of the political and economic system – democratic – and the economic system – capitalist. This consensus is not questioned in any radical sense by any of the major groups within society.[22]

3 However, within this consensus and within the bounds of acceptable political activity, groups representing different interests within society compete for influence. In fact pluralist society consists of different groups competing for the allocation of scarce resources.[23]

4 No one interest can dominate society because for each interest there exists a balancing, competing interest. This notion of balance is crucial.[24] If one group argues a particular case there will inevitably be, the pluralists argue, some existing group or 'potential' group which will contradict it and argue the opposite case. If the group is 'potential' rather than actual the stimulus which the competing group provides will cause it to be organised and formalised.[25] The result is that no one interest will dominate in all issues, and no one interest will achieve the complete fulfilment of any one radical proposal. So, while change is possible, as one group gains a slight temporary ascendancy, it will be gradual and not radical.

5 Within a complex pluralist industrial society all individuals will be members of many groups. This overlapping group membership will help to ensure that no one group dominates, as each individual and each group will be subject to competing interests. No group will push any one

interest too strongly when many of its members may have competing interests as members of other groups.[26]

6 The state or, perhaps more accurately, the government acts in this model as an arbiter between interests. It decides on the validity of each interest and of its representations on each issue. The implication is that the government chooses the strongest or best argument in each case, that it adjudicates each case on its merits. In a pluralist state the government is not associated with any particular interest but acts as an independent arbiter. It also has a conception of the 'national interest' which is independent of the interests of any one group. At the same time if any interest is not adequately represented – for example the consumers as compared with the producers – the government in a sense represents those interests itself, weighing them against those of the more forcefully represented groups. This model then implies that all decisions taken by a government are 'political' and that the autonomy of politics is complete as the state is independent of any particular interests.[27]

7 So in pluralist society groups act as mediators between individuals and the society. In this way groups are beneficial to society by: ensuring that there is some measure of government responsiveness to the wishes of the citizenry; making it possible to resolve conflicts through negotiation; preventing one group dominating and promoting stability while encouraging gradual change.

There are a number of problems with such a model of society. In particular, while attempting to refute elitism it retains an important element of it. The whole notion of pluralism relies on functional specialisation and interdependence among well organised intermediate organisations. This in itself implies the necessity for societal-wide, and highly centralised, coordination, regulation and control of special activities.[28]

In addition the pluralist model tends to imply that all actors and groups within the political system have access to all necessary information about the operation of that system. This is of particular relevance to the crucial notion of balance between competing groups. If group B is threatening the interests of group A, group A (or under some circumstance the government) must be aware of its own interests, aware of the threat to them and must act to neutralise that threat. Otherwise group B is in danger of achieving its ends totally and destroying the essential balance. An assumption of perfect rationality has little validity in actual decision-making situations, in which individuals or groups are faced with imperfect or incomplete information or decision-making schemes.[29]

However, our aim in this book is not to criticise the internal logic of the pluralist model but rather to see how far such a model represents an accurate description of the distribution of power in Britain. Pluralism is of course a response to various elitist theories of the distribution of power in a society. It represents an attempt to refute the Marxist belief that power in a capitalist society is concentrated in the hands of a ruling class, which has one unifying common interest. At the same time the pluralists are attempting to show that while certain elites do exist within society this notion is not incompatible with democracy, because these elites compete with one another and do not represent a tight, unified ruling class.

The most appropriate presentation of the Marxist model for our purposes is that of Miliband,[30] both because he is consciously attempting to refute the pluralist model and because he concentrates upon the role of the state in capitalist society, that is on the relationship between the political and economic spheres. However, we are well aware that Miliband's work has been subject to substantial criticism by some Marxists, notably by Poulantzas, and we shall return to this criticism later. Miliband's presentation of the Marxist model can be summarised as follows:

1 Power in a capitalist society is concentrated in the hands of the owners and controllers of the means of production.[31]

2 This elite or ruling class has a common interest in preserving the economic and political system which protects its own socio-economic position.[32]

3 There may be certain differences of interest among the various elements of the ruling class over the detailed operation of the system, but not over the nature of the system itself.

4 The ruling class ensures that the mass accepts the nature of the system in Western capitalist democracies through the process of political socialisation. So, a consensus on the nature of the system (to the Marxist a false consensus or rather acceptance) exists in such capitalist societies.[33]

5 It is very likely that members of the ruling class will have similar social and educational backgrounds, will interact, and will have common interests on policy issues. However, this is by no means inevitable. The basic position of the ruling class is the result of an objective relationship to the means of production. Shared backgrounds and shared short-term policy interests are merely reflections of that relationship.[34]

6 The state in capitalist society is thus the agent of this tightly-knit ruling class, acting in its interests and on its behalf. Members of govern-

ment and the administration are likely to be linked by shared social and educational backgrounds and shared attitudes with the owners and controllers of the means of production. The state is not an arbiter because it is of its nature committed to protecting and forwarding one interest. However, the state is not necessarily totally subservient to the ruling class as, on the details of the operation of the political and economic system, it can have a great deal of discretion. The level of autonomy which the state has will vary from one type of capitalist system to another.

7 This means that political decisions are not totally determined by the economic pressures of the capitalist system. On the details of the operation of the system the individual elites, including the government, may have different views. So the state can have considerable independence of action on individual policy decisions. However, in the British system, Miliband's analysis suggests that the political sphere is closely related to, and its decisions are influenced by, the economic sphere.

These two models raise a number of questions which need to be asked about any given political system. Is there a ruling class? How much autonomy does the political sphere have from the economic sphere? How much interaction is there between the occupiers of various elite positions? In studying the peak organisation of manufacturing industry, which represents the views of a large section of the economic sector to government, including the vast majority of the large industrial firms, we hope to throw light on these questions. Do CBI leaders share common social and educational backgrounds with political leaders and civil servants? What is the extent of their interaction with civil servants and senior politicians? Does the CBI have a great deal of influence over government policy?

However, before we can answer these questions there are a number of reservations which must be acknowledged and problems which must be faced. Initially it must be accepted that many Marxists would deny the whole utility of an analysis which relies largely on behavioural evidence. Poulantzas in his critique of Miliband warns: 'the procedure chosen by Miliband – a direct reply to bourgeois ideologies by the immediate examination of concrete fact – is also to my mind the source of the faults of his book.'[35] In more detail Poulantzas' criticism is based upon

the difficulties that Miliband has in comprehending social classes and the state as *objective* structures, and their *relations* as an *objective system* of regular connections, a structure and a system whose agents, 'men', are, in the words of Marx, 'bearers' of it. Miliband constantly gives the impression that for him social classes or 'groups' are in some way reducible to interpersonal relations, that the State is reducible to interpersonal relations of the members of the diverse 'groups' that constitute the State, and finally that the relationship between social classes and the State is itself reducible to the interpersonal relations of 'individuals' composing social groups and individuals composing the State apparatus.[36]

Poulantzas is arguing that Miliband's evidence, which is of the same type as the material we shall consider, is irrelevant to the real basis of Marxist analysis. If the real basis is an objective one, resulting from the nature of the system itself, only historical and comparative analysis can form the basis of relevant empirical evidence. In this book we accept Miliband's point that it is crucial to examine the background and decisions of the individuals who occupy economic and political elite roles, but we are aware that this approach is open to criticism.

Even if one is willing to accept the utility of behavioural evidence in studying the influence of the CBI there are still a number of problems. It is not possible to give a precise, quantifiable answer to the key question: how much influence does the CBI have over government policy? As yet we have no acceptable measure of influence and many people would argue that it will not be possible to devise such a measure. Indeed, there have been a number of methods used to examine the influence of pressure groups but all have considerable limitations. Perhaps the most common form of analysis has dealt with the social and educational backgrounds of group members and with the similarity between their backgrounds and those of senior politicians and civil servants. In addition researchers using this type of analysis have searched for patterns of social and political interaction between group leaders and politicians. This is the type of analysis which is perhaps stated in its most extreme form by Guttsman[37] but which is also heavily relied upon by C. Wright Mills[38] and Miliband. The assumption behind this analysis is of course that common backgrounds and interaction are related to shared political and economic attitudes and shared policy objectives. This is a dubious assumption because while common backgrounds and interaction may facilitate contacts with, and access to, government they do not ensure influence.

One might, in contrast to this approach, rely upon a variation of the type of reputational analysis which has been used in studies of community power in America.[39] In this case one might rely upon the observations and experience of the individuals most involved in the political process. They would presumably include interest group leaders and activists, politicians, civil servants and informed observers such as political journalists. However, this method has obvious limitations. How would you choose your observers? In the British system, politicians and particularly civil servants are unwilling to talk in detail about, or to admit to, interest group influence. They will talk about the 'general patterns' of influence but certainly active civil servants will not talk in detail about current, or recent, legislation. On the other hand, if one concentrates upon the interest groups concerned one is likely to receive an unbalanced view as they are prone to overestimate their own influence.

Probably the most rewarding method, although it is the most expensive in terms of resources, is the decision-making approach. Within this method one can distinguish two distinct alternatives. First, the specific approach: a case study which examines in depth the passage of one piece of legislation; second, the general approach, which considers a policy area over a considerable period of time. Each approach has its disadvantages and its strengths.

The specific approach provides more detail and, it is to be hoped, a more accurate assessment of influence on one piece of legislation; it also usually has more scope to consider the role of other competing groups.[40] However, the case study chosen may well be atypical and one may therefore over-estimate or underestimate the overall importance of a given group. The second method reduces this problem but is less detailed and tends to con-centrate upon one group to the exclusion of others. This more general approach is the one which has formed the basis of most studies of interest groups in Britain.

This discussion of the decision-making approach brings us face to face with another important problem. This approach almost inevitably tends to embody a basic methodological assumption crucial to the pluralist model, that 'power is totally embodied and fully reflected in "concrete de-cisions" or in activity bearing directly upon their making.'[41] This method, as Bachrach and Baratz have pointed out, by concentrating on decisions actually made often fails to analyse the power which a group can exercise in limiting the scope of decision-making 'by influencing community value systems and political procedures and rituals, notwithstanding that there are in the community serious but latent power conflicts'.[42]

This point is well made. If we are looking at community or societal power structure we must be aware of the 'dynamics of non-decision-making'. This brings us fairly close to Poulantzas' position as this type of power is difficult to study on the basis of behavioural evidence. However, in any study of power in Britain the researcher must be aware of this limitation and try to examine the influence of various groups in maintaining the parameters of decision-making.

In our study we shall incorporate all these methods of assessing influence. We shall present a socio-economic background analysis of key CBI officials and chairmen of CBI committees. We have also looked in depth at the interaction between the CBI and politicians and civil servants. At the same time, we have interviewed at length civil servants, politicians, CBI officials, TUC officials, representatives of Trade Associations, Chambers of Commerce and the Retail Consortium and senior industrialists and trade unionists. We cannot claim that our interviewees represent a random sample of political influentials, indeed they were not chosen to do so. However, the people we have talked to represent a wide range of interests and opinions and almost all had specialised knowledge of, and interest in, the field of industrial representation. Each gave us his opinion of the influence of the CBI, and so we have built up a form of reputational analysis.

Despite all this our main concern has been with the decision-making approach. We will be presenting case studies of four specific pieces of British legislation: the 1967 Iron and Steel Act, the 1968 Clean Air Act, the 1972 Industry Act and the 1972 Deposit of Poisonous Wastes Act. However, it is evident that these cases may be atypical and studies of other legislation might reveal different patterns. Therefore, we shall also examine the influence the CBI had, as compared with other groups, upon general industrial and economic policy from 1965 until February 1974. In addition we present one case-study dealing with the CBI's attempt to influence policy in the EEC on economic and monetary unity.

It is clear then that the major aim of this book is an examination of the influence of the CBI, particularly in relation to pluralist and Marxist models of power. However, this problem can only be dealt with in the context of a comprehensive study of the organisation. We shall examine: the history of industrial representation and of the CBI in particular; its place in the system of business representation; its internal organisation and membership; and its contacts with government. This will give depth and perspective to our consideration of its influence over government. It is especially important to avoid the risk of exaggerating the influence of the CBI by ignoring the constraints which are imposed on its operations by its limited resources, its internal conflicts and the wider political context in which it operates.

Notes and References

1 See D. Marsh, 'Political socialisation: the implicit assumptions questioned', *British Journal of Political Science*, **I** (1971), pp. 453–65. Also D. Kavanagh, *Political Culture* (London: Macmillan, 1972) especially p. 61.

2 *Report of the Commission of Inquiry into Industrial and Commercial Representation (Devlin Report)* (London: Association of British Chambers of Commerce and Confederation of British Industry, 1972), p. 5.

3 See review by John Dearlove in *Political Studies*, **XXI** (1973), pp. 403–4.

4 R. D. Coates, *Teachers' Unions and Interest Group Politics* (London: Cambridge University Press, 1972).

5 T. R. Marmor and D. Thomas, 'Doctors, politics and pay disputes: "Pressure-group Politics" revisited', *British Journal of Political Science*, **2** (1972), pp. 421–42.

6 P. Peterson, 'British interest group theory re-examined' in *Comparative Politics*, **3** (1971), pp. 381–402. See also S. Beer, 'Pressure groups and parties in Britain', *A.P.S.R.*, **L** (1956), pp. 1–23.

7 M. Olson Jnr, *The Logic of Collective Action: Public Goods and the Theory of Groups* (New York: Schocken Books, 1968).

8 H. Eckstein, *Pressure Group Politics* (London: Allen and Unwin, 1960).

9 P. Self and H. J. Storing, *The State and the Farmer* (London: Allen and Unwin, 1962).

10 Coates, op. cit.

11 V. L. Allen, *Trade Unions and the Government* (London: Longmans, 1960).

12 G. A. Dorfman, *Wage Politics in Britain* (Ames, Iowa: Iowa State University Press, 1973). In fact the trade unions have recently been an object of a great deal of study for obvious reasons. See I. Richter, *Political Purpose in Trade Unions* (London: Allen and Unwin, 1973); M. Moran, *The Union of Post Office Workers* (London: Macmillan, 1974); T. May and M. Moran, 'Trade unions as pressure groups', *New Society*, 6 September 1973, pp. 570–3; S. E. Finer, 'The political power of organised labour', *Government and Opposition*, (1974), pp. 391–406; and T. May, *Trade Unions and Pressure Group Politics* (Farnborough: Saxon House, 1975).

13 S. Blank, *Government and Industry in Britain* (Farnborough: Saxon House, 1973).

14 B. L. R. Smith, 'Accountability and independence in the contract state' in B. L. R. Smith and D. C. Hague (eds), *The Dilemma of Accountability in Modern Government* (London: Macmillan, 1971), pp. 3–69, p. 3.

15 The Chapman Report shows that a number of courses on government-industry relations are taught in British universities, but in the discussions about the academic future of public administration in the United Kingdom it has not been argued that there is a need to create a subject which is something more than a subsidiary branch of public administration. R. A. Chapman, *Teaching Public Administration* (London: Joint University Council for Social and Public Administration, 1973). See also

'Teaching Public Administration: Report of the Special Meeting of the Committee', *Public Administration Bulletin* No. 16.

16 S. Brittan, *Capitalism and the Permissive Society* (London: Macmillan, 1973), p. 241.

17 Premises in Carlton House Terrace were offered to the British Mechanical Engineering Confederation (BRIMEC) and its associated bodies at a rent far below that which would be normal for such a prestige site.

18 See Marvin E. Olsen (ed), *Power in Societies* (New York: Macmillan, 1970), for an excellent analysis of power as the central concept in political sociology.

19 One only needs to look at the range of definitions of 'politics' which are prevalent to show the validity of this point. Most definitions of politics stress consensus, conflict and compromise, a very pluralistic conceptualisation of the 'political'.

20 D. B. Truman, *The Governmental Process* (New York: Knopf, 1962); R. E. Dahl, *A Preface to Democratic Theory* (Chicago: The Chicago University Press, 1956); R. E. Dahl, *Who Governs?* (New Haven: Yale University Press, 1961). However, the father of pluralism, and a very neglected one, was A. Bentley, *The Process of Government* (Chicago: University of Chicago Press, 1908).

21 'The balance of group pressures is the existing state of society' in Bentley, op. cit., p. 259.

22 The notion of consensus has to be crucial given the pluralists' definition of 'politics' in pluralist societies as involving compromise and conciliation as well as conflict. Compromise and conciliation and the ordered solution of differences implies a considerable basic agreement about the 'rules of the game'. See Olsen, op. cit., p. 186; and Joseph Gusfield, 'Mass society and extremist politics', *American Sociological Review*, **27** (1962), pp. 19–30.

23 Truman, op. cit., p. 33; and Dahl, *Who Governs?*, op. cit., p. 224.

24 Truman, op. cit., pp.26–7.

25 ibid., pp. 51–2.

26 ibid., pp. 509–10.

27 See J. K. Galbraith, *American Capitalism* (Boston: Houghton Mifflin, 1952), especially pp. 108–34.

28 There have, of course, been a great number of criticisms of pluralism. One of the best expositions is that of Shin'ya Ono, 'The limits of bourgeois pluralism', *Studies on the Left*, (1963). See also P. Bachrach and M. Baratz, 'The two faces of power', *A.P.S.R.*, **LVI** (1962), pp. 947–52, and S. Lukes, *Power* (London: Macmillan, 1974).

29 See J. Watkins, 'Imperfect rationality' in R. Berger and F. Ciofi (eds), *Explanations in the Behavioural Sciences* (London: Cambridge University Press, 1970), pp. 167–217.

30 R. Miliband, *The State in Capitalist Society* (London: Weidenfeld and Nicolson, 1969).

31 'In the Marxist scheme, the "ruling class" of capitalist society is that class which owns and controls the means of production, which is able, by virtue of the economic power thus conferred upon it, to use the state as its instrument for the domination of society.' Miliband, op. cit., p. 23.

32 'The economic and political life of capitalist societies is *primarily* determined by the relationship, born of the capitalist mode of production, between these two classes – the class which on the one hand owns and controls, and the working class on the other.' Miliband, op. cit., p. 16.

33 ibid., pp. 183 ff.

34 The whole tenure of Miliband's debate with Nicos Poulantzas supports this point. See R. Miliband, 'The capitalist state: reply to Nicos Poulantzas', *New Left Review*, (1970), pp. 53–60.

35 N. Poulantzas, 'The problem of the capitalist state', *New Left Review*, **58** (1969), pp. 67–73, p. 69.

36 ibid., p. 70.

37 W. L. Guttsman, *The British Political Elite* (London: MacGibbon and Kee, 1963).

38 C. W. Mills, *The Power Elite* (New York: Oxford University Press, 1959).

39 F. Hunter, *Community Power Structure* (Chapel Hill: University of North Carolina, 1953).

40 In Britain the best example of this type of approach can be found in the work of J. Barnett, *The Politics of Legislation: The Rent Act 1957* (London: Weidenfeld and Nicolson, 1969).

41 Bachrach and Baratz, op. cit.

42 ibid., p. 948.

2

The emergence of the CBI

THIS CHAPTER PLACES THE EMERGENCE OF THE CBI IN A HISTORICAL perspective, with particular emphasis on the development of the three associations which merged to form the new national employers' organisation: the Federation of British Industries (FBI), British Employers' Confederation (BEC) and National Association of British Manufacturers (NABM). However, although we shall be outlining the histories of these organisations, it should be pointed out that the development of the FBI in particular has been carefully analysed by Blank in his *Industry and Government in Britain*.[1] We do not wish to duplicate Blank's analysis, although later in the chapter we shall be critically examining his account of the later years of the FBI. Rather in this chapter we shall be concerned with examining how far the pattern of development of industrial representation in Britain can be better explained and understood in terms of the theoretical perspectives offered by writers like Nettl, Olson and Salisbury. Our primary concern is with the growing body of theory which attempts to explain the formation and survival of interest groups.

The 'by-product' theory of interest groups developed by Olson represents an important contribution to our understanding of the processes whereby interest groups attract and retain members and are thus enabled to survive and develop as organisations. In order to understand Olson's theory, it is necessary to appreciate the distinction he makes between collective and noncollective goods. Olson states: 'A common, collective, or public good is . . . any good such that, if any person X_i in a group X_i . . . , X_i, . . . , X_n consumes it, it cannot feasibly be withheld from others in that group. In other words, those who do not purchase or pay for any of the public or collective goods cannot be excluded or kept from sharing in the consumption of the goods, as they can where noncollective goods are concerned.'[2] Olson argues that large organisations which are unable to make membership compulsory have to provide 'some attraction distinct from the public good itself, that will lead individuals to help bear the burdens of maintaining the organisation'.[3] This is because 'the individual in a latent group has no incentive voluntarily to sacrifice his time or money to help an organisation obtain a collective good; he alone cannot be decisive in determining whether or not this collective good will be obtained, but if it is obtained because of the efforts of others he will inevitably be able to enjoy it in any case.'[4] Thus, in Olson's view, 'the common characteristic which distinguishes all of the large economic groups with significant lobbying organisations is that these groups are organized for some *other* purpose. The large and powerful economic lobbies are in fact the by-products of organisations that obtain their strength and support because they perform some function in addition to lobbying for collective goods',[5] such as offering advisory services. Olson uses historical evidence to attempt to show that the formation and continued existence of the largest economic interest groups in the United States are explained by his by-product theory.

Nettl argues that 'the British consensus' is 'a social institution with its own structure, procedures, attitudes, beliefs'.[6] It sucks in members from the periphery, emasculating groups 'while preserving their outward shell of autonomy and independence'.[7] Nettl maintains that 'the flow of influence is greater from the government towards organised industry than from industry inwards'.[8] The formation of representative industrial organisations has been encouraged by government. In his view 'the whole point' about industrial representation in Britain is that 'it is so largely government sponsored or at least government encouraged'.[9]

Nettl stresses that the government's growing interest in regulating the economy has not been the only reason for the formation of industrial organisations. Often, organisations which were formed to operate price-fixing or market-sharing agreements later came to be actively involved in a dialogue with Whitehall. As we shall see, it was the government's involvement in the economy during the First World War which led to its first significant and systematic attempts to influence the development of the system of industrial representation.

Although Olson and Nettl stress very different aspects of interest group formation, it should be emphasised that their models are not mutually exclusive. Nettl's emphasis on the importance of government encouragement and assistance in stimulating interest group formation is not inconsistent with Olson's model. If government assists an interest group by seconding skilled officials or providing low-cost accommodation (both practices which have been employed in Britain), it can reduce the operating costs of the organisation and thus the costs of membership. Government assistance may affect the costs and benefits of group membership and thus influence interest group formation and survival.

Salisbury has developed an 'exchange theory' of interest groups which he regards as 'partially parallel' to the work of Olson.[10] His argument is that 'interest group origins, growth, death and associated lobbying activity may all be better explained if we regard them as exchange relationships between entrepreneur/organisers, who invest capital in a set of benefits which they offer to prospective members at a price-membership'.[11] Particular emphasis is placed on the role of the entrepreneur/organiser in group formation. Salisbury argues that Olson 'does not examine how groups are first organised but assumes a going system'.[12] In so far as Salisbury is particularly concerned with 'group development through time',[13] his approach is particularly relevant to the concerns of this chapter.

A number of unsuccessful attempts were made to form a national industrial organisation before the Federation of British Industries came into being during the First World War.[14] The one 'peak association' which did exist in the late nineteenth century, the Association of British Chambers of Commerce (ABCC), founded in 1860, was to a large extent a loose confederation of local business interests maintaining a central office in London and hiring the services of a parliamentary agent. As Alderman points out, 'The Association of British Chambers of Commerce was hampered by the fact that many of its constituent chambers were small, weak and incessantly suspicious of each other.'[15] A few of the larger member chambers, such as Manchester, Liverpool and Glasgow, were of sufficient individual significance to be able to gain direct access to ministers, but the attitude of government to the organisation as a whole was perhaps revealed by Sir Hubert Llewellyn Smith, Permanent Secretary to the Board of Trade, who told a meeting of the ABCC in 1914 that, whilst he appreciated the large chambers' highly developed machinery for consultation and investigation, he could not shut his eyes to the fact that at the other end of the scale there were still a few member chambers whose organisation 'did not go much beyond a brass plate and an annual banquet'.[16]

Perhaps the fundamental underlying problem which weakened the

ABCC was that it attempted to represent both traders and the often divergent interests of industrialists. These different sectors of business did, of course, have some things in common: they might unite to decry the supposedly iniquitous scale of charges of the railway companies, and to some extent the ABCC could pursue the particular interests of both groups at the same time – for example, its continuing interest in the law of bankruptcy was a response to the concerns of traders, whilst its support for changes in the law relating to patents and trade marks was primarily a response to the concerns of its manufacturing members.[17] However, serious divisions existed between traders and manufacturers within the organisation on some fundamental questions, in particular tariff reform.[18] The organisation must have been weakened by these internal divisions and, in explaining the formation of the rival Federation of British Industries, the historians of the ABCC have concluded, 'it is likely that many of the bigger industrialists found themselves out of sympathy . . . with the smaller manufacturers, traders and professional men who in the main constituted the membership of the local chambers.'[19]

Thus, in Britain, the emergence of organisations serving the interests of particular industries, such as coal-mining and engineering, and of locally-based groupings such as Chambers of Commerce, predated the development of associations claiming to speak for industry as a whole. One or two modern associations representing particular industries can trace their lineage back to the eighteenth century, but permanent, nationally-organised trade associations (dealing with commercial matters) and employers' organisations (dealing with industrial relations) did not develop on an extensive scale until the last quarter of the nineteenth century.

The growth of large-scale joint stock companies serving extensive markets made agreements between enterprises on price or output control feasible; fears of growing foreign competition often made such agreements seem a necessity. As Alderman points out, 'falling profits and higher costs produced a greater sense of urgency'[20] about the need for national representative bodies for industry towards the end of the nineteenth century. The need to match the growing strength of labour also provided a stimulus for the formation of associations designed to defend the interests of capital. This was certainly a predominant motive for the formation of one of the most important of the new employers' associations, the Engineering Employers' Federation, established in 1896. At the time of its establishment, 'every other function of the Federation was subordinated to the primary purpose of defending the employers against attack from the trade unions.'[21]

In so far as they had representations to make to the government, most industrialists were apparently content to act through their trade association or approach the appropriate department themselves. There was little popular support for organisations claiming to speak for industry as a whole; the common interests of industrialists were not of sufficient importance to overcome the rivalries which many saw as a healthy aspect of free competition. Moreover, as Blank has pointed out, the continuation of a free trade policy meant that there was no incentive for industrialists to combine to influence tariffs.[22]

It is possible to find examples of industrial associations formed in the nineteenth century as a response to government action. For example, the railway companies united in the Railway Industries Association after the passage of regulatory legislation in 1868. However, although one can cite isolated examples of such associations, there were no systematic attempts by government to encourage the formation of representative industrial organisations. It is not until the First World War, and the emergence for the first time of a comprehensive system of industrial representation in Britain, that Nettl's model begins to acquire explanatory value.

The First World War led to substantial changes in the nature of the relationship between government and industry, which created a need for new organisations for the representing of industrial interests. By the end of the war, most major sectors of the economy were the subject of some form of governmental intervention, even if the measures used were not as extensive or efficient as the controls developed in the Second World War. Trade associations played an important role in the administration of wartime controls, and a much closer relationship developed between the various associations and government departments as a consequence. A number of new industry associations were formed, but of potentially greater importance was the formation of three new 'peak associations' designed to represent the interests of industry as a whole – the Federation of British Industries (1916), the National Union of Manufacturers (1916) and a distinct body for industrial relations, the National Confederation of Employers' Organisations (1919) (later the British Employers' Confederation).

The way in which the Federation of British Industries (FBI) was formed conforms closely to Nettl's model. As Blank notes, the support of the government for the new organisation was of crucial importance.[23] The two most senior officials of the FBI were seconded from the Foreign Office, which forecast an important role for the FBI in promoting overseas trade after the war. However, Nettl's model only offers a partial explanation of what happened. Salisbury emphasises the role of the entrepreneur/organiser in interest group formation. Certainly, no account of the formation of the FBI would be complete without mentioning the part played by Dudley Docker, chairman of the Metropolitan Wagon, Carriage and Finance Company, in setting up and mobilising support for the new organisation.

Some of the employers' organisations, particularly the key Engineering Employers' Federation, were suspicious of the quasi-syndicalist ideas of some of the FBI's leaders and eventually formed a separate organisation to deal with labour matters, latterly called the British Employers' Confederation (BEC). In this case, the Salisbury model is helpful. The initiative for the formation of a separate industrial relations organisation came from the Engineering Employers' Federation and, in particular, from its chairman, Sir Allan Smith.[24] The government took little direct interest in these developments and the BEC was heavily reliant, at least initially, on the financial support of the Federation, in whose headquarters it was housed. Thus the Salisbury model offers a better explanation of the formation of the BEC than that of Nettl or Olson.

The separate existence of the BEC posed recurring problems for the FBI. Between 1942 and 1949, a sustained attempt was made to merge the two organisations, but, although the majority of the membership of both bodies apparently favoured a merger, it was impossible to agree on terms. As Sir Norman Kipping, Director General of the FBI from 1946 to 1965, recalls: 'I cannot pretend that we in the FBI found our relations with the BEC either easy or particularly congenial.'[25] Kipping argues that relationships between the two organisations had been relatively straightforward when the BEC had concentrated on labour matters, but as the TUC became involved in a wider range of economic problems the BEC had also widened its range of concern so that it began to trespass on the preserves of the FBI. Relationships were complicated by the fact that 'the BEC lived a predominantly defensive life, the FBI a largely promotional one'.[26] Certainly, the BEC was a secretive organisation, though it can hardly be said that the FBI distinguished itself for most of its history by its outgoing attitude. The important point as far as the pattern of industrial representation is concerned is that the government was able to 'play off' the FBI against the BEC. This seems to have happened in 1955 when the BEC was more willing to discuss price stabilisation with the government than the FBI.[27]

The third 'peak association', the National Union of Manufacturers (later the National Association of British Manufacturers), always had a larger proportion of small firms among its membership than the other two major industrial organisations. Both its policies and subscriptions were tailored especially so as to appeal to the small firm. Again, the Salisbury model is helpful in explaining its formation. Disgruntled with the FBI, Dudley Docker turned his entrepreneurial attentions to the NUM. The NUM did not provide the range of services offered by the FBI and it is difficult to explain its survival in Olsonian terms. Rather one must focus on its overtly political stance in defending business interests and on the satisfactions its members derived from participation in its active local branches. As far as its impact on the system of industrial representation is concerned, Kipping argues that 'The existence of the NABM was not a menace to the FBI, but it was certainly a nuisance. . . . We often felt that the need to carry them along with us put a brake on our speed of action.'[28]

Finally, to complicate the system of representation still further, the ABCC remained in existence. Fearful that it might be 'snuffed out' by the FBI, the ABCC set about reorganising itself to meet this new challenge. It increased its subscription to supplement its meagre finances, moved into new offices and reorganised its internal decision-making structure.[29] Whereas the FBI tended to take a protectionist stance, the ABCC continued to advocate liberal trading policies.[30] However, although it received a substantial influx of new members during the Second World War, it remained a body that was stronger in the regions than at the centre.

The First World War had led to a much closer relationship between government and industry, but there was considerable uncertainty on both sides about the form this relationship should take in future. The government acknowledged the contribution made by the trade associations towards the war effort but was also concerned about their monopolistic aspects and their effect on free competition. The industrialists, on the other hand, whilst appreciating the benefits of a continuous dialogue with government, were concerned about what they saw as the dangers of interference by meddling bureaucrats in their activities. As it happened, the advocates of a return to normality prevailed. The decline in contacts between government and industry posed problems for organisations like the FBI.

As Blank has shown, the FBI was in no sense 'the brain-centre of British capitalism' as it was portrayed by its opponents in the inter-war period. In Blank's view, 'the FBI was never very effective as a pressure group'.[31] In particular, 'the leadership almost always felt that it was more important to avoid alienating any sector of their constituency than to provide leadership of industry as a whole by producing a statement of policy or by taking a stand on an issue.'[32] Blank's assertion that the FBI exerted limited influence on British politics is supported by other analysts of the organisation's activities. In his examination of the first British application to join the European Economic Community, Lieber argues that the FBI was weakened by 'a relative lack of discipline and resources'.[33] He concludes, 'there is no doubt that in the crucial phase of decision-making the FBI as an organisation lagged behind the British Government'.[34]

Although the FBI languished in the inter-war period, the drive for industrial 'reconstruction' in the 1930s did lead to greater government involvement in industry. However, these developments took place on an industry by industry basis and the main beneficiaries were the individual trade associations rather than the FBI. A number of new industry associations were formed; for example, the Iron and Steel Federation which acted in consort with the government's Import Duties Advisory Committee.[35] These developments at the industry association level in the 1930s are consistent with Nettl's emphasis on the role of government in the formation of industrial associations. As far as the FBI was concerned, its membership and income fell and 'its use to members was primarily as a provider of services'.[36] Thus, the FBI's survival in the inter-war period can largely be explained in Olsonian terms. Certainly, in terms of Salisbury's approach, the effects of 'hard times' in which 'group membership may be one of the first luxuries to be sacrificed' was not compensated for by 'leadership vigour'.[37]

The FBI was probably more effective after the Second World War than during the inter-war period. As Blank comments, 'just as the First World War had been directly responsible for the formation of the FBI, so the Second World War brought about its revitalisation'.[38] Government and industry cooperated closely in the wartime organisation of production and distribution. Interchanges of staff between government and trade associations helped to break down mutual suspicions and led to a number of friendships which facilitated closer cooperation on the return of peacetime conditions. Under the leadership of its new Director General, Norman Kipping, the FBI's internal structure was reshaped. Acting in the Salisbury mould of an entrepreneur/organiser, Kipping helped to reinvigorate the organisation. Membership rose from 4,478 firms in 1946 to 6,226 in 1950, 8,096 in 1960 and 8,607 in 1964.

The interventionist policies of the 1945 Labour government created new areas in which consultation between government and industry was necessary. The government ministers most closely concerned with matters affecting industry made every effort to maintain good relations with industrialists and their representative organisations. As Chancellor of the Exchequer, Sir Stafford Cripps is said to have 'made himself available to industry to a degree which few ministers can have equalled', whilst Mr Harold Wilson at the Board of Trade is said to have 'maintained constant contacts in industrial circles'.[39] Towards the end of the government's period in office, relationships between government and industry began to deteriorate. Nevertheless, despite particular disagreements over matters such as steel nationalisation, the whole nature of government–industry relations undeniably underwent a major change during and after the Second World War. This period marks the final establishment of what has been variously referred to as 'collectivism', 'corporatism' or 'the new group politics'. Whatever terminology is used, the basic pattern of relationships is clearly apparent. Government intervention in the economy has created a situation in which a close and continuing relationship between government departments and organisations representing industrial interests has been found to be indispensable to both sides.

On the return of a Conservative government with neo-liberal sympathies in 1951, there was 'a drawing apart of government from the FBI and BEC'.[40] The Conservatives were anxious to 'avoid any risk of being identified with "big business" '[41] both for electoral reasons and because they wished to establish a good working relationship with the unions. Kipping recalls of this period: 'The fact is that we were out of touch with economic policy-making, and the government was out of touch with us. For outside advice, it relied mainly on private consultation with men of its own choosing, more of whom, I suspect, were men of the City than of industry.'[42]

A new phase in the FBI's history began with its conference on The Next Five Years, held at Brighton in 1960. The conference accepted both the desirability of growth as a means of attacking the balance of payments problem and, perhaps more significantly, 'the connection was accepted between an objective of growth and the necessity for some degree of planning'.[43] In his analysis, Blank talks of the ' "Brighton revolution" in industrial attitudes'.[44] Blank argues that these events had an important impact on the FBI. He maintains that, 'in its last years, the Federation underwent major changes. Its leaders were far more willing than in the past to take a leading role in industry. . . . Its influence increased dramatically during this period.'[45]

Undoubtedly, important changes did take place both in the FBI's outlook and its effectiveness. However, one should not exaggerate the FBI's role in the movement towards some form of national economic planning. As Kipping points out, 'diverse influences were pushing in the same direction.'[46] Blank tends to make a little too much of the Brighton revolution. His analysis is at its weakest when he tries to trace linkages between changes in societal attitudes and values and changes in the attitudes and activities of the FBI. Blank argues that 'the public image of businessmen and industrialists has changed enormously. From being a suspect character at the very edge of the stage, the businessman has become a manager . . . very modern, professional and efficient.'[47] Undoubtedly, there was a 'cult of management' in Britain in the 1960s. However, although social democratic theorists like Crosland might be able to make much of the separation of ownership and control and the emergence of a new managerial class, it is questionable whether this kind of subtle distinction was made by the general public. One suspects that they probably still recognised 'bosses' rather than 'owners' and 'managers'.

It could, of course, be argued that it was a change in the climate of 'informed opinion' rather than in public opinion which was significant and which affected the outlook of the FBI. However, if this is the point Blank is trying to make, he does not make it explicit. Instead he argues, 'the Federation's greater initiative in developing new policies, in accepting new responsibilities, and in encouraging industry to take on a new role in the formation and execution of government policies was strongly supported by the "new respectability" of business in British society'.[48] The evidence which he produces in support of this argument is primarily derived from Sampson's *Anatomy of Britain* and relates to a rush of able young graduates into industry and to the number of people taking courses in management. The empirical evidence which is available would seem to suggest that British society is characterised by 'a combination of populist hostility to big business, the City, financiers etc. with general support and trust of management and private enterprise'.[49] Although the degree of hostility towards big business is neither great nor widespread, the available empirical evidence does not really support Blank's analysis. It is important to differentiate between changes in what may loosely be termed 'elite opinion', which is to some extent tapped by books such as that by Sampson, and general public opinion which can only be tapped by sample surveys to which Blank does not refer.

In the context of the renewed interest in economic planning after 1960, the need for more effective arrangements for the representation of industrial opinion became more pressing. Thus, in July 1963, the Presidents of the FBI, the BEC and the NABM appointed Sir Henry Benson and Sir Stephen Brown to prepare a report on the way in which the three organisations could be merged into one 'National Industrial Organisation'. When the Labour government was returned to power in 1964, it actively encouraged the process of amalgamation, another illustration of the usefulness of Nettl's model. Mr George Brown, First Secretary of State and Minister for Economic Affairs, made it clear soon after taking up his appointment that he wished to discuss industrial affairs and pursue his productivity policy with one body, not three. In particular, it has been suggested that the work carried out by the National Economic Development Council and the Department of Economic Affairs on incomes policy revealed 'more clearly and urgently than before the harm done by dealing with wage questions through the BEC and non-wage matters through the FBI and NABM'.[50]

The FBI was generally in favour of the Benson–Brown proposals. After all, the new organisation was to operate under a revised FBI charter. The BEC quickly encountered opposition to the merger proposal from its leading member, the Engineering Employers' Federation. The Federation argued that if companies paid subscriptions to the new body 'they might not also wish to pay to their employers' organisation, particularly if they could exert influence through the labour committee'[51] of the national industrial organisation. At the root of the EEF's objections was its dislike of 'non-federated firms', that is (generally small) engineering firms not in membership of the Employers' Federation. Undoubtedly, the EEF leaders felt that if these firms could obtain information on labour problems through the new national industrial organisation they would have an additional excuse not to join the EEF. According to Kipping, the EEF eventually withdrew its objections because 'it did not wish to be made a scapegoat'[52] for a breakdown of the negotiations. Wigham emphasises the more positive argument that many members of the EEF were in favour of a single employers' organisation 'as a counterweight to the TUC, because they believed it would increase their power to influence the ever more extensive intervention by the Government in industrial affairs'.[53] Undoubtedly, both arguments helped to make an agreement possible. What is significant is that, whereas the EEF was able to promote a separate organisation to deal with industrial relations in 1919, it was not able to pursue an independent line in the changed climate of industrial opinion in 1964.

In many ways, the NABM proved the hardest of the three organisations to fit into a new merged association. A number of NABM members, in particular a group of small manufacturers in the Midlands, felt that the special problems of smaller businessmen would not be taken sufficiently into account by the new organisation. They were inclined to see the merger as an attempt by the government to impose control on business and industry. In particular, they were opposed to the proposal to admit the nationalised industries to membership. A number of smaller businessmen were so concerned that the new industrial organisation would 'become a tool of government policy'[54] that they decided to form their own Society of Independent Manufacturers. Although only two dozen people attended the inaugural meeting of this body, it now claims twenty thousand firms as members under its new title of the Smaller Businesses Association.

The formation of a united organisation of industrialists removed one major impediment to the attempts of industry to influence government decisions in Britain, although until such time as the Confederation of British Industry becomes a Confederation of British Business, representing all sectors of finance, commerce and retailing, as well as industry, it is not realistic to refer to what may alternatively be termed a common organisational front among capitalists or an organisation which can speak for managers in all sectors of British business. Organisational problems have to some extent limited the influence of British industry on policy-making in the past, but good organisation is a necessary not a sufficient condition of being able to influence the content of government decisions.

Nevertheless, the leaders of the new Confederation of British Industry felt confident that 'this major unification of activities, experience and resources has put the CBI in a unique and unprecedented position to promote and protect the interests of management'.[55] The new organisation conformed less well to Olson's model of interest group formation and survival in so far as it was decided to place less emphasis on services to members. Of course, one of the difficulties of applying Olson's model is that leaders of industrial organisations see the service and representational aspects of their activities as essentially complementary. As Kipping notes, 'services' work . . . brought FBI staff hard up against some of the practical problems of industrial life, with benefit to the way they dealt with their work in the office'.[56]

It might appear from the analysis contained in this chapter that Olson's model is most useful in explaining the formation and early development of interest groups before they attain organisational maturity. Such an explanation, although not inconsistent with the history of the FBI and CBI, is a little too simplistic. It would not, for example, fit in with the recent changes which have taken place in the functions of employers' organisations dealing with industrial relations. The development of work-place bargaining 'took away from many employers' organizations their traditional role and created for them the new one of providing information and advice to their members on their individual local problems'.[57] On the basis of a sample survey of forty-five employers' organisations, Gospel et al concluded that 'their advisory functions, as distinct from their regulatory and other functions, have expanded and will play in the future a still more important part in their services to members'.[58] Olson's theory would seem to be most applicable when an organisation faces a crisis of survival. Such crises are particularly likely to occur in the early years of its existence, and they were exacerbated in the case of the FBI by the slump in world trade that overshadowed the early years of its existence. However, any change in the operational environment of an organisation, such as that recently faced by the employers' organisations, may lead the organ-isation to devote more resources to the development of selective incentives for its members.

Olson's model does enhance our understanding of interest group activity by emphasising the importance of the services which a group provides to its members, an aspect of group activity which might otherwise be neglected or overlooked. However, perhaps it should be emphasised that this problem was not always ignored by earlier writers.[59] Nevertheless, Olson does provide for the first time a coherent theoretical framework for the analysis of the importance of services as compared with an interest group's representational activities. The usefulness of his model is enhanced by a consideration of Salisbury's emphasis on the entrepreneur/organiser. As we have seen, such individuals have played an important role in the history of British industrial representation, both in terms of interest group formation and the resuscitation of groups after periods of difficulty.

Nettl's model is useful in so far as it draws attention to an important aspect of the history of industrial representation in Britain, the part played by government in the formation of the supposedly independent organisations of industry. As we have seen, the government played an important role in the establishment of the FBI, encouraged the formation of the CBI and has more recently seconded staff to the Devlin Commission which reviewed the future of business representation. Government has done little actively to encourage the implementation of the Devlin Report's findings. Moreover, the active interest taken by government in the system of industrial representation does not, of itself, prove that the 'emasculation' of industrial representation foreseen by Nettl has taken place. The membership of a representative organisation may not accept a situation in which it becomes a satellite of Whitehall as docilely as Nettl implies.

Despite their limitations, the theoretical perspectives offered by Olson and Nettl do considerably enhance our understanding of the development of the system of industrial representation in Britain. However, the development of an effective representative organisation for industry cannot be seen simply as a product of the initiative of industrialists; government encouragement has played its part. Moreover, the survival and development of the FBI and the CBI owe as much to the provision of services to their members as to their performance as spokesmen for manufacturing industry.

Notes and References

1 S. Blank, *Government and Industry in Britain* (Farnborough: Saxon House, 1973).
2 M. Olson Jnr, *The Logic of Collective Action* (New York, Schocken Books, 1968), pp. 14–15.
3 Olson, op. cit., pp. 15–16.
4 Olson, op. cit., p. 134.
5 Olson, op. cit., p. 132.
6 J. P. Nettl, 'Consensus or elite domination: the case of business', *Political Studies*, **13** (1965), pp. 22–44, p. 22.
7 ibid., p. 22.
8 ibid., p. 31.
9 ibid., p. 30.
10 R. H. Salisbury, 'An exchange theory of interest groups' in R. H. Salisbury (ed), *Interest Group Politics in America* (London: Harper and Row, 1970), pp. 32–67.
11 ibid., p. 33.
12 ibid., p. 54.
13 ibid., p. 54.
14 For example: the General Chamber of Manufacturers of Great Britain (1785); the National Association of Federated Employers (1873); the Employers' Parliamentary

Council (1898); the Manufacturers' Association of Great Britain (1905); the Employers' Parliamentary Association (1915).

15 G. Alderman, *The Railway Interest* (Leicester: the University Press, 1973), pp. 99–100.

16 A. R. Ilersic and P. F. Liddle, *The Parliament of Commerce: the Story of the Association of British Chambers of Commerce, 1860–1960* (London: Newman Neame, 1960), p. 165.

17 ibid., p. 93.

18 ibid., pp. 168–9.

19 ibid., p. 170.

20 Alderman, op. cit., p. 13.

21 *Royal Commission on Trade Unions and Employers' Associations, Written Evidence of the Engineering Employers' Federation* (London: HMSO, 1968), pp. 378–478, p. 429.

22 Blank, op. cit., p. 12.

23 ibid., p. 14.

24 E. Wigham, *The Power to Manage: a History of the Engineering Employers' Federation* (London: Macmillan, 1973), pp. 103–4.

25 Sir N. Kipping, *Summing Up* (London: Hutchinson, 1972), p. 49.

26 ibid., p. 49.

27 Blank, op. cit., pp. 131–2.

28 Kipping, op. cit., p. 50.

29 Ilersic and Liddle, op. cit., p. 185.

30 *Report of the Commission of Inquiry into Industrial and Commercial Representation (Devlin Report)* (London: Association of British Chambers of Commerce and Confederation of British Industry, 1972), p. 21.

31 Blank, op. cit., p. 7.

32 ibid., p. 51.

33 R. J. Lieber, *British Politics and European Unity* (Berkeley: University of California Press, 1970), p. 104.

34 ibid., p. 97.

35 N. Harris, *Competition and the Corporate Society* (London: Methuen, 1973), p. 43.

36 Blank, op. cit., p. 30.

37 Salisbury, op. cit., p. 42.

38 Blank, op. cit., p. 31.

39 Sir R. Streat, 'Government consultation with industry', *Public Administration*, **37** (1959), pp. 1–8, p. 3.

40 Kipping, op. cit., p. 84.

41 ibid., p. 85.

42 ibid., p. 90.

43 ibid., p. 85.

44 Blank, op. cit., p. 153.

45 ibid., p. 216.

46 Kipping, op. cit., p. 95.

47 Blank, op. cit., p. 209

48 ibid., p. 209.

49 R. Jessop, *Traditionalism, Conservatism and British Political Culture* (London: Allen and Unwin, 1974), p. 95.

50 A. Denton, M. Forsyth and M. Maclennan, *Economic Planning and Policies in Britain, France and Germany* (London: Allen and Unwin, 1968), p. 267.
51 Wigham, op. cit., p. 216.
52 Kipping, op. cit., p. 228.
53 Wigham, op. cit., p. 216.
54 *The Times*, 3 March 1965.
55 *Your Company and the CBI* (London: CBI, 1972), p. 3.
56 Kipping, op. cit., p. 42.
57 Commission on Industrial Relations, *Employers' Organisations and Industrial Relations* (London: HMSO, 1972), p. 36.
58 ibid., p. 36.
59 For example, see A. Potter, *Organised Groups in British National Politics* (London: Faber and Faber, 1961).

3

Membership

THE ABSOLUTE SIZE OF AN INTEREST GROUP'S MEMBERSHIP IS ONLY one of many factors that may be related to its effectiveness. However, size, particularly if a group has a large actual membership in relation to its eligible membership and if it is backed by strong and efficient organisation, is likely to ensure that the group has frequent contacts with government. As Presthus points out: 'Among the most crucial of an association's socio-economic resources is probably the size and quality of its membership.'[1] In the consideration of any interest group it is clearly essential to analyse the composition of its membership.

In the first section of this chapter we will analyse the size and quality of the CBI's membership. Subsequently we will consider the reasons why firms join the CBI. We shall be relying upon data collected from a sample of firms who are members of the CBI. Our aim will be to review this data in the light of the explanations of interest group formation and membership advanced by the pluralists[2] and by economists.[3]

Membership size and range

The range of the CBI's membership has been considerably enlarged since its formation in 1965. In the three organisations which existed prior to 1965, membership was restricted to what were broadly called manufacturing industries. This term was taken to include the transport and construction industries, although these industries were under-represented in the FBI's actual membership. The retail sector and the nationalised industries were not eligible for membership. However, in the FBI ancillary services such as banks and insurance companies and brokers were admitted as commercial associate members. The NABM in contrast existed almost exclusively for small manufacturing firms, while the BEC was composed of national employers' organisations and trade associations. The memberships of the three organisations in 1964 (the last year of their existence) is analysed in Table 1.

	Name of organisation		
	FBI	BEC	NABM
Large and medium companies	1,660*	—	31
Small companies (less than 200 employees)	2,412	—	4,800
Trade associations and employers' organisations	280	53	53

TABLE 1: ANALYSIS OF MEMBERSHIPS OF FBI, BEC AND NABM IN 1964

SOURCE. Devlin, op. cit., pp. 20–1

* The FBI also had 4,535 subsidiary companies in membership whose subscriptions were covered by their parent bodies.

The structure of the CBI was closely modelled upon that of the FBI and the BEC. In particular the division of membership between companies and organisations was continued in the new organisation. In addition, as had been the case in the FBI, a category of membership, commercial associate, was provided for organisations such as banks, finance houses, advertising agencies and organisations representing the distributive trade.

However, one major constitutional innovation distinguished the CBI from its predecessors. A new category of membership, industrial associate, which granted all the rights and privileges of full members but excluded representation on the governing body, was created primarily for the nationalised industries, in accordance with the recommendations of the Benson/Brown report.[4] In 1969 the category of associate membership was abolished and all associate members were admitted to full membership. Thus the CBI at present has five categories of members: industrial companies; trade associations and employers' organisations; public sector members; and commercial companies and commercial associations.[5]

The number of members in each category of membership in 1973–5 is outlined in Table 2.

	At 31/12/73	At 31/12/74	At 31/12/75
Industrial companies	11,242	10,234	10,112
Commercial companies	379	425	488
Public sector members	18	16	15
Employers' organisations and			
trade associations	196	172	163
Commercial associations	39	31	34
Industrial/commercial			
companies	9	NS	NS

TABLE 2: THE CBI'S MEMBERSHIP 1973-5

Thus we see that the CBI has a membership of under eleven thousand companies and organisations. However, this figure excludes those subsidiary companies of member firms which do not receive CBI literature. The CBI itself estimates that if all these firms were counted the membership figure would be nearer fifteen thousand. It is also obvious from Table 1 that the CBI has extended the foothold established by the FBI in the City, as well as taking the nationalised industries into membership. Thus, all the clearing banks as well as twenty merchant banks and ten major insurance companies are members. Indeed, since its formation the range of the CBI's membership has been considerably extended beyond the field of manufacturing industry. An interesting reflection of this can be found in the membership of the CBI's Economic Committee, which had representatives from merchant banking, stockbroking, nationalised industries, mining, finance, farming and construction, as well as from manufacturing industry.

Nevertheless, despite this development the CBI is still, and is likely to remain, primarily concerned with the interests of manufacturing industry. Indeed, although the retail organisations have been eligible for full membership since 1969, neither the Retail Consortium, which is the peak organisation, nor any of its constituent elements have joined the CBI. In fact, the Consortium has discouraged any retail organisation or company from joining partly in order to strengthen its own position and partly because it believes that the CBI could not represent both the manufacturing and the retail sectors, whose interests differ on some occasions. In addition there is a history of animosity between the two organisations. All this has meant that only a few purely retail companies have joined the CBI and there seems little likelihood that the situation will change much in the forseeable future.[6] At the same time, although the CBI has made some headway in the City, its initiatives have been largely unsuccessful. Thus at a working dinner the CBI gave in April 1968 for leading representatives of the City of London, as part of an initiative to create a more widely-based organisation, they met with a lukewarm, if not hostile, response. Subsequent advances have received similar reactions. Whilst many City bodies have welcomed in principle the idea of closer links with the CBI, they are anxious not to sacrifice the channels of access to the government which they have developed for themselves over the decades. Indeed, as Devlin notes, City interests 'appear not to rely on the CBI as their main channel of representation, but rather to see it as a useful means of keeping themselves informed of what is happening in manufacturing industry and its related industries'.[7] There is little doubt that in the near future the membership of the CBI will continue to be drawn largely from the manufacturing sector.

The quality of membership

The absolute size of an interest group's membership is not usually as crucial as the quality of its membership.[8] Of course, it is not always easy to define or measure quality. However, in the case of the CBI it is particularly significant that the great majority of *large manufacturing* companies are in membership. In fact, its membership includes 75 per cent of the companies in *The Times* list of two hundred leading companies. In addition the majority of those who are not members come from the commercial sphere, although GEC/AEI has never joined the CBI, and more recently Alcan resigned and a number of other companies temporarily suspended membership. At the same time half the top thousand companies are in membership. All this does not mean that the CBI represents only large companies. Indeed, as Table 3 shows, most companies in membership are small firms.

Size of company	% of CBI's industrial company membership
Under 50 employees	40%
51–200 employees	31%
201–1,000 employees	16%
Over 1,000 employees	13%

TABLE 3: THE CBI'S INDUSTRIAL COMPANY MEMBERSHIP (1975)

Nevertheless an enormous number of small firms are not members of the CBI, nor indeed members of their Trade Associations. One informed observer has calculated that there are one and a quarter million small businesses in Britain.[9] Most of those take little part in organisations of industrial representation.

The CBI is divided into twelve regions[10] and inevitably its membership is largest in those areas which are most heavily industrialised. In Table 4 a breakdown of the CBI's membership by region is presented.

Scotland	1,053
Northern	523
Yorkshire and Humberside	1,339
North Western	1,197
East Midlands	608
West Midlands	1,468
Wales	609
Eastern	426
Southern	385
London and South Eastern	2,801
South Western	543

TABLE 4: CBI COMPANY MEMBERS BY REGION
(as at September 1975 excluding Northern Ireland)

The quality of an interest group's membership cannot only be measured in terms of absolute or relative size. It is significant that the CBI has in membership most large manufacturing firms, but other factors are also important when considering the quality of membership. A group may have a large number of members but few who are willing or able to be active. This is very important as most large interest groups rely heavily upon the work of committees, particularly for the discussion and evolution of group policy. Indeed, such committees are crucial if any interest group is to function efficiently. Yet such committees are most often composed of unpaid members. Thus if a group only has a small *active* membership willing to serve unpaid on committees this can severely limit its effectiveness.

With its limited resources the CBI is no exception. It relies very heavily on the work of its committees. Indeed it is one of the strengths of the organisation that many of its members play an active role in a

regional and/or national council and in various committees. The amount
of skilled, unpaid manpower that the CBI is able to mobilise is considerable. Of course not all member firms play an active role. In general,
larger firms, who have more executives available, are more active, but
there are enormous differences between companies. Some companies play
almost no part while the Imperial Tobacco Company seemed to have one
director who spent almost all of his time on CBI matters. Nevertheless
the CBI can rely on skilled unpaid aid and this is an important indication
of the quality of its membership.

The cost of membership
The monetary cost of membership can readily be calculated. Until
October 1973 each firm paid a subscription on a sliding scale in relation
to the number of its employees. If a company had a number of subsidiaries each subsidiary automatically became a member and the fee
payable by the central company was calculated on the basis of the total
workforce in all group companies. Costs in monetary terms were not high.
At that time an industrial company with a thousand employees would
have paid £275. Even a firm employing 120,000 people would have paid
a subscription of only £7,650 in 1972. Moreover, up to forty per cent of
these subscriptions can be written off against tax. Costs were then, and
still are, small. These levels are typical of the costs of all organisations of
industrial representation in Britain. Indeed, the report of the Devlin
Commission on Industrial Representation found that the rates that six
major groups paid to organisations of industrial representation here varied,
as percentages of their turnover, from 0.014 to 0.0396 per cent. This was
considerably lower than similar groups paid in other European countries.
The rates of medium- and small-sized firms, as percentages of their
turnover, were higher (varying from 0.022 to 0.12 per cent) but were still
relatively low.[11]

However, the CBI was unhappy about the level of subscriptions and
about the fact that the old system discriminated against labour–intensive
industries. The new system introduced in 1973 for industrial and public-
sector members is based upon the member's total United Kingdom salary
bill and upon its United Kingdom turnover. This change meant that
a few firms' subscriptions trebled, or even quadrupled. In addition
subscription costs have also increased inevitably as a result of inflation. This has meant that the CBI's subscription income increased from
£1.4 million to £2.4 million. Many firms were not happy about the

1973 changes but at an extraordinary general meeting of the Council the overwhelming majority accepted the increases. Despite this a certain number of firms, mainly small ones, ceased to be members as a result of these increases in subscription. Thus the CBI's annual income has grown substantially since its formation, from £800,000 in 1965 to £1.6 million in 1973 and £2.4 million in 1975. In Table 5 the main sources of income are examined in more detail.

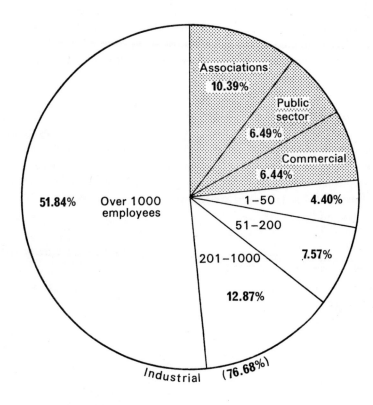

TABLE 5: THE CBI'S SOURCES OF MEMBERSHIP REVENUE

It is obvious from this analysis that most of the CBI's revenue comes from large industrial companies. Indeed, 50 per cent of the whole income of the CBI comes from member companies listed in the top 500 in *The Times* list of a thousand leading companies. Once again this illustrates the dominant importance of manufacturing industry within the CBI and the strong position of large companies. The change in the basis of subscription has considerably increased the CBI's income without materially changing the source of that income.

Recruiting members

The CBI is obviously very concerned to attract and retain members. However, a shortage of resources means that its membership secratariat is relatively small. In the headquarters in Tothill Street there are two officers, two research assistants, two secretaries and one clerk. Much of the recruitment is done by the Regional Offices; each Assistant Regional Secretary has a defined territory and most of his job is taken up with the recruitment and retention of members. Despite this relatively small staff the CBI is 'marketed' in a much more efficient way than the old FBI, which was sold, as one of our contacts put it, 'like a golf club'. The membership department at headquarters keeps a list of sectors of industry in which membership drives might take place. Before any approach is made a considerable amount of market research is undertaken to discover what are the problems of the sector and what services it might need. Thus when an Assistant Regional Secretary makes an approach he is provided with a fairly full brief. A very careful study is made of why firms leave the organisation and if a company threatens to resign it is immediately visited in the hope that its directors can be persuaded to change their mind. Despite all this the CBI's membership, after rising very slowly up to 1973, fell dramatically in 1974, and fell slightly again in 1975.

In Table 6 below we can see the changing membership pattern in the years from 1970–1975.

1970	+ 1%
1971	+ 1½%
1972	+ 2%
1973	+ 1%
1974	− 8%
1975	− ½%

TABLE 6: MEMBERSHIP PATTERN (1970–5)

Future membership patterns

Obviously it is difficult to speculate about the future membership patterns of any organisation. In the case of the CBI at present (May 1976) the problem is complicated by the fact that the organisation is in a vulnerable position. As we point out elsewhere the CBI walks a tightrope. It has to cooperate with government, without becoming too identified with it in the eyes of its membership. In 1974 there was evidence of considerable unrest among its membership, many of whom believed that the CBI was accepting too passively increased government intervention in the economy in general and in industry in particular. This unrest was accentuated by an unfortunate occurrence during the campaign leading up to the February 1974 election. Campbell Adamson, then Director General of CBI, was widely reported (supposedly on the basis of an off-the-record comment) as being in favour of the repeal of the 1971 Industrial Relations Act by the next government. This was seen, by some CBI members, as both a reason for the Conservatives' narrow defeat and an illustration of the CBI's 'radical' attitudes.

Many members were in an unhappy frame of mind which was not helped by the new minority Labour government's apparent renewed commitment to nationalisation. The unrest resulted in some resignations, and in some companies, notably Guest Keene and Nettlefold, 'suspending' membership, although in reality suspension of membership amounted to very little, as membership subscriptions had been paid and the CBI still sent these firms literature and provided them with services. In addition, the rising costs of membership along with the deteriorating economic situation led to a number of companies, particularly small companies, ceasing membership. The result was a substantial decline in membership in 1974, as Table 6 shows. This loss was not recovered in 1975 and many firms, particularly smaller firms, who left because of economic pressures, have not rejoined, and seem unlikely to do so.

The majority of the larger firms who left have rejoined and those who to date have not seem likely to rejoin in future. In this way GKN, who 'suspended membership' in a blaze of publicity, paid their subscription to remain members in the following year. There appear to be two main reasons why large firms have rejoined, or are likely to rejoin. Firstly, the CBI responded fairly quickly and firmly to this challenge to its position. In 1974, statements by CBI became increasingly opposed to intervention generally and nationalisation in particular. In addition, the deteriorating economic situation caused the Labour government to rethink its policy and attempt to re-establish better contacts with industry and the CBI. At the same time, the membership secretariat kept in close contact with those companies who had resigned or suspended membership, not only sending literature and offering services, but also visiting them.

Second, and more importantly, the CBI has the great advantage of having no real rival. There is no other peak organisation for manufacturing industry and most CBI members we talked to, including a number who subsequently suspended membership, stressed that some such organisation was essential. Thus, with no alternative to the CBI, companies who have resigned face the prospect of approaching government alone, or through trade associations, many of which are weak, or of returning to the fold. Perhaps the CBI will lose permanently a few members because of its supposedly conciliatory stance towards government, but it seems unlikely to lose many firms for this reason. Indeed, it appears to us that the real significance of this unrest was that it indicated once again the problems integral to any large interest group which represents a very diverse membership. The leadership of the group cannot hope to please all the members all the time. In addition, interest groups rely very heavily on close contacts with government departments, usually advocating conciliation and compromise rather than confrontation. Yet many interest group members will at some time, if not always, favour confrontation, so it is easy for the leadership to be out of step with the membership at such times. The outburst among members in 1974 and the subsequent substantial decline in membership seems to be a symptom of a recurrent and inevitable, if not necessarily terminal, disease.

In our view, then, the CBI is likely to retain most large manufacturing firms as members. However, it is quite feasible that these firms will rely less heavily on the CBI's contacts with government and approach departments directly more often than in the past. This is inevitable if such firms lose confidence in the CBI. At the same time it seems unlikely that the CBI will substantially expand its membership.

The CBI itself seems most anxious to increase its membership among those firms in *The Times* Top Thousand who are not members. However, it seems unlikely they will have much success, for many of these firms are outside the manufacturing sector. This is a crucial point. There seems little likelihood that they will make much ground in the retail sector, where the Retail Consortium is attempting to establish itself and where the retail organisations are advising their members not to join the CBI. The CBI has had more success in the commercial sphere and indeed this has been the fastest growing section of the CBI's membership. However, further progress seems unlikely while the City has its own direct contacts with government. Indeed, if an expansion of membership is to take place, it seems most likely to be among small- and medium-sized firms. Such firms, unless they are in a field such as engineering which has a strong employers' organisation/trade association, could be attracted by the range of services which the CBI has to offer.

On joining the CBI

So far in this chapter we have looked at the changing patterns of CBI membership without asking why people join the organisation. Yet this is a matter of great interest both to interest group researchers and to the CBI. Indeed in recent years the question why people join interest groups has attracted increasing attention. This is largely because certain theorists, notably Olson and Frohlich *et al*, have adapted economic models in order to question certain of the assumptions and conclusions of the pluralist writers.

The pluralists have been primarily concerned with the problems posed by the activities of interest groups for democratic theory rather than with any consistent explanation of why groups exist. Nevertheless, pluralists make certain assumptions, either explicitly or implicitly, about the origins of associations. In essence they believe that group members share public policy related interests which preceded the existence of the organised group and that they join the group in order to forward these policy objectives. This explanation of the formation of interest groups has one crucial limitation which Olson has cogently pointed out.

The pluralists assume not only that interest groups are formed to pursue common interests but also that an individual will join a group to pursue his own individual interests. In doing so the pluralists ignore the fact that the individual may not materially affect his own interests by joining an association when the benefits that groups negotiate with government are available to him as an eligible member even if he does not join the organisation. In fact, Olson demonstrates that in many circumstances an individual's strict self-interests are not likely to be served by joining an interest group. The pluralists' approach to the formation of interest groups is essentially superficial. They tend to assume that because a group exists its potential members have a common interest that takes precedence over their own individual interests. Their theory has more to do with an ideological commitment to democracy than with empirical evidence or logical rigour.[12]

In contrast, Olson has developed what he terms a 'by-product theory' of interest group activity. He says: 'The common characteristic which distinguishes all of the large economic groups is that they are also organised for *some other* purpose.'[13] The lobbying activity of the association is seen as a by-product of its other activity: 'The lobbies of large economic groups are the by-products of organisations that have a capacity to "mobilise" a latent group with "selective incentives".'[14]

Olson's model is based upon the rationality principle. It is not rational for a firm to join an interest group to benefit from its lobbying or 'collective good' when that good is equally available to non-members. Thus if an interest group is to attract members it must offer 'selective incentives' which are available only to members. These 'selective incentives' may be negative, taking the form of coercion or the enforcement of a closed shop, or positive, taking the form of services. It will only be rational for a firm to join the CBI, in Olson's terms, if the benefits it receives from membership outweigh the costs of membership. Thus, except in certain cases,[15] one would expect most firms to join the CBI for its services.

Why do firms join the CBI? Do they join for its lobbying activities or for its services? In Olson's terms, do they act rationally? Before we can answer this question, a crucial qualification of Olson's model must be considered. In a model based upon the rationality principle, the individual (or firm) is assumed to have certain aims, desires or preferences, or perhaps one single aim, and to make a factual appraisal of the problem situation. The rationality principle involves an assumption that he will act in a way consistent with his aims and his situational appraisal. All perfect rationality models assume an optimal decision-making situation in which sufficient information about the decision-making situation is available to the individual.[16] In effect they assume that it is possible to construct an objective decision-making situation, an evaluation of the individual's aims and desires, and therefore a necessary prediction of the outcome in terms of his actions.

Watkins points out the limitations of the principle of perfect rationality in a lucid and stimulating article.[17] He notes, 'an ideal decision-making scheme is pictured as being presented to the agent's mind in its entirety, a completed whole in which the several components simultaneously play their due role.'[18] In fact, 'an actual decision-making scheme is something like a crude caricature, drawn with a few bold strokes, of the complete situational picture and preference map of normative decision-theory.'[19]

In an actual decision-making situation, the individual does not have access to complete information about that situation nor does he pay equal attention to all information. The main criticism therefore of the perfect rationality model is that it is inappropriate and cannot be applied to most practical decision-making situations. Watkins in contrast develops what he calls an 'imperfect' rationality principle. What becomes important is the individual's reconstruction of the decision-making situation. An individual may be acting rationally in terms of his reconstruction and of his preferences (desires), although he is actually acting irrationally in terms of the objective decision-making situation. However, the use of the imperfect rationality principle is not without its problems. How does one reconstruct the individual's perception of the decision-making situation? Olson himself is far from clear about his assumptions concerning the individual's decision-making scheme. Yet this obviously becomes a crucial area when one attempts quantitatively to test the hypotheses from the model. There is likely to be a considerable difference between the actual costs and benefits of membership and the perceived costs and benefits. This point is acknowledged but insufficiently developed by Olson.

In the rest of this chapter we shall be referring to data collected in a series of interviews with CBI member firms and CBI officials. We asked each firm why it had joined the CBI (or one of its predecessors) and why it remained in membership, and we paid particular attention to the way it perceived the costs and benefits of membership. This is of course only one type of evidence relevant in tests of Olson's model. Olson himself concentrates on an analysis of the historical formation and development of various interest groups. We have already used such an approach[20] and found that Olson's model was most useful in accounting for the survival of groups in situations of organisational crisis. Here we are concerned to examine the actual decisions of individual companies.

The sample

In elite interviewing it is almost impossible to obtain a representative sample of an organisation's membership. As Dexter argued cogently: 'The population cannot be satisfactorily randomised or stratified in advance.'[21] In addition, as our resources were limited, we could not hope to interview a large number of respondents. However, we did attempt to interview a meaningful cross-section of the membership. With the cooperation of Regional Secretaries in four CBI regions (Wales, South-West, South-East and West Midlands) a list of potential respondents was drawn up containing a cross-section of the CBI's membership in those areas, particularly in terms of size of firm and type of industry. Care was taken to see that the list included firms which took little interest in the work of the CBI as well as those represented upon the Regional Council.

We interviewed ninety-one firms or nationalised industries, speaking in most cases to the chief executive and/or the person chiefly responsible for the firm's relations with the CBI.[22] We have excluded consideration of the nationalised industries from this section,[23] and so, in effect, the following analysis is based upon interviews with eighty firms; thirty-one of these were large (over a thousand employees), twenty-seven medium and twenty-two small (under two hundred employees). Of the individuals interviewed, forty-eight were Regional Council members, thirty-two were not. The sample thus overrepresents larger firms and firms with representatives on Regional Councils. However, such an emphasis was inevitable given the other concerns of this research.

Clearly, the data has considerable limitations, but we believe that it provides a means of assessing the utility of Olson's theory and of examining Watkin's critique of the limitations of the perfect rationality principle. The data does focus attention on certain problems which could be followed up by subsequent, larger-scale studies. In hour-long interviews we covered a great deal of ground, although we concentrated on the firms' reasons for being members of the CBI. We were particularly concerned to discover in the case of larger firms how far they thought their involvement influenced the supply of the collective good. This was especially important because it would be rational for very large firms to join for a supply of the collective good if they felt that their membership would bring the CBI more lobbying power which would, in turn, result in that large firm receiving an increased supply of the collective good sufficient to outweigh the cost of membership.

The costs and benefits of membership
We have already dealt at some length with the monetary cost to firms of membership of the CBI. It is very low. Indeed the managing director of a small firm in Wales commented: 'My subscription is very small because I have few employees. One doesn't need to get much back at all to get one's money worth.' It is true that people do incur greater costs by playing an active role in the organisation. However, it should be stressed that they do not always perceive this involvement as a cost. One member of the Midlands Regional Council commented that he attended the Regional Council partly because 'one of the problems of the small firm is the intense loneliness of management. There is very rarely anyone of similar

mental capacity in the organisation that the director of a small firm can talk to.' Other respondents stressed that they found CBI activities rewarding in terms of their career strategies or business opportunities. Generally, respondents found the costs of involvement difficult to calculate but regarded them as low.

The CBI provides a wide range of what may loosely be termed 'services' for its members. These range from advice and assistance on industrial relations problems to background intelligence on foreign countries and information on technical translation services. The CBI will even draft letters to government departments for members. Its recruitment literature heavily stresses the financial advantages that individual firms have derived from CBI membership. The organisation is particularly proud of the case of the company in Scotland that 'collected an unexpected windfall of £6000' when the CBI drew attention to its entitlement for training grants and that of the firm which was able to collect Regional Employment Premium after it had been restructured into separate companies on CBI advice.

Are such services the main reason why companies join the CBI? There is no doubt that a great deal of information is available elsewhere, either from government departments or from trade associations serving particular industries. One industrialist commented: 'There always seems to be a degree of overlap between Department of Employment information, Economic Development Council information and CBI publications. At the same time, as part of the engineering industry, we are already well served by our own employers' federation.' Selective incentives may only be available to CBI members, but they are often available to members and eligible members from other sources.

We stressed earlier that one of the problems with Olson's theory is that it is assumed that eligible group members have access to, and pay attention to, all the information necessary to make a rational decision. Indeed it quickly became apparent from our interviews that many member firms were not aware of the range of services offered by the CBI. This finding fits in well with Watkins' critique of the perfect rationality model. The members of the CBI have less than complete knowledge about the organisation and its services.

When we asked our respondents how important a part services played in their decision to join and remain members, a distinct pattern emerged. Services were a far more important factor in the reasoning of small companies than in that of large companies. The reason for this pattern of responses is not hard to discover. Most larger firms have ample supplies of information about legislation, foreign markets etc. from within the company. They employ large numbers of people specifically to supply them with such information. A director of one of the largest companies in Britain commented: 'We make minimal use of CBI services. We don't remain members for that reason. Large firms know most things the CBI could tell us or have ways of finding out. Indeed, the CBI sometimes comes to us for information.'

In fact, none of the respondents from large firms whom we interviewed thought that the services the CBI provided were the major, let alone the only, reason why their firms had joined, and remained members of, the organisation. Among smaller and medium-sized firms, however, the picture was different. Almost all the small firms interviewed saw the services offered as a main stimulus to their joining and remaining in the CBI. They were particularly important to 'non-federated firms', that is, firms in the engineering industry outside the Engineering Employers' Federation which relied on the CBI for information on industrial relations. Indeed, the Engineering Employers' Federation's intense dislike of non-federated firms was one reason why, for a time, it opposed the formation of the CBI.[24]

Small firms, then, used the services of the CBI much more than larger firms, and seventeen of the twenty-two small firms we interviewed gave the availability of a wide range of services as their main reason for membership. Often these small firms considered that the benefits derived from these services outweighed the costs of CBI membership. A managing director of a small firm in Wales commented: 'I have few employees so membership doesn't cost me much. I use the CBI services fairly often. The really important saving is in time and effort and at times money. They can get me information I need quickly, where it would take me hours.' It was certainly not the case, however, that all small firms felt that the usefulness of the services outweighed the costs of membership. Indeed at least eight of the small firms we spoke to doubted that the selective benefits of membership outweighed the costs. Many felt that the services the CBI offered were often available elsewhere, either from their trade association or the relevant government departments.

It can hardly be said on the basis of our interviews that it is the services which attract and retain most members of the CBI. One of the problems is, of course, to define precisely what is meant by a service. For example, the CBI sometimes takes up problems affecting particular firms with government departments. This type of activity is treated by the CBI as a service in its recruitment literature, but in some ways it is closer to a collective benefit. In trying to influence the administration of a policy, the CBI may affect the policy itself. If a concession is negotiated it will subsequently apply to non-members as well as members. A number of respondents did mention the CBI's role in taking up their particular problems with government and with local authorities. As such, this is an incentive, and in most senses a selective one. However, even if we accept it as a selective incentive, it does not seem to be particularly significant in explaining why members join. Olson treats social incentives and contacts as selective benefits. Clearly, such incentives are selective in that one must be a member of an organisation in order to meet people in it and through it. In smaller firms, directors did view these contacts as important. These respondents valued the CBI as a forum for meeting other business-men for three distinct reasons:

1 Purely socially: one might make new friends or meet people with similar interests and outlooks;

2 As a way of building up a picture of the 'state of trade'. As one respondent put it: 'One tends to feel a little closer to what's happening. You meet people in other industries which is more valuable than meeting people in one's own industry. People in one's own industry tend to be reticent. By exchanging information with non-related industries one gets a much better picture of what is happening.'

3 As a source of business opportunities. One respondent commented: 'Business results from contacts and the CBI is a wonderful source of contacts, it has such a wide membership.'

These selective incentives seem in most cases to be of marginal importance. However, once again they seem more important to small than to large firms. Large firms did not value the CBI as an opportunity to meet other industrialists. A number of respondents from large firms echoed the remark of one respondent who commented, 'I wouldn't learn much about the state of trade through the CBI.'

It is difficult to see how Olson's notion of the importance of coercion or negative sanctions has any significance when considering the CBI (although it may be applicable to trade associations such as the Society of Motor Manufacturers and Traders, which controls major exhibitions).[25] The CBI has no closed shop and can impose no sanctions on firms which do not join. Sometimes companies did report that the recruitment efforts of the CBI Regional Secretary had influenced their decision to join, and the director of one large company said rather cynically: 'It's easier to pay than have the CBI pester us over the next five years to join.' Such reactions are few and far between and this influence hardly amounts to negative sanctions in the sense in which Olson uses the term.

In addition, some of our respondents did report pressure on companies from other industrialists to join the CBI. A director of a medium-sized firm explained: 'We are members because it is the accepted thing to do. There is a certain amount of pressure from one's friends.' An industrialist in the south-west commented: 'People join or stay as members partly because their fellow industrialists are involved. There is some pressure to join or remain members, particularly if the local business community is a tight one. Industrialists don't like to see others getting benefits out of the CBI's actions without paying for them or supporting them.' In contrast several respondents reported unsuccessful attempts to persuade other local industrialists to join, and one respondent commented: 'There is not to my knowledge any attempt by firms to influence non-members to join, no pressure is put on firms by other firms to join the CBI. This contrasts with the situation in the Engineering Employers' Federation where such pressure is common.' Although no straightforward pattern emerges, pressure of the kind described hardly amounts to a negative sanction in Olson's terms.

On collective goods

Our interviews indicate that many companies join the CBI because of the collective goods it offers rather than for any selective benefits. The large firms are particularly concerned with the CBI's representative function even though they are likely to have direct contacts with government departments. The CBI seems to be valued by its members largely for its influence on government and as a counter-balance to the trade union movement. A response from the managing director of a large firm was fairly typical of the pattern of replies:

If the CBI didn't exist we would need to create it. We need someone to stand up and talk for industry. The CBI knows what industry thinks because their channels of communication are good. They can keep government informed in the myriad of contacts they have with departments. They may not always directly influence policy but they make sure government knows the bounds within which they can work in the industrial sphere, and they act as a check on the power of the trade unions.

Another director of a large firm said:

> The main reason we are members is because the CBI represents the views of industry to government. They are often successful. If the CBI helps to improve the condition of the economy by as much as one per cent, and in the field of taxation it is quite successful, this makes thousands of pounds' difference to the profits of big firms. It is the presence of big firms like us that makes the CBI influential.

It was not only respondents from the large firms, however, who stressed the representative role of the CBI. Almost every respondent mentioned its role as a counter-balance to the TUC.

Thus, many firms seem to behave irrationally. They make little use of services, and other selective incentives they claim to value would be available to them even if they were non-members. Why then do they join? There is no doubt that one or two of the very large firms we talked to (firms in *The Times* Top Thousand companies) believed, probably quite accurately, that their membership strengthened the CBI's position and ensured a larger proportion of the collective good. However, there are few firms in this position. Much more common was a response from an industrialist which illustrates a typically irrational argument: 'Whether we were members of the CBI or not we would derive some benefit from the part it plays for industry. You get that type of benefit whether you are a member or not, but if nobody was a member you would be worse off.'

This argument is irrational in Olson's terms unless the industrial firm's decision will directly affect the decisions of others when it comes to joining[26] to such an extent that the supply of the collective good is materially improved. This industrialist, like a number of others, was misperceiving the decision-making situation.

As far as the CBI members we have interviewed are concerned, collective benefits seem to be the major incentive for membership, particularly, although not exclusively, among the larger firms. Olson's analysis seems to have limited utility as far as this particular interest group is concerned.

For many industrialists, the question of whether to join and to remain in membership of the CBI is a relatively minor matter. It is hardly worth expending the effort to cross the 'rationality threshold'. As one Welsh industrialist remarked:

> I don't know in real terms what it has meant to us one way or the other. The amount we have subscribed has not been large and the

amount of direct benefit we have had we can't really measure. One cannot really say what difference it would have made to this company or to the influence of the CBI if we had not been members. One tends perhaps to drift into situations and it is only when people like you come along and ask questions that one is forced to try and rationalise one's position.

Industrialists have far from perfect information about, nor do they pay perfect attention to, the CBI. Many believe it is an important means of articulating the views of industry even though it may not benefit each company equally. Such a spokesman is regarded as essential, and most respondents seem to see it as their duty to support it, even though the cost of membership may outweigh the direct benefits gained from it.

We also interviewed officials in the CBI's central offices and in six Regional Offices who were responsible for membership recruitment and retention. This provided useful supplementary information about why firms join the CBI, for after years of experience any association is likely to have adapted its recruitment policy to meet the demands of eligible members.

Representatives of the CBI always stress both their policy role and the services they have to offer when they attempt to solicit members. In fact, the membership secretariat issued a directive to Assistant Regional Secretaries, who are responsible for recruitment in the regions, which stressed that each must receive attention. However, services are stressed when a small firm is being approached, whereas the representative function is emphasised rather more when the quarry is a large firm. In other words, the CBI does not sell itself largely on selective benefits as Olson's analysis would imply. It varies its approach according to the 'sales target', but it never stresses services to the exclusion of the organisation's representative function. Indeed, this would seem sensible, as most members seem to value the supply of the collective good at least as much as the supply of selective incentives. Perhaps the CBI's membership secretariat has a better idea of its members' beliefs and requirements than do the political economists.

Conclusion

Our data represents a far from perfect test of Olson's theory or extensions and critiques of it. Olson's theory is difficult to test because some of the definitions and assumptions incorporated in it are imprecise and because many of the variables involved are difficult to quantify. At the same time, with a small sample of CBI members, our results can at most only be suggestive of possible patterns.

Olson's model would seem to be most applicable to the smaller firms who are members of the CBI. In their case, the services the CBI offer seems to be an important reason why they join, although not all small firms thought that the benefits they derived from CBI services equalled the cost of their membership fee. Such a perception did not deter them from paying and renewing their subscription. Thus, many CBI members are either acting irrationally in Olsonian terms or else their perception of their actual decision-making situation is a different one from that constructed by Olson – in other words, they are acting rationally but operating with an imperfect decision-making scheme.

If the latter were found to be the case, then Watkin's model would provide a more useful framework for analysis. Some firms were aware that they made little use of services but believed that the collective benefits they received would be greater as members than as non-members. Their behaviour can be explained in terms of Watkins' model because to them the collective benefits outweighed the cost of membership; they did not perceive or believe that such benefits would be theirs if they were non-members. However, a large number of CBI member firms were aware that even non-members obtained collective benefits but made little use of the available services. Some of these were large firms who, as we have said, believed that their involvement with the association would materially improve their supply of the collective good.

Nevertheless many firms, particularly medium- and large-sized firms, did not believe that they received value for money from the services. They were, in Olson's or Watkins' terms, acting irrationally. Why did they act in this way? In our view they had two related reasons. The costs involved in membership were very low in terms of most firms' turnover and the benefits of membership were often difficult to calculate. This meant that very few firms we talked to had attempted a cost-benefit anaylsis of CBI membership. Most felt that they should join or were persuaded to join, and the costs involved were not sufficiently high to impel them towards the rationality threshold.[27] Most of the large- and medium-sized firms we talked to had not really considered the costs of membership.

It is possible, of course, that managers in large firms do not consider costs because they are spending the money of shareholders. We are not, however, convinced by such an argument. We did find that managers undertook crude 'cost-benefit' analysis of fees paid to other associations in which costs and benefits were easier to calculate. In addition, we talked to a number of private companies, including one very large one, and there seemed to be no evidence that the managers or shareholders of these firms viewed CBI membership in a more cost-conscious way. Nevertheless, it would be worthwhile in any future study to examine how the separation of ownership and control influences decisions on joining associations. Despite this qualification, there is little doubt that the contributions of large- and medium-sized firms to the CBI fall below the rationality threshold. One might argue that this merely indicates that the association studied does not meet the preconditions Olson establishes as necessary if his theory is to operate. However, Olson himself admitted that his model is inappropriate to the study of altruistic interest groups[28] and to the study of many small groups.[29] If we now deny its applicability when costs are low, can it apply to any interest group? A deductive model is of little utility if its preconditions can never be met.

In our view, neither Olson's model nor Watkins' notion of imperfect rationality is sufficient to explain why companies join and remain in membership of the CBI. The analytical frameworks provided by both authors help us to account for some aspects of the behaviour of some of the firms which are CBI members, but both models seem most, if not only, appropriate when costs are high.

Notes and References

1 R. Presthus, *Elite Accommodation in Canadian Politics* (Cambridge: Cambridge University Press, 1973), p. 131.
2 See especially A. Bentley, *The Process of Government* (Chicago: University of Chicago Press, 1908) and D. B. Truman, *The Governmental Process* (New York: Knopf, 1962).
3 See M. Olson Jnr, *The Logic of Collective Action* (New York: Shocken Books, 1969) and N. Frohlich, J. Oppenheim and O. Young, *Political Leadership and Collective Goods* (Princeton: Princeton University Press, 1971).
4 Sir H. Benson and Sir S. Brown, *Report on the Formation of a National Industrial Organisation* (London: Federation of British Industries, British Employers Confederation and National Association of British Manufacturers, 1964).
5 There is in theory another category of membership: combined industrial/commercial members, for companies which have 50 per cent industrial and 50 per cent commercial activities. However, there are at present few, if any, members of this type.
6 The formation of the Retail Consortium and its relations with the CBI are dealt with

at length in W. Grant and D. Marsh, 'The representation of retail interests in Britain', *Political Studies,* **22** (1974), pp. 168–77.

7 Devlin Report, p. 59.

8 See, for example, K. Hindell and M. Simms 'How the abortion lobby worked', *Political Quarterly,* **39** (1968), pp. 269–82.

9 See P. Clarke, *Small Businesses* (Newton Abbot: David and Charles, 1972), especially pp. 347–8.

10 Although one region, London and the South-East is subdivided into three.

11 See the Devlin Report, p. 76.

12 It is crucial to the pluralists' conception that individuals with latent common interests can at any time form an actual association if their interests are threatened. If they do not assume this to be so, then existing strong associations might dominate the polity. The pluralists thus stress the ease of establishing a formal organisation and ignore the problems of the incentives necessary to encourage people actually to form such an association.

13 Olson, op. cit., p. 132.

14 Olson, op. cit., p. 135.

15 Olson argues that it might be worth an individual joining an interest group for its collective goods if the group is very small (see Olson, op. cit., pp. 33–6) or if an individual's presence is likely materially to increase the supply of the collective good.

16 Although, of course, in decision-making theory even optimal decisions may be made under different conditions, known as conditions of certainty, conditions of risk and conditions of uncertainty. This distinction is lucidly developed by John Watkins, 'Imperfect rationality' in R. Berger and F. Cioffi (eds), *Explanation in the Behavioural Sciences* (London: Cambridge University Press, 1970), pp. 167–217, especially pp. 179–96.

17 ibid.

18 ibid., p. 206.

19 ibid., p. 208.

20 See above, pp. 27–8.

21 See in particular, L. A. Dexter, *Elite and Specialised Interviewing* (Evanston: North-western University Press, 1970), p. 39.

22 It is generally recognised that there are special problems in interviewing 'elite' groups such as businessmen. Kincaid and Bright maintain that: 'To a greater extent than is probably the case in most types of interviewing, interviews with the business elite must be flexible. It is more sensible – indeed often inescapable – to shape the interview around the respondent rather than conduct it in a certain specified manner.' We did not use a questionnaire in our interviews with CBI members but simply had a list of topics which we pursued in an open-ended discussion. Although we found that this technique had many advantages, it does present problems with the comparability of responses. See H. V. Kincaid and M. Bright, 'Interviewing the business elite', *American Journal of Sociology,* **62** (1957), pp. 304–11, p. 309.

23 This is because nationalised industries have little choice about membership. The government expects them to be members of the CBI. This is another example of the way government has encouraged the formation and growth of employers' organisations.

24 See Sir N. Kipping, op. cit., pp. 227–8.

25 One respondent commented: 'We pay an even larger subscription to SMMT than to CBI. We are members of SMMT because otherwise you can't participate in the annual motor show.'

26 It is not only the industrialists joining the CBI who are irrational in this way. In the recent (1974) power crisis many people justified their economies of electricity by a similar argument.

27 A similar point is made concerning the 'cost' of voting by Brian Barry in his extremely useful critique of Downes in B. Barry, *Sociologists, Economists and Democracy* (London: Macmillan, 1970).

28 Olson, op. cit., p. 160.

29 ibid., pp. 33–6.

30 The material dealt with here is presented in a more detailed form in D. Marsh, 'On Joining Interest Groups: An Empirical Consideration of the Work of Mancur Olson', *British Journal of Political Science*, **6** (1976), pp. 257–71.

4

The system of
industrial representation

THE CONFEDERATION OF BRITISH INDUSTRY IS ONLY ONE OF THE channels through which the views of industrialists are forwarded to government in Britain. There is also a large and complex system of associations which look after the interests of individual industries or, in some cases, the interests of manufacturers of particular products, and many large firms deal directly with government. Moreover, this somewhat chaotic system of industrial representation forms only one part of a larger and even more incoherent system of business representation. Finance and the retail sector have their own representative structures and arrangements which stand in isolation from, and sometimes in opposition to, the representative organisations of industry. In this chapter, we shall examine the ways in which the activities of these other business organisations impinge on the operations of the CBI. We shall also be considering, in the light of the 1972 report of the Devlin Commission on Industrial and Commercial Representation, possible future developments which may transform the CBI into a different kind of organisation.

The large firms
Most commentators agree that large firms tend to enjoy direct contacts with government, and one might expect these contacts to become more significant as the larger companies (and nationalised industries) come to assume a dominant role in the economy. Perhaps it should be stressed that firms cannot always readily be classified as 'large' or 'small' on the basis of the size of their workforce or the amount of capital employed. A firm may have a relatively small number of employees but may enjoy close contacts with government because it dominates a particular industry or market.

C.B.I.—3

However, cases of this kind are the exception rather than the rule. The data we collected in our interviews with the directors of companies in membership of the CBI confirmed our expectation that larger firms, primarily measured in terms of size of workforce, would tend to have more direct contacts with government than smaller firms; and the larger the firm, the higher the level within government at which access would be available if necessary. As a director of a motor manufacturing company commented: 'There is a very natural sort of relationship between people like ourselves and government. We have direct contacts at ministerial level. On routine matters we deal with the permanent officials, but because of our size and scope it's generally at a senior level.' Most respondents in large firms who had direct contacts with government took a position not unlike that of the managing director of a subsidiary of one large company who commented: 'When we wanted to influence government after the last power strike, we didn't mess about with the CBI. We went straight in at ministerial level and after that at senior civil servant level.' Apart from those firms which have relationships with government as a customer, frequent contacts between smaller firms and government are unusual. When a smaller firm contacts government, it is usually to ask for information and advice rather than to attempt to exert influence.

The Devlin Report pointed out that there are limits to the extent to which a big company can make its sole voice heard in a democracy. The report argues that the minister will want to tell Parliament that he has consulted the representative organisation of a particular industry, not some large company. However, although he may want to legitimise the process of consultation by talking to the appropriate trade association, the minister may also decide to consult the big companies in an industry separately. The managing director of a leading construction company commented: 'In our industry the trade associations tend to reflect the interests of the smaller companies but their experiences are not always typical. So it is not uncommon for ministers to send for the leaders of the larger companies to get their views. In this field it's the big boys who have the muscle and are therefore listened to by the government.'

The industry and product associations

Devlin discovered 865 functioning associations claiming to represent employers. Of these 865 only seventy-three met the committee's test of effectiveness, a minimum subscription income of £70,000 a year. Many of these associations are in the financial sector, and the representation of manufacturing industry is dominated by half a dozen or so giant organisations such as the Engineering Employers' Federation, the Society of Motor Manufacturers and Traders and the Chemical Industries Association.

Most trade associations evolved as price rings or market-sharing arrangements. They were largely a defensive reaction to increased external competition. Since the passage of the Restrictive Trade Practices Act in 1956 they have had to find new functions to justify their existence.[1] Their activity was not, of course, confined to price-fixing, though this was the main purpose of the majority of the associations. One resultant problem is that 'many of the associations would have had different membership boundaries had they originally been formed for purposes other than price and market agreement.'[2] Nowadays, in addition to making more general representations to government, the more effective associations concern themselves with a range of problems such as cost comparisons, trade missions, customer–supplier relationships, metrication, training, standardisation of contracts, safety and negotiations with the British Standards Institution. Many of these matters are highly technical, but they may be of considerable importance to the firms concerned. A slight change in a standard may mean retooling an entire production line.

In general, large companies, particularly those which dominate an industry, are not very interested in the work of the appropriate trade association (if one exists). As one manufacturer in such a position commented, 'there is no one to tell us about our technologies except ourselves'. Another large manufacturer told us: 'We don't feel that we need a trade association merely to hold us by the hand and take us to the door of the Department of Trade and Industry or the Department of the Environment.' Nevertheless, there may be particular reasons why large manufacturers stay in trade associations. A director of a motor manufacturing company commented: 'We are in the Society of Motor Manufacturers and Traders because otherwise you can't participate in the annual motor show.' A director of another motor manufacturing company also felt that his company did not need a trade association to defend itself. Although it was useful for 'mundane administration like tariff changes in Nicaragua, we're so big we can go directly to government, or all the motor manufacturers could have dinner together and say what we should do is "x".' He did, however, see the Society of Motor Manufacturers and Traders as a useful forum for meeting suppliers: 'Two-thirds of our turnover is accounted for by bits we buy in. We have an infrastructure that we depend on and which is dependent on us. If suppliers have something to say, the Society of Motor Manufacturers and Traders is the appropriate place to say it.' The other motor manufacturer we talked to was not persuaded by this argument. He pointed out that he had a supply manager and a supply department who spent their lives purchasing materials. The way in which the strengths and weaknesses of a particular firm match with the strengths and weaknesses of its trade association is an important factor in determining the usefulness of the one to the other.

Trade associations are of particular importance to firms in industries where the actions of government (or, now, the EEC) have a significant impact on the operational environment. For example, the managing director of a firm dealing in food and malt products commented: 'The trade associations are pretty vital to us. We are dealing in raw materials subject to varying marketing conditions and government constraints. If somebody sets the restitution price on barley at the wrong level, it could halve our profits.'

The report of the FBI Organisation of Industry Committee published in 1944 suggested that 'adversity has provided the principal stimulus to the formation of associations'.[3] Although this is less true now that trade associations perform rather different functions, it is still a factor of some importance in accounting for changes in industrial representation. For example, the threat posed by Japanese competition has helped to stimulate closer relationships among the trade associations concerned with electronics. The managing director of a firm manufacturing a product developed in the last ten years complained to us that the industry was 'run by physicists who have weird design ideas, the result is a proliferation of designs'. Design rationalisation would save the industry a lot of money, but in the absence of a trade association, it was difficult to 'get hold' of the industry. During the preceding year the industry had gone through 'a very rough time and this did enable us to get something done, but it took nine months to get agreement with customers on rationalisation of a very simple product'.

It was suggested to us by several respondents that a number of associations which are too small to be really effective are kept going because members enjoy taking their turn as president or because members are worried about what would happen to the secretary if the association were wound up. Sheer inertia is also a factor in keeping in being associations which have outlived their useful purpose. As the Devlin Report comments, it is often less trouble to go on subscribing than to stop.[4]

When, however, there is a change of ownership, sentimental attitudes towards the trade association may be swept aside. For example, in one industry a series of mergers left two big companies in a dominant position. The head of the larger company decided that he was paying too much for the services of the industry's trade association. The trade association had to accept a reduced subscription and as a result was forced to cut its staff by about half.

Admittedly, the company concerned has a reputation for the aggressive pursuit of larger profits. However, some people we talked to thought that the trend towards larger companies would pose problems for trade associations in the next decade. Many associations are kept going by donations from big companies. For example, in 1972–73, the British Plastics Federation spent £166,805, but subscription income was only £114,244. The difference was largely made good by voluntary donations of more than £46,000 from companies. An official of another trade association told us:

> These big companies can talk direct to government. If there are two big companies in a particular sector they may keep a trade association going just to keep an eye on each other. But if one is confident that it can outstrip the other, it may not bother; the trade association is just another charge which hinders its competitiveness. The head of our largest company is on personal terms with the Prime Minister, the director of a medium-sized trade association just can't hope to be.

Employers' organisations concerned with industrial relations face similar problems. A study carried out for the Commission on Industrial Relations notes: 'Large companies, with an increasing proportion of total employing power, have been more concerned independently to control their production costs and many large multi-plant companies, especially those which are also multi-product, have felt the need to develop their own company wages structures and disputes procedures. This has in some cases led to resignation from their employers' associations.'[5] The report suggests that, in some circumstances, 'employers' organisations may find that their main function is to service small and medium sized firms and develop more as advisory bodies.'[6] Most employers' organisations have expanded the range of advisory services they offer in recent years, but reliance on the subscriptions of the smaller firms may limit the range of services that can be offered. This may, in turn, make membership less attractive to the smaller firms, and a vicious cycle of decline will set in.[7]

Most employers' organisations and trade associations are members of the CBI (the most important exceptions are the Chamber of Shipping and the Retail Consortium). In its recruitment literature, the CBI claims that its activities 'in no way duplicate the essential work' of the individual industry associations. In explaining the distinction between the functions of the trade associations and employers' organisations and the CBI, it is stated that 'a great deal of the CBI's work is "horizontal" rather than "vertical". It concerns national questions which cut across industries and affect groups of firms (or all firms) which have certain interests in common; such as being close companies, overseas investors, water consumers, involved in Britain's membership of the EEC, or taxpayers.'[8]

In fact, matters are a little more complicated than the bland statements of the recruitment literature would imply. It is not always easy to distinguish between a national question and an industry question. Moreover, because the CBI has both individual companies and associations in membership, 'the CBI must also find it difficult to give appropriate weighting to the views of individual companies and to those which have been reached within associations and represented to it in that form'.[9] The associations, of course, have the majority of the seats on the CBI Council, even though they contribute only 14 per cent of the CBI's revenue.[10] However, as the Devlin Report frankly admits: 'The CBI is not controlled simply by voting strength. . . . There are certain sources of power which its policies must accommodate if they are to be workable. One of these is the big companies.'[11]

A number of mechanisms have been used from time to time to coordinate the work of the CBI and the individual industry associations. When the CBI was established, a series of formal quarterly meetings was held to discuss general policy questions with the directors of trade associations and employers' organisations. After a while, these regular, formal meetings were discontinued, but in 1973 they were revived in the hope of detecting 'any possible overlap or duplication of activity'.[12]

The large trade associations and employers' organisations tend to make relatively little use of the CBI. A senior official of one of the major trade associations told us: 'We could do without the CBI. They are too government-oriented and their span of activities is too wide.' We heard similar views from other large associations. Wigham notes in his study of the Engineering Employers' Federation that they found it necessary to approach the Chancellor of the Exchequer and ministers directly 'rather than leave the representation of the employers' point of view entirely to the CBI, which because of its comprehensiveness had to compromise between the various shades of opinion among employers in many different industries'.[13]

The smaller associations tend to use the CBI to fill gaps in their expertise and, when necessary, to reinforce their representations to government. On a strict interpretation of its functions, the CBI should not involve itself in the problems of a particular industry, but it is often willing to lend a helping hand on the grounds that the particular problem raises wider issues of interest to its membership. For example, in 1972, the CBI became actively involved in the problems of the ball-bearing industry on the grounds that 'a sharp increase in imports from Japan, concentrated on a narrow range of products, was a source of major concern to industry'.[14] This example illustrates how difficult it is to make a precise distinction between the role of the CBI and the various industry and product associations.

The retail sector
In general, the CBI contains a good cross-section of the larger manufacturing companies in its membership – and many of the smaller ones as well. However, its coverage of other sectors of business is patchy. Although retailers have been eligible for membership since 1969, most of the companies that have joined are also manufacturers (such as Boots and Burtons). The one department store group in membership of the CBI that we interviewed seemed to regard its membership as being something of an experiment. The absence of many leading retail groups from the CBI's membership lists would not be so serious if the retail trade associations were in membership, but neither the Retail Consortium nor its constituent members have joined the CBI. Indeed, the first Chairman of the Retail Consortium (Lord Redmayne) criticised the then Director General of the CBI, Campbell Adamson, for making 'ill-founded'[15] criticisms of the retail trade, and the two organisations cannot be said to have enjoyed a close relationship recently. In order to understand fully the nature of the relationships between the CBI and the retail sector, it is necessary to examine the way in which the system of retail representation in Britain has evolved.[16]

In comparison with other sectors of business, retailers have exerted relatively little influence on the British political process at the national level.[17] It was not until 1967 that a general retail organisation (the Retail Consortium) was formed, and even this body was limited in the extent to which it could act as a general spokesman for retailers. However, the retail sector is now emerging from the position of political obscurity which it has for so long occupied.

Until the belated formation of the Retail Consortium, the interests of retailers were looked after by a number of small and generally ineffective trade associations. In his analysis, *Retail Trade Associations*, published in 1942, Levy noted that retail trade associations 'seldom show the degree of organisational combination exhibited in general by industrial organisation'.[18] In 1969, the Economic Development Committee for the Distributive Trades estimated that 'at least one hundred and fifty trade associations were in existence; most are small and weak'.[19] The two major exceptions to this pattern of ineffectiveness are the Multiple Shops Federation (founded in 1935), which has most of the supermarket chains in membership, and the Retail Distributors' Association (founded in 1912), which represents the interests of the department stores.

Before the formation of the Retail Consortium, the major retail trade organisations acted together from time to time, but they had to 'start from cold' on each occasion. Many retail trade associations felt that some more permanent machinery was needed. What emerged in 1967 was a loose confederation of the Multiple Shops Federation, the Retail Distributors' Association, the Cooperative Union and the National Chamber of Trade (a body largely representing small retailers). Initially, the Consortium did not have a secretariat of its own, facilities being provided by each association for two years in turn. However, in the spring of 1974 it was announced that a permanent secretariat was to be established with the aid of subscriptions from more than thirty store groups. The first permanent Director General of the Retail Consortium, R. S. Weir, took up office in January 1975. He was formerly a member of the Consumer Protection Advisory Committee which has acted as a 'buffer' between the Office of Fair Trading (formerly headed by John Methven, the third Director General of the CBI) and the Department of Prices and Consumer Protection.

The Retail Consortium has a long way to go before it will be a retailers' equivalent of the CBI, although it was certainly strengthened by the decision of the Retail Alliance to join the grouping in 1971. The Retail Consortium was initially formed from 'general associations' not limited to particular commodities, and the Retail Alliance was set up in 1967 to coordinate the work of a number of organisations of specialist retailers such as the Drapers' Chamber of Trade, the Radio and Television

Retailers' Association and the Menswear Association of Great Britain. The decision of the Retail Alliance to join the Retail Consortium and act as a 'clearing house' for the views of the leading specialist associations helped to clear up the confusion which the existence of two general retail associations with similar names had caused in many quarters, although the position has been complicated again recently by the formation of a Retail Food Confederation in 1975. In 1972 the Retail Consortium was further strengthened by the admission into membership of the Mail Order Traders' Association (many members of the Multiple Shops Federation are also involved in this organisation). Finally, the geographical scope of the Consortium was widened by the admission of the Scottish Retail Federation in 1973. The Scottish Retail Federation was formed to exert pressure on the Scottish Office in Edinburgh in relation to matters in which Scottish legislation differs from that of England.

Why was the formation of a 'peak association' for retailing so long delayed, and why did the Retail Consortium come into existence when it did? Perhaps the most important reason for the delay in the formation of a 'peak association' was the relatively slow development of government intervention in the retail sector and thus the lack of an important stimulus to the retail sector to become better organised. The retail trade has been one of the 'last strongholds of competition'.[20] The activities of government have generally impinged less on the retail sector than on manufacturing industry and the City of London. If we accept that government intervention is the stimulus which produces the response of business organisation, then the rudimentary state of retail representation in Britain becomes less surprising.

Government intervention is not, however, the only form of external pressure that can lead to the formation of employers' associations. Such organisations have often been formed in response to developments in the trade union movement. Gospel et al note that 'historically, trade union organisation has been one of the main factors persuading employers to create their own organizations'.[21] However, the major retail trade union, the Union of Shop, Distributive and Allied Workers, has until the mid-1970s had a declining membership.[22] The Union blamed this trend on 'continuing rationalization' in the cooperative and private retail trade sectors.[23] The Union has estimated its eligible potential membership at 750,000; at the end of the first quarter of 1975 it had 364,146 members.[24] These figures, however, probably exaggerate the proportion of retail trade workers in union membership; other sources estimate that less than one-fifth of employees are members of a trade union.[25] Clearly, with a high proportion of women workers, a high proportion of part-time workers, a high labour turnover, and with the majority of employees dispersed in a large number of relatively small units, the retail trades are not easy to unionise. In addition, it is interesting that unionists in retailing are also concerned by what has been described as 'the sheer incapacity of those who are representing distribution (on the employers' side) to get "with it" . . . in the same way that employers in industry get "with it" through the CBI'.[26]

There was therefore little external stimulus for retailers to organise more effectively until recently. However, as the Economic Development Committee for the Distributive Trades has pointed out, 'imperfect communication between the trades and government has been as much their (the retailers) fault as that of Whitehall'.[27] Many retail outlets are owned by small entrepreneurs who are often openly hostile to the idea of any close relationship with government. Even the larger outlets are often headed by highly individualistic entrepreneurs who, even if they accept the idea of a strong retailers' organisation, may find it difficult to co-operate with their fellow businessmen in practice. As the EDC for the Distributive Trade has noted, 'there is still a strong spirit of enterprise and independence'[28] which is inimical to the formation of strong representative organisations.

It is not difficult, then, to see why effective organisation in the retail sector has been so long delayed, although it should be stressed that the delay can only be partially understood in terms of the relative lack of government intervention in this area. Nevertheless, as the government began to intervene more in the retail sector, particularly through the imposition of new or higher indirect taxes (such as the Selective Employment Tax), the retail sector became increasingly aware that it needed to be able to bargain with government.[29] The need for such bargaining meant that an effective 'peak association' which could speak for all sectors of retailing was necessary. At the same time, government was becoming increasingly aware of the significance of the retail sector in the economy, an awareness that was heightened by the attempts of the Heath administration to control prices.

It seems fair to conclude that government intervention in the economy considerably stimulated the formation of a peak association in the retail sector. However, the government did little *directly* to encourage such developments. Indeed, there is a clear difference between the case of the retail sector and that of the manufacturing sector. As we have pointed out, the formation of both the FBI and the CBI was actively encouraged by the governments of the day. In the retail sector, government intervention and the other factors we have mentioned, rather than direct governmental encouragement, stimulated changes in the system of representation.

The Devlin Report argued that the Retail Consortium was 'having some difficulty in becoming established as an effective body for the retail sector'.[30] Certainly, the Retail Consortium has suffered from limitations in terms of organisational resources and cohesion. Most economic pressure groups find it difficult, even with a large and expert staff, to reconcile the divergent interests of their members in such a way as to evolve policies which contain something more than vague and platitudinous generalisations unlikely to impress anyone – especially government. These difficulties are compounded for a federation of interest groups such as the Retail Consortium and policy formation involves two stages, the formation of policy by the constituent associations and the development of a federation policy. The Consortium has operated an unanimity rule to avoid downgrading any of its constituent members, so each member association has an effective veto over the Consortium's actions. As the Consortium has evolved, a presumption that it will tackle any general problem has developed, but this is an attitude not a rule.

The ability to gain access to government is not, of course, simply a function of organisational resources or cohesion. As an active member of the Consortium we interviewed pointed out: 'All you can hope to do in a trade organisation is to get into one room at the right moment with the right people and the Retail Consortium has done that. You can either do what the Retail Consortium has done with a big, expensive organisation like the CBI or you can do it more cheaply. The Retail Consortium concentrates on a few key issues; it skims the cream.' The Retail Consortium does now enjoy access to government right up to Prime Ministerial level and it has become involved in intensive consultations on a number of key issues such as industrial relations policy, Value Added Tax and, more recently, prices and incomes. It has been suggested that a proposal by the Price Commission for much stricter control of shop prices was dismissed by the Conservative government after representations from the Retail Consortium.

However, unlike the CBI, the Retail Consortium cannot monitor the whole range of government policy. Organisations like the CBI are generally unable to reverse or even substantially to modify major government policy decisions, but they are in a position to obtain detailed concessions on behalf of their members. The cumulative effect of these concessions may be quite considerable. By continually monitoring decisions with the aid of the expertise of its permanent officials, and by sifting these decisions through its extensive network of specialist committees, the CBI is able to exert influence on government at the crucial formative stages of policy-making. The opportunities to exert influence open to the Retail Consortium are necessarily more limited.

Eckstein emphasises that: 'The pattern of policies enforced in a political system is an important determinant of the effectiveness of pressure groups simply because it is one of the situational elements which selects among the objective attributes of groups those which are of special political account.'[31] The Retail Consortium's importance was greatly enhanced by the 1970 Conservative government's urgent need to develop a credible and effective counter-inflation policy, although the Consortium was probably also helped in its dealings with the Conservatives by the fact that its chairman was Lord Redmayne, a former Conservative Chief Whip.

It was widely felt in the retail trade that one reason for the collapse of the tripartite talks on a voluntary prices and incomes policy held in the autumn of 1972 was the fact that retail interests were never invited to become directly involved. Outlining his proposals for a voluntary policy in September 1972, Mr Heath spoke of embarking upon 'the management of the economy by the three parties, the government, the CBI and the TUC'[32] without mentioning the retailers. It quickly became apparent that the control of retail prices would be a major issue when the tripartite talks resumed. Both the Leader of the Opposition, Mr Wilson, and trade union leaders criticised the lack of specific proposals to curb increases in retail prices in Mr Heath's plan. In an effort to demonstrate its determination to bring retail prices under control, the government invited leaders of the Retail Consortium for talks with Mr John Davies, then Secretary of State for Trade and Industry, on 10 October 1972.[33] The Consortium gave an undertaking that the retail trade would exercise price restraint, but not all sections of the trade felt that the Retail Consortium was in a position to give such an undertaking. The managing directors of three joint purchasing organisations for independent grocers – Mr Stewart Whatmore of Mace Marketing, Mr Michael Reynolds of Spar–Vivo and Mr Richard Branston of VG Management – demonstrated their dissatisfaction with what they saw as a usurpation of their right to self-determination by going to see Campbell Adamson of the CBI to give their own independent undertakings on price restraint. More recently, Mr Reynolds again acted on his own initiative when he proposed a scheme for price ceilings on basic foodstuffs which was successfully opposed by the Retail Consortium.

The retailers' concern at their exclusion from the tripartite talks in the autumn led the government to make a special effort to consult them over the arrangements for later stages of the prices and incomes policy. At the beginning of January 1973, the Prime Minister, accompanied by three senior ministers, held discussions at Downing Street with the Retail Consortium. It is interesting that at these talks the leaders of the Retail Consortium were joined by the Chairman of J. Sainsbury Ltd and by Sir Marcus Sieff of Marks and Spencer Ltd. There has been no separate representation of big companies on CBI delegations to Downing Street. The Retail Consortium was closely involved in subsequent discussions on prices and incomes policy, thus replacing a tripartite system of consultation on major economic issues with what was effectively a quadripartite system.[34]

One strategy that the Retail Consortium might follow in an attempt to enhance its effectiveness would be to develop a closer relationship with the CBI. Certainly, the Devlin Commission was anxious to see the retail sector more actively involved in the work of the CBI and in the new Confederation of British Business proposed in the report. However, as we have pointed out, relatively few retailers have joined the CBI, and relationships between the Retail Consortium and the CBI have not been particularly good. Lord Redmayne recently emphasised: 'It is a basic belief of the very great majority of the retail trade that the problems of retailing require representation separate from that of industry and commerce.'[35]

The majority of the industrialists we interviewed were not enthusiastic about closer involvement of the retail sector in the CBI. Some were willing to admit the larger retail firms into membership, particularly those with manufacturing interests, but were anxious to exclude small retailers. Many respondents were concerned about the 'dilution' of the CBI and stressed that manufacturers had research, development and marketing problems which were not shared by retailers. These reservations about a closer relationship were echoed by a retail trade association official who commented: 'The CBI has a long tradition of representing manufacturing industry. It can't be expected to be equally concerned about the problems of distributors and industry. If we were to combine with them, our interests would be swamped. CBI activities do not come close to the particular interests of retailers. There can never be a complete identification as they are sellers and buyers.'

It would seem unlikely that the Retail Consortium will join the CBI in the foreseeable future. The developments within the Retail Consortium itself are of more immediate importance. It is not envisaged that the Retail Consortium will have direct company members (unlike the CBI) and the new permanent secretariat will be as much a creature of the member associations as their master. However, it may be that eventually the member associations will be absorbed within the Consortium and thus become functional divisions of a general retail organisation. The present structure of trade associations reflects past rivalries as much as present realities. The Retail Distributors' Association and the Multiple Shops Federation, for example, share many common problems, and it may be argued that the historical rivalries which existed between department stores and multiples are not a sufficient reason for the two types of shop to have separate trade organisations. A merger of the two organisations is not contemplated at present, but it is the kind of development which might flow from a strengthening of retail representation at the 'peak association' level.

The Retail Consortium has achieved a great deal on a limited budget, to some extent because of the present policy concerns of government, but it is doubtful whether it could achieve much more without engaging in a more systematic coverage of government activity. The proposals for providing the Retail Consortium with a permanent secretariat represent the first step towards providing retailers with the kind of organisational resources that are required to make any sustained impact on the decisions of government. In the long run, one may see a strengthened Retail Consortium, incorporating some of the trade associations, playing an important role within the CBI. Certainly, it is unlikely that retailing will ever again be insulated from the world of politics; whether retailing exerts a substantial influence on the political process will in part depend on whether the structure of retailer representation is further changed to meet the new demands being placed upon it.

The City of London

If the retail sector has for a long time lacked access to government at a senior level, this could not be said of the City of London. Industrialists are suspicious of what they often see as the undue influence exerted by City interests on government. A senior industrialist we interviewed commented: 'There is a false assumption that all businessmen have common interests. Yet to me it is patently obvious that the interests of manufacturing business and the City are sometimes not coincident. In many cases the interests of the TUC and CBI are much closer than the interests of business, the retail trade and the City.' Looking at the problem from a somewhat different perspective, Nairn has commented: 'It is wrong to imagine "capitalism" in Great Britain as a undifferentiated bloc . . . It shows rather a profound (and often contradictory) division into two major sectors: a relatively "undynamic" industrialism with feeble political leadership, and an enormously over-grown financial elite with world-wide aspirations and the strongest influence upon the State.'[36]

The Governor of the Bank of England has traditionally been regarded as the general spokesman for City interests, although it should be stressed that the relationship between the Bank and the Treasury is now much closer than it once was. The Governor of the Bank can no longer regard himself as a 'totally independent potentate',[37] and a recent report of the Inter-Bank Research Organisation maintains that 'the Bank is an agency of government . . . it must, therefore, be inhibited from representing their [financial institutions'] interests forcefully to the government, especially in potentially embarassing circumstances.'[38] The former Governor of the Bank of England, the Rt Hon. Sir Leslie O'Brien, GBE, made it clear in evidence to the Select Committee on Nationalised Industries that he 'filtered' the representations made to him. He would only represent City interests when he thought it right and proper to do so.[39] However, he stressed that he did not see any difficulty in being both 'an arm of authority and the Bankers' best friend'.[40] This view was supported in the evidence given to the Select Committee by other City institutions. The Stock Exchange Council felt that 'the wearing of more than one hat is a common experience in the City as elsewhere, and presents few problems in practice.'[41] The Finance Houses Association stated that 'there are clearly advantages in having the Bank act as a spokesman for the City and for individual financial interests, since it carries the authority of independence and of a unique breadth of knowledge and experience of the whole financial sector.'[42]

As Roy Jenkins, then Chancellor of the Exchequer, pointed out in his evidence to the Select Committee, 'The idea that the Governor arrives with some great representations to present . . . each week . . . is a totally false one.'[43] However, the meetings between the Chancellor and the Governor are supplemented by a wide range of contacts between their subordinate officials. The Select Committee heard that the Bank was represented on nearly every economic committee operated by government and practically every day the Bank was attending a meeting at one level or another in Whitehall.[44] There are also, of course, direct contacts between the city's various 'trade associations' (the Accepting Houses Committee, the British Insurance Association, the Stock Exchange Council, etc.) and various sectors of government. The Finance Houses Association explained to the Select Committee on Nationalised Industries that whether it approached the Bank or a government department depended largely on the nature of the matter under consideration.[45]

The IBRO report did stress that the City was not generally well regarded by industry, and certainly it has not been easy to build up a satisfactory working relationship between the CBI and financial institutions. Regretting the absence of an 'FBI of the City' which the old FBI could have consulted, Kipping notes in his memoirs that 'our only recourse was to talk with individual bankers, brokers, insurers and others, and to invite a few of them to work on some of our committees.'[46] When the CBI was first formed, financial institutions were admitted to a category of associate membership, and in 1969 they were made eligible for full membership. Since then a wide range of financial concerns has joined, including all the acceptance houses and clearing banks, the Corporation of Lloyd's and the Baltic Exchange, fourteen shipping and forwarding agencies and almost half the major stockbroking firms. Perhaps the most tangible evidence of a better working relationship between the CBI and the City has been the work of the Watkinson Committee on the role and responsibilities of the public company. Chaired by Lord Watkinson of Cadbury–Schweppes, the committee included representatives of the clearing banks, the Stock Exchange and the British Insurance Association. Further evidence of the CBI's intention to concern itself rather more in future with problems that affect both the City and industry was the formation of a new Company Affairs Directorate in 1972. As far as the City itself is concerned, there have been two interesting innovations: the appointment of an industrial adviser to the Bank of England (Sir H. Benson) and the establishment of a City Communications Centre to improve external relations.

It should be stressed, however, that although the City is prepared to assist the CBI in its work, it does not regard the CBI as an additional channel of access to government but rather as a means of liaising with industry and learning about industrial problems. Even though the formation of the CBI gave the structure of industrial representation greater coherence than before, this does not really counterbalance the links developed over the centuries between the City and government. Moreover, these links are reinforced by the effective possession by the City of a range of sanctions, movement of capital, influence on sterling, for instance, for which industry has no real counterpart.

The chambers of commerce movement and other organisations

To a limited extent, the separate systems of industrial, retail and financial representation are brought together in the chambers of commerce movement. However, this is much more effective in some parts of the country than in others. The chambers of commerce in London, Birmingham, Glasgow and some other major centres enjoy a well-deserved reputation for the standard of service they provide for their members. But many 'chambers of commerce' are, as the Devlin Report emphasises, 'chambers of trade'; that is to say, they are largely concerned with representing the interests of small retailers in their areas. Moreover, despite a recent revitalisation, the Association of British Chambers of Commerce has limited resources and 'when it mixes the regional views and turns them into a national policy, the result is inevitably defective because it is reached in isolation from all the powerful elements that at present make up the CBI and are outside the Chamber movement'.[47] In fact, the chambers have been most active and effective on the regional and international levels, a curious combination which 'is due to history rather than logic'.[48] Many of the chambers organise frequent trade missions abroad and are empowered to issue certificates of origin for goods being exported. These industrialists we interviewed whose firms were members of a chamber of commerce appreciated primarily their international work. In 1966 the CBI discontinued certain export services such as status reports, agency enquiries and detailed market information on individual products.

In addition to the organisations we have already discussed, there are a number of other general associations to which industrialists belong. The Institute of Directors has individuals, not companies, in membership. It generally takes a more right-wing stance than the CBI, and its journal, *The Director*, has from time to time printed statements criticising the close relationship between the CBI and government. Most of the industrialists we interviewed did not see it as a politically influential body, referring to it in such terms as a 'club in London where you can get a good lunch'. The Institute also provides an excellent executive health service. For some industrialists it may be a 'safety valve', where, away from the collectivist environment in which their companies find themselves obliged to work, they can give vent to their feelings about taxation, socialism and the unions.

The British Institute of Management is primarily concerned with such matters as management education, but, as a senior civil servant told us: 'It does perform more general representative functions somewhat unintentionally. Because it has members all over the country there is a feedback of information.' However, the extent and importance of its contacts with government clearly come nowhere near those of the CBI.

Nevertheless, under the chairmanship of Sir Fred Catherwood, the BIM is attempting to develop into something more than simply a professional organisation. Catherwood has made it clear that he sees the role of the BIM as that of putting forward the views of the manager at a national level. Catherwood is attempting to get away from what he sees as the clash of labour and capital represented by the TUC and CBI. How successful he will be in this rather ambitious objective remains to be seen.

There are also a number of other organisations which receive financial support from certain sectors of industry. Some of these, like Aims of Industry, set up in 1942, are essentially concerned with warning public opinion about the iniquities of nationalisation, 'infiltration' of the trade unions by Communists and other supposed dangers. Aims of Industry has about four thousand members, with a preponderance of middle-sized companies. Whereas the CBI strenuously endeavours to avoid becoming too closely involved in matters of party controversy, Aims of Industry is not afraid of a political scrap. It does not have to worry about relationships with Labour governments, and it can indulge in the sort of criticism of Labour policies that the CBI has to forego. It is therefore a useful supplement to the work of the CBI, offering, like the Institute of Directors, a 'safety valve' for industrialists. If these two bodies did not exist, the CBI might find itself lured into political rows which might seriously damage its day-to-day relationships with government.

The Devlin Report and future developments

It was concern about the untidiness and shapelessness of the British system of industrial and commercial representation that led the Confederation of British Industry and the Association of British Chambers of Commerce to commission an enquiry into its effectiveness. The subsequent report of the Devlin Commission noted the contrast between the 'duplication and confusion' which the committee found in many areas of industrial representation with the 'orderly and logical pattern' prevailing in other European countries.[49] The report was critical not only 'of the absence of connecting links between organisations operating in the same industrial field' but also of 'the existence of links where hierarchically they ought not to be'.[50] However, even the 'coherent and rational'[51] system of representation envisaged by Devlin involves a triple-tiered hierarchy of associations.

Many people hoped that the Devlin Report would offer a blueprint for the future development of the system of industrial representation. However, most of the industrialists we interviewed after the publication of the report criticised its findings in vigorous terms. The CBI rejected some of the report's main recommendations, in particular that relating to the establishment of a Confederation of British Business. The CBI stressed that they were not 'politely shelving the Devlin Report',[52] but there has not been much noticeable progress towards implementing its recommendations.

In the next few pages, we shall be assessing the proposals contained in the Devlin Report. Our own general verdict is that, although the report represents a painstaking and thorough analysis of the system of industrial and commercial representation in Britain, the remedies it proposes are unrealistic at the present time. Of course, any report that vigorously attacks the *status quo* is bound to have its critics. However, criticism of Devlin was not limited to those businessmen who wish to see the state take a minimal role in the economy. Certainly, many of our respondents felt that Devlin was trying to change too much too quickly. One managing director commented: 'Creating a large representative body is fine in principle, but finding out what employers want could be more difficult in a more diversified organisation. If you diversify too much, you could weaken the organisation.'

The basic theme of the Devlin Report is the need for 'the formation of a Confederation of British Business and the rationalisation of the structure of employers' organisations and trade associations within it'.[53] The Confederation of British Business would incorporate the chambers of commerce and represent 'industry and commerce in every form, including financial services, shipping and the distributive trades'.[54]

The report argues: 'From the recognition that there is no real division between industry and commerce, there follows inexorably the fact that what is wanted as the top representative organ is . . . a Confederation of British Business.'[55] We would question the basic premise that 'there is no real division between industry and commerce'. The links between industry, finance and the distributive trades may be closer than they once were, but the majority of the industrialists we interviewed believed that they faced different problems which required different representative organisations.

A significant minority of our respondents did favour the creation of a Confederation of British Business, and it may be that such an organisation will eventually evolve from the CBI. Certainly, the widening of the CBI's membership represents the first step in that direction. In view of this possible future development, it is unfortunate that the Devlin Report did not make more precise proposals about the form a CBB might take. The committee felt that anything more than 'an indication of possibilities' would be 'premature and likely to do more harm than good'.[56] Having admitted that its proposals asked a good deal of the CBI and meant a 'period of rather difficult adjustment'[57] for the organisation, perhaps the committee felt that it had grasped enough nettles.

Certainly, nothing in the Devlin Report annoyed the industrialists we interviewed more than the proposal for a closer association between the CBI and the chambers of commerce. A not untypical comment was that of a Welsh industrialist who remarked: 'The Devlin Report was biased in the direction of chambers of commerce. What they failed to do was to go out into the country and find what the chambers of commerce could do. They went to areas where the chamber of commerce was strong like London, Birmingham and Glasgow, but didn't come to areas like North Wales where there are no chambers of commerce.' Some industrialists were clearly worried about the standing of the sort of person they would have to associate with in chambers of commerce. One respondent commented: 'I was chairman of our local chamber of commerce ten years ago. My successor was an ice cream merchant, followed by a furniture trader who has sold out. I wouldn't be prepared to sit under that sort of chairmanship.' Most of our respondents detected something more than 'the semi-tones of difference'[58] between the ABCC and the CBI noted by the Devlin Report. A senior member of the Midlands Regional Council of the CBI commented: 'I have always regarded the chamber of commerce as a place where the retail trade meets and the CBI as a place where manufacturers meet. The chamber of commerce is the place for retailers, garage proprietors, service industries. They should do more about things like the adequacy of roads in Birmingham. Their job is to see that the retail trade of Birmingham goes well.'

It would seem that a closer relationship is unlikely to develop between the chambers of commerce and the CBI. However, we do not think that this is as serious a matter as the Devlin Report implies. Even allowing for the fact that some of the continental chambers perform functions which are handled by other bodies in Britain (e.g. training), the existence of a chambers of commerce movement alongside a system of industrial representation does not seem to pose serious problems in countries such as Federal Germany. It is, of course, undesirable to have directly competing systems of representation, and the closer contacts which are now developing between some CBI Regional Councils and some chambers of commerce may lead to some reduction in the overlap that does exist. It would seem sensible for the chambers of commerce to concentrate on matters concerned with international trade and matters of a purely local nature, leaving the CBI to deal with national policy using its regional councils as a 'sounding board'. Clearly, there will be some regional problems on which both the chambers of commerce and the CBI Regional Council will wish to take a view, but given closer contacts this should not pose too many problems.

Although, in general, there is better coordination between the CBI and the individual industry associations than the apparent incoherence of the system of industrial representation might lead one to expect, difficulties do arise from time to time. The Devlin Report wanted to see the CBI placed firmly at the head of a hierarchy of associations. Under its proposals the trade associations and employers' organisations would be expected eventually to provide one-half of the CBI's income as against less than one-sixth at present. No company would be allowed to belong to the CBI if it was not a member of the appropriate industry association. Whether this would be an adequate *quid pro quo* for the associations' increased contribution to the CBI is doubtful. The report talks of the CBI providing a 'back-up service' for the associations, but it provides such a service already. Indeed, it is clear from our investigations that the CBI often draws on the specialist knowledge of the associations. There is nothing wrong with such a state of interdependence, but it is doubtful whether some of the larger associations would want to pay substantially more for the privilege of participating in a two-way exchange of information with the CBI. Indeed, the Chamber of Shipping went so far as to tell the Devlin committee that it felt it would gain very little – and might lose its own close relationship with government departments – by joining the CBI. Undoubtedly, associations find the broader perspective offered by the CBI helpful to them in their own more specialist work, but this does not mean they would be prepared to pay for a greater part of the substantial running costs of the CBI.

The Devlin Report was also anxious that there should be a rationalisation of the structure of employers' organisations and trade associations. We have a certain sympathy with the viewpoint of an industrialist who told us: 'It is obvious that there are some trade associations that cannot give an efficient service, but I don't think this is necessarily a function of size. Devlin was bemused by the virtues of size, by an assumption that something big is good and that something small is hopeless.' There are many small trade associations who, by accepting the CBI's advice to 'concentrate in depth on a few issues which particularly affect their members',[59] are performing a service of real value. We are not saying that there is not room for a certain tidying up of the existing system of trade associations and employers' organisations. Many employers are eager to bring about improvements. For example, the managing director of an East Anglian firm told us: 'The trade association structure has many inadequacies. At the moment I am trying to develop a group view on the ones we are involved in, then I will go and talk to a few key people who, along with us, provide most of the money for the associations involved.' Developments of this kind will be assisted by the formation in 1973, in accordance with the recommendations of the Devlin Report, of an Advice Centre serving 'as a source of information for . . . trade associations contemplating rationalisation and as a continuing spur to change'.[60] The Advice Centre is headed by Mr T. C. Fraser, CB, MBE, TD, who was director of the Devlin inquiry.

Many of our respondents echoed the Devlin Report's criticisms of the large number of small and ineffective trade associations. However, our research suggested that in certain cases very small associations can bring a stream of benefits to their members which considerably outweigh the costs incurred in membership. We interviewed the chairman of a medium-sized firm in the Midlands who had recently helped to form a new trade association with only six members. A retired executive served as the chairman and the secretarial work was looked after by a firm of accountants. Although this is exactly the kind of arrangement of which

Devlin is critical, the respondent felt that his firm had gained a number of specific advantages from membership of the trade association. It provided comparative sales statistics, so he could see where his firm was in the 'league table', information which had not been available to him before. The formation of the association had permitted the rationalisation of entertainment at conferences. Entertainment was provided by the association instead of each firm providing its own. Finally, it gave the firm 'an organised base to resist exhibition promoters'. Exhibitions were now held every four years instead of every two, with consequent cost savings. This example suggests that small associations may often confer direct and specific benefits on their members in return for a relatively small outlay, which may explain their persistence.

The Devlin Report wanted to see small firm members 'phased out' of the CBI and a new Small Business Council formed which would involve the Smaller Businesses Association, a body which considers that the CBI cannot adequately represent the interests of the smaller company. It has not always been easy to represent the interests of small and large industrialists in one organisation, but most of the CBI members we talked to felt that the CBI should try to represent both large and small companies. The Devlin Report's proposals on small firms aroused strong opposition within the CBI and the organisation has stressed that 'everyone eligible who wishes to join the CBI should remain free to do so'.[61]

It cannot be said that a great deal has been done to implement the recommendations of the Devlin Commission since 1972. The Association of British Chambers of Commerce has moved into a vacant part of the CBI's building and a special liaison group at Presidential level has been set up to coordinate the work of the two organisations. However, sharing the same offices does not necessarily lead to good relations, as the precedent of the Federation of British Industries and the British Employers' Confederation shows. Although the CBI and the ABCC are potentially complementary organisations, there is also a sense in which they are competitive. This competitive edge between the organisations has been sharpened by the efforts of the ABCC to gain a seat on the National Economic Development Council.

In January 1976, the CBI published a new reappraisal of its role prepared by Lord Plowden, Sir John Partridge and Sir Philip Allen. The recommendations of the Plowden Report, which included a strengthening of the two deputy director generals, are being considered by the CBI. Whether any dramatic changes will result remains to be seen. In many ways, the British system of industrial representation still bears the stamp of its Victorian origins. There have been important changes in recent years, particularly since the formation of the CBI, but there is still a long way to go before the creation of a unified and coherent system of business representation.

Notes and References

1 One or two associations continue to operate agreements which have been approved by the Restrictive Practices Court, e.g. the Publishers' Association.
2 Sir N. Kipping, *Summing Up* (London: Hutchinson, 1972), p. 49.
3 *The Organization of British Industry* (London: Federation of British Industries, 1944), p. 17.
4 Devlin Report, p. 68.
5 *Employers' Organizations and Industrial Relations* (London: HMSO, 1972), p. 45.
6 ibid., p. 46.
7 This is not, of course, always the case. The Engineering Employers' Federation expanded its staff from sixty to one hundred in five years, mainly in the advisory and research departments. Despite the higher costs incurred, membership continued to rise. Wigham, *The Power to Manage* (London: Macmillan, 1973), p. 228.
8 *Your Company and the CBI* (London: CBI, 1972), p. 5.
9 Devlin Report, p. 55.
10 From information supplied to us by the CBI dated 4 July 1972. The Devlin Report (p. 22) states that associations provided only 12.3 per cent of the CBI's income in 1971–72. However, this figure relates only to *industrial* associations.
11 Devlin Report, p. 11.
12 *CBI Annual Report*, 1973, p. 31.
13 Wigham, op. cit., p. 234.
14 *CBI Annual Report*, 1972, p. 13.
15 Letter in *The Times*, 23 February 1973.
16 For a more detailed analysis see W. P. Grant and D. Marsh, 'The Representation of Retail Interests in Britain', *Political Studies*, **22** (1974), pp. 168–177.
17 The influence of retailers may be greater in local than in national politics, but this question is outside the scope of our analysis.
18 H. Levy, *Retail Trade Associations: a New Form of Monopolist Organization in Britain* (London: Kegan Paul, 1942), p. 41.
19 *Distribution Efficiency and Government Policies* (London: Economic Development Committee for the Distributive Trades, 1969), p. 1.
20 N. Harris, *Competition and the Corporate Society* (London: Methuen, 1972), p. 46.
21 *Employers' Organizations and Industrial Relations*, op. cit., p. 7.
22 331,597 in 1947; 356,038 in 1962; approximately 325,000 in 1973.
23 *The New Dawn*, official journal of the Union of Shop, Distributive and Allied Workers, January 1972.
24 The estimate of an eligible potential membership of 750,000 was given by Mr A. W.

Allen in *Minutes of Evidence* to the *Royal Commission on Trade Unions and Employers' Associations* (London: HMSO, 1966), vol. 29, p. 1132.

25 *Distribution Efficiency and Government Policies*, op. cit., p. 1.

26 Evidence of Mr A. W. Allen to the *Royal Commission on Trade Unions and Employers' Associations*, op. cit., p. 1133.

27 *Distribution Efficiency and Government Policies*, op. cit., p. 3.

28 ibid., p. 1.

29 Selective Employment Tax was a major topic at the Distributive Trades Conference at Brighton in 1966 which discussed the improvement of retail representation.

30 Devlin Report, op. cit., p. 34.

31 H. Eckstein, *Pressure Group Politics* (London: Allen and Unwin, 1969), p. 36.

32 *The Times*, 27 September 1972.

33 At the same time the leaders of some eighteen retail and wholesale food trade organisations took part in talks at the Ministry of Agriculture.

34 The Retail Consortium was closely consulted by the Department of Prices and Consumer Protection set up by the 1974 Labour government.

35 *The Times*, 7 March 1974.

36 T. Nairn, *The Left Against Europe?* (Harmondsworth: Penguin, 1973), p. 19.

37 Evidence by the Rt Hon Roy Jenkins, M.P. to the Select Committee on Nationalised Industries, *First Report from the Select Committee on Nationalised Industries, 1969–70, Bank of England* (London: HMSO, 1970, HC 258), p. 314.

38 Inter-Bank Research Organisation, *The Future of London as an International Financial Centre* (London: HMSO, 1973), Section 1, p. 41.

39 Select Committee on Nationalised Industries, op. cit., p. 273.

40 ibid., pp. 295–6.

41 ibid., p. 371.

42 ibid., p. 375.

43 ibid., p. 327.

44 ibid., p. lxvi.

45 ibid., p. 375.

46 Kipping, op. cit., p. 51.

47 Devlin Report, op. cit., p. 61.

48 ibid., p. 54.

49 ibid., p. 7.

50 ibid.

51 ibid., p. 55.

52 *The Times*, 22 March 1973.

53 Devlin Report, op. cit., p. 15.

54 ibid., p. 16.

55 ibid., p. 14.

56 ibid., p. 62.

57 ibid., p. 57.

58 ibid., p. 13.

59 Confederation of British Industry, *A Review of Mechanical Engineering Trade Assocations* (London: CBI, 1966), p. 8.

60 *CBI Annual Report*, 1973, p. 31.   61 ibid.

5

Decision-making in the CBI

THE ACCUSATION THAT 'GROUP SPOKESMEN ARE UNREPRESENTATIVE OF an apathetic membership'[1] is one that has frequently been levelled at interest groups. In the case of the CBI, arguments that the organisation is essentially undemocratic acquired a new significance as the Heath government of 1970–74 moved towards a 'tripartite' style of government in which the CBI and TUC were involved alongside the government in the making of major economic decisions. One of the arguments used by those who disapprove of the tripartite style of government is that the CBI and the TUC are 'irresponsible oligarchies', that 'it is questionable whether organisations such as the CBI and TUC reflect the desires of their members at all satisfactorily; they are far less democratic, even within their limits, than our own parliamentary democracy'.[2] In this chapter we are concerned to examine whether the internal decision-making arrangements of the CBI result in policies which reflect the general state of industrial opinion.

The internal decision-making structure of the Confederation of British Industry was closely modelled on that of the Federation of British Industries. In particular, the CBI, like the FBI, is ultimately responsible for its actions to a council of some four hundred members drawn from member companies and employers' associations. The CBI likes to think of its Council as the 'parliament of British management'.[3] Like its counterpart round the corner in the Palace of Westminster, industry's parliament in Tothill Street is as much a debating and legitimising body as a forum where crucial decisions are taken. However, an effort is made to make the CBI Council representative of the organisation's membership in terms of sectors of activity, size and location. Under the original arrangements for the selection of Council members, two hundred representatives were nominated by trade associations; one hundred and thirty-five members were elected by individual firms, each firm being a member of one of forty-two 'electoral panels' covering a sector of industry, the number of Council members elected by each panel being related to the number of employees of member firms in the industry; thirty-six members were elected by the Regional Councils; the past presidents, President, Vice-President and committee chairmen were ex-officio members, and up to twenty members could be coopted.

Some difficulties were encountered in operating this system for the selection of the Council. In particular, the electoral panels were criticised by some members. A number of firms complained that they did not know other members of their panel and were therefore unable to make a meaningful choice in elections. It was felt that, as a consequence, the system tended to work in favour of the large firms with 'household names'.

Under changes introduced in 1969, the trade associations were still allowed to nominate two hundred members to the CBI Council.[4] However, the electoral panels were abolished and, as part of a more general effort to strengthen the regional organisation, the CBI's twelve Regional Councils were given a new role in the selection process. The Regional Councils now have fifty representatives of their own membership on the central body and also select another fifty Council members from individual firms who need not be members of a Regional Council. Thus, the Regional Councils are responsible for the selection of a hundred members, compared with thirty-six under the old arrangements. In addition, the General Purposes Committee can now nominate a minimum of seventy-five and a maximum of one hundred Council members. The proportion of coopted members has thus increased under the new arrangements. Some fears were expressed at the time of these changes in the composition of the Council that they might reflect and reinforce a trend towards oligarchal 'big business' domination of the CBI. However, it is in the CBI's interests to recruit and retain as large a proportion of its eligible membership as possible, and the organisation's leadership is concerned to ensure that small firms are given an adequate opportunity to participate in decision-making.

The eleven meetings of the Council which take place every year attract an average attendance of between one hundred and fifty and two hundred. Occasionally, special meetings are held in times of crisis, after devaluation for instance. Most of the industrialists we spoke to who were members of the CBI Council were somewhat sceptical about its value. As the chairman of one Regional Council commented, 'it is impossible for a body of that size to do any original thinking, it can only react'. A number of respondents stressed that debates in the Council tended to be dominated by a few authoritative speakers. A small firm member commented: 'A lot of people don't speak because they feel inadequate in front of such a body of well-informed people, so you get the experts talking all the time, the chairmen of committees, not the rank-and-file. You don't get the cut and thrust of debate.' Some respondents, however, made it clear that they were quite happy to sit back and listen and that they primarily appreciated Council meetings as an educative experience. Among comments of this kind were two from former chairmen of regional councils: 'It's a very good education, I regard it chiefly as an education, I'm sure it broadens people's minds, you get a much better idea of how other sections of industry are being run', and 'the interest was in listening to others more skilled than oneself and seeing how they make points'. A new member of the Council remarked enthusiastically, 'It's most impressive to hear the captains of industry debating points.'

A senior trade association official told us that he thought that the CBI Council was 'a waste of time' and expressed the view that 'the President and the Director General are very skilful at crushing opposition'. Kipping recalls in his memoirs the fascination of the interplay between 'the backwoodsmen and the progressives' on the FBI Council and notes that 'the progressives almost always won'.[5] The Devlin Report acknowledged the limitations of the Council but felt that its approval of a proposal was 'a fair indication of it being acceptable to the greater part of industry and commerce'.[6]

It is clear that the CBI Council is too large a body to carry out the detailed formulation of policy, and that the main task of policy-making rests with the Council's standing and special committees. However, the Council does perform two important functions in the process of decision-making within the CBI. First, it gives general guidance to the committees by debating from time to time the principles involved in a subject under general study. Secondly, it scrutinises and endorses policies which have been formulated by the committees. Before the CBI actively promotes a new policy, the support of the Council is always obtained; like any legitimising body, it is not without a certain amount of influence. As one industrialist who had been on the CBI Council since its inception told us:

'There have been six or seven major issues since the CBI was set up when the President has sensed the mood of the meeting and changed his mind by the end.'

Nevertheless, the committees inevitably play a key role in policy formulation within the CBI. Two committees which are of central importance in the determination of the CBI's internal policies are the General Purposes Committee and the Finance Committee, which is concerned with the control of the CBI's income and expenditure. The General Purposes Committee, of which the President is chairman, gives advice and guidance on a number of crucial matters 'such as the handling of issues facing the CBI, relations with other organisations, and the deployment of CBI resources'.[7] The General Purposes Committee's concern with the tactics of persuasion may be seen to complement the Council's concern with long-term policy.

The CBI now has thirty-four standing committees concerned with particular subject areas, six more than when the organisation was formed. In addition, there are a number of special study groups. One of the most important standing committees was the Economic Committee, which has provided the basis of CBI representations on such important topics as domestic monetary policy, the economic aspects of the Budget and the role of profit in the economy. However, in 1973 the Economic Committee was replaced by three committees, the most important being an Economic Policy Committee. Below this policy committee is an Economic Situation Committee which keeps a watching brief on the economic situation and also oversees the quarterly CBI Industrial Trends Survey. Aspects of domestic and international monetary policy which are of interest to industry are handled by a Financial Policy Committee. The CBI's explanation for these changes is that they result from the increasing diversity of its economic activities, and certainly there has been a tendency for CBI committees to proliferate as the organisation has become more involved in economic policy at all levels. However, the changes may not also be unrelated to an upheaval in the CBI's Economic Directorate following the resignation of its director in January 1973.

Major problem areas often require a complex committee structure to deal with them, as is illustrated by the case of industrial relations. The committee at the top of the 'functional pyramid' in the industrial relations field has been the Employment Policy Committee, which formulates the CBI's broad policy on industrial relations and coordinates the technical consideration of policies carried out by the Industrial Relations Committee, the Safety, Health and Welfare Committee, the Social Security Committee and a number of special study groups. The chairman of the Employment Policy Committee is also usually chairman of the Labour and Social Affairs Committee, which is seen by the CBI as providing a wider and broadly based forum for the discussion of major policy questions in the field of industrial relations. It has one hundred and thirty members who are mainly representative of employers' organisations, although it also includes members from the nationalised industries and from a number of large companies which negotiate directly with the trade unions.

A 'representative' committee of this kind is not, however, suitable for the performance of the overseeing functions carried out by the Employment Policy Committee, nor can it deal with the detailed questions of industrial relations policy which are the responsibility of the Industrial Relations Committee and, in specific areas, the Social Security Committee and the Safety, Health and Welfare Committee. Moreover, there are many problems in industrial relations which employers may wish to be discussed on a highly confidential basis, and the Wages and Conditions Committee provides a medium for confidential discussions between persons engaged in collective bargaining. This system of committees is completed by the International Labour Committee, which coordinates CBI work at the International Labour Organisation and by a number of working parties and panels on such matters as labour statistics and equal pay.

Although the various committees which have been discussed are all concerned with the same problem area, it is clear that they perform distinct functions. Some are concerned with 'collecting the voices' of members as an aid to the formulation of CBI policy, others are concerned with detailed work on particular aspects of industrial relations policy, whilst the Employment Policy Committee helps to ensure that CBI policy on industrial relations retains the overall coherence necessary if it is to make the required impact on government and informed opinion. In his study of the FBI, Finer noted the existence of 'an important distinction between the "specialist" and "representative" committees',[8] and this distinction seems to have been perpetuated by the CBI, with the addition of coordinating committees to ensure that the policy proposals of the enlarged industrial organisation's committees are not out of line with one another.

When industrial relations policy is being formulated, proposals from a government department or a member are normally referred to all member employer organisations and nationalised industries before being put to a committee. As much time as possible is allowed for member organisations to consult their constituent firms. The proposal is then put to the appropriate committee with an analysis of the replies from member organisations. However, in industrial relations events often move so quickly that it is not possible to go through this lengthy procedure of 'collecting the voices' of members and then processing the results through the elaborate committee machinery. Urgent matters may be dealt with by the chairman of the Employment Policy Committee acting in consultation with a select group of leading members. These will normally include the representatives of the largest employers' organisations, although, according to Wigham, the giant Engineering Employers' Federation has not always been satisfied with its treatment in this respect. He notes that the Federation 'were extremely critical of the CBI/TUC "productivity initiative" which they complained had been concluded without any detailed consultation with the Federation'.[9] However, Wigham implies that the EEF influenced the CBI's evidence to the Donovan commission,[10] although pressure from the CBI helped to persuade the EEF not to proceed with a 'lock out' of staff employees.[11] Although the difficulty of consulting a cross-section of CBI members when the pressure of events demands a quick reaction is particularly apparent in the area of industrial relations, it is a more general problem for the CBI, particularly as it has come more into the limelight and is expected to comment on every major domestic issue affecting industry.

Clearly, chairmen of committees are key figures within the CBI. The chairman of each committee is appointed by the CBI's President, and the ordinary committee members are appointed by the Director General. These arrangements might seem designed to maintain in power a self-perpetuating oligarchy. However, the President and the Director General cannot appoint committee chairmen and members in accordance with their personal whims. If anything, they are in the position of buyers of a scarce resource rather than sellers of a highly desired good. The CBI is naturally anxious to secure the services of eminent and experienced businessmen with considerable knowledge of a particular field as committee chairmen and members. Such men are not, however, in plentiful supply. They already have many demands on their time, and companies may be reluctant to allow their directors to take on the demanding task of being a CBI committee chairman. It is usually, of course, the larger companies who have the men with the necessary expertise and can afford to 'spare' them without putting their business in jeopardy. Committee chairmen in the CBI are usually the directors of major national or multi-national companies (some companies such as Imperial Tobacco and Delta Metal have made a particularly strong contribution), although or or two are drawn from trade associations and nationalised industries.

It is interesting to note some of the changes which took place in key CBI committee chairmanships after Campbell Adamson became Director General. Mr Alex Jarratt, a former civil servant with some moderately radical ideas about business life, replaced Sir Hugh Weeks, a more traditional guardian of private enterprise, as chairman of the key Economic (now Economic Policy) Committee. He has, in turn, been replaced by Adrian Cadbury. Industrial relations is in the hands of the 'progressive' chairman of the Employment Policy Committee, Richard O'Brien, like Campbell Adamson at one time a civil servant in George Brown's Department of Economic Affairs.

The chairmen of the major committees are important figures in the CBI, but the key position is that of President. The President is usually drawn from a major industrial company, although the CBI's second President, Sir Stephen Brown, was chairman of Stone-Platt Industries, a firm which ranks 235th in The Times 'Top Thousand'.[12] Although the President's appointment for a two-year period has to be endorsed by the CBI's annual general meeting, he is in fact nominated by the General Purposes Committee. The President in office from 1974–76, Mr Ralph Bateman of Turner, Newall Ltd, had a difficult two years in office. He was faced with a Labour government which initially seemed set to pursue more interventionist and left-wing policies than its predecessors and which, despite some conciliatory statements, seems more anxious to develop its links with the trade union movement than with the CBI. The President's difficulties were compounded by the fact that many CBI members felt that the organisation had been insufficiently outspoken in its defence of industrial interests. Although a more combative approach towards government is clearly attractive, it could lead to accusations that the CBI is a partisan organisation and to a complete breach in relationships with Whitehall. Mr Bateman's first task was to reassure the membership that he understood their problems and sympathised with their point of view. Some members at least felt that the traditional balance between a conservative President and a liberal Director General was restored. It seems likely that this balance will be maintained by Bateman's successor,

Lord Watkinson, a former Conservative cabinet minister and former chairman of Cadbury-Schweppes.

Given the constraint of the limited supply of suitable candidates, the CBI must try to ensure that all sectors of industry and all types of firm play some part in its policy-making process. As Political and Economic Planning commented in its report on trade associations: 'If some part of an industry is under-represented it is likely to suspect that the consensus of opinion on the council does not properly reflect the attitude of the industry.'[13] It is in the interests of the CBI to ensure that the views it puts forward as those of industry are acceptable to the vast majority of its members and that none of them feel that they are being excluded from the organisation's decision-making machinery.

The fulfilment of these objectives does not necessarily require 'democratic' elections. One or two non-governmental organisations (such as the Church of England) have internal 'parties' which assist members in their acts of voting choice. In the absence of such parties, it is difficult to operate an electoral system within an interest group – we have already noted that the CBI had to abandon its system of 'electoral panels' because it was unworkable. The disruptive costs of fostering such a party system within the CBI would probably outweigh the benefits of creating a nominally more democratic organisation. The formal provisions of its constitution may give the CBI the appearance of being an oligarchy, but in practice the responsible officials are anxious to ensure that the views of all sections of industry are heard.

However, the CBI must not only be concerned with giving its members an opportunity to voice their opinions; it must also ensure that these opinions are aggregated into a policy which is well-informed as well as representative of industrial opinion. The problem of balancing these requirements has been a recurrent one for the CBI. The CBI's first President, Sir Maurice Laing, commented in 1965: 'There are those who feel that despite our short existence we should nevertheless have done even more and that we should constantly "fight" the Government. Whatever our personal views we see it as the duty of the CBI to be non-political and to endeavour to assist the Government of the day whatever its colour wherever they take action or consider taking action that we see to be in the interest of industry and the nation.'[14] This 'strategy of responsibility' has, however, not continued to be without its opponents. In a major speech at Cardiff in March 1973, the then President of the CBI, Sir Michael Clapham, denied that the CBI enjoyed a 'cosy relationship' with the government. Sir Michael made it clear that he considered that 'to bawl abuse at governments across a chasm of misunderstanding is popular but uncreative'. It could lead to 'a breakdown of that continuous and constructive dialogue with ministers and civil servants out of which mutual understanding grows'. Wilful non-cooperation was 'a weapon which can only be used by those whose enemy is democracy itself'.[15]

The CBI must therefore choose men to fill positions of responsibility who will command the respect of government. This consideration must be balanced against the desirability of having a leadership which is representative in the microcosmic sense of all sections of industry, and the final choice will always be constrained by the limited supply of men whose qualifications and qualities make them acceptable to the industrialists they represent and to the politicians and public officials they talk to.

The permanent staff
The Director General heads the CBI's staff of some four hundred, most of whom work in its Tothill Street offices just round the corner from Whitehall and Westminster. When the first Director General, John Davies, took over the job, he apparently had clear conceptions about his role and the direction in which the CBI should develop. He is reported to have thought that the CBI 'had become too much like its own sort of civil service' and that 'it had not taken a strong enough line on major issues'.[16] Certainly, a number of similar complaints were made about the FBI by the industrialists we interviewed. Davies put the CBI on its feet (he subsequently became a member of the Heath government), but it was left to the second Director General, Campbell Adamson, to build on the structure that Davies had helped to create and to bring the CBI to full maturity. Davies had spent his working life in the oil industry; Adamson came from a rather different background. Educated at Rugby and Cambridge, he had worked for most of his life with the nationalised steel company, Richard Thomas and Baldwins. In 1967 he was seconded to the Department of Economic Affairs as Deputy Under-Secretary of State and Co-ordinator of Industrial Affairs. His successor, John Methven, has also had a career which has combined industrial and government experience. Having spent most of his working life with ICI, he became Director General of Fair Trading in 1973.

The Director General is perhaps the most prominent public figure in the CBI, and Adamson helped to steer the CBI away from any suggestion that it is an organisation of hidebound reactionaries selfishly pursuing its own interests. Adamson showed himself to be sensitive to the changing climate of social and political thought, perhaps a little too sensitive for the liking of some of the CBI's grassroots members. Some of the controversy which surrounded Campbell Adamson arose from the basic dilemma facing the CBI. If it takes a reactionary line on contemporary public issues, it is unlikely to win much sympathy from public opinion. On the other hand, if its stance appears to be too 'progressive', it may lose the support of its own membership.

Campbell Adamson managed to balance these conflicting requirements remarkably well. He enjoyed a high reputation in Whitehall and among his own staff. Unfortunately, his position as Director General was called into question by some off-the-cuff remarks he made a few days before the general election of February 1974. Replying to a question at a panel session at the Industrial Society two days before the election, Adamson commented on the Industrial Relations Act: 'I should like to see the next government saying right from the beginning – We will repeal the Act, but we will repeal it only when we have some joint agreement that would succeed it.'[17] Many industrialists were privately in agreement with these remarks, but they naturally became an element in the election campaign: 'CBI slips an ace into Wilson's hand' was the *Guardian*'s lead story the next day. It is difficult to estimate what impact, if any, Adamson's remarks had on the electorate, but in a close contest there was naturally concern that the CBI had appeared to depart from the neutral stance it had striven so hard to maintain throughout the campaign. Certainly, there was an adverse reaction from some CBI members. Group Captain J. P. Cecil-Wright, Chairman of the CBI's Midlands Regional Council, declared, 'the suggestion that the Act should be repealed has angered many influential Midlands businessmen'.[18] A major carpet company, Brintons of Kidderminster, announced that it was resigning from the CBI in protest. Sir Tatton Brinton, chairman of Brintons, also complained about earlier remarks by Adamson about the distribution of wealth. He commented: '[Adamson] is taken by the media to speak for British industry. He does not speak for our company, and we have today therefore resigned our membership of the CBI.'[19]

The difficulties created by Adamson's remarks about the Industrial Relations Act were complicated by a more general disquiet in some quarters about Adamson's political stance. Following Adamson's remarks about the distribution of wealth in Britain, the *Daily Telegraph* published an editorial under the heading 'Leveller at the CBI?' in which a comparison was made between Adamson and 'some progressive Duchess on an ILP platform or one of those clergymen who used to add respectability to Communist front organisations in the thirties'.[20] Although one should not take remarks of this kind too seriously, their jocular tone does reveal a more serious underlying concern about the CBI's stance on the major issues of the day. Following his remarks at the Industrial Society meeting, Adamson twice offered his resignation to Sir Michael Clapham, then President of the CBI. After consultations with senior industrialists, the offer of resignation was not accepted. Adamson's announcement of his intention to resign in 1975 was unexpected and reflected the demands placed on any person who is Director General of the CBI for a long period of time. Undoubtedly, Adamson's successes with the voluntary prices initiative and in developing a dialogue with Len Murray of the TUC weighed in his favour. If nothing else, the stir caused by Adamson's remarks indicated the extent to which the CBI had become accepted as an important part of British national life.

The role of the permanent staff in general in organisations such as the CBI does raise some wider issues which have been explored by writers on interest group theory. In a provocative contribution to the literature on interest groups, Nettl has argued that 'the flow of influence is greater from the government towards organised industry than from industry inwards'.[21] In particular, Nettl argues that association officials are 'temporary civil servants for much (an increasing part) of the time. They see and hear from their opposite numbers in Whitehall much more frequently than from many of their own members.'[22] These comments were echoed by some of the industrialists we interviewed. Not all respondents were as emphatic as the chairman of one large company who commented: 'CBI has become an arm of government, it's a tool of the civil service. I have seen CBI people more at home with members of ministries, junior members of government than they were with fellow industrialists.' Doubts about the CBI's ability to resist civil service pressure were held most widely by those industrialists who were not actively involved in CBI work. The more active members took the line that the involvement of large numbers of senior industrialists in the CBI's extensive network of specialist committees ensured that the permanent staff were in touch with, and responsive to, the latest trends in industrial opinion. In particular, a number of respondents stressed that the senior industrialists who served on these committees were often of higher calibre than the permanent officials that serviced them. There is no doubt that many of the senior staff in the CBI are of a very high calibre and are widely respected both in government circles and in industry. This cannot be said, however, of all the supporting staff. Some of these were acquired by the CBI from the BEC and NABM. Some of them are very good, but some are less outstanding. In time, of course, they will retire, and the CBI has managed to recruit some extremely able junior staff. However, the organisation does not pay very good salaries and it is questionable whether it will be able to retain them. In short, many of the CBI staff are not capable of dominating the committee members even if they wanted to.

However, the extent of the involvement of many of the committee members in the work of the CBI is such that they too are exposed 'to the pressure of the consensus emanating from Whitehall'.[23] This is reinforced by the fact that there is a tendency for CBI activists to be involved in the work of other public bodies. One Welsh respondent noted: 'There are a handful of people in this area who are not just on the CBI, but are on the Development Corporation, Welsh Council, Industrial Development Boards because we are seen to be interested.' One interpretation of the present state of the CBI is that it is dominated by a 'progressive coalition' of senior officials and key committee chairmen. It is not necessarily a correct interpretation (a point to which we shall return later), but there is considerable force in the argument of one industrialist we interviewed who commented, 'the CBI, because of its professionalism and its ability to discuss things intelligently, is exposed to the danger of being used and getting satisfaction from being used'.

The regional organisation of the CBI

The CBI sees its regional organisation as an important means of keeping its head office staff and committees in touch with grass roots feeling. When the FBI was first set up in 1916, it was intended that it should be an organisation with a strong sense of central direction in contrast to the Association of British Chambers of Commerce, which was essentially a confederation of autonomous local bodies continually beset by centrifugal tendencies. When Sir Norman Kipping became Director General of the FBI in 1946 he undertook a complete revision of its regional organisation, setting up regional councils in each of the government's standard regions. The National Association of British Manufacturers had a strong regional organisation and the Benson–Brown report which led to the formation of the CBI stressed the importance of involving the regions in the work of the new organisation. Since its formation the CBI has attempted to place its

Regional Councils more in the mainstream of policy formation. The abolition of the Regional Directorate at head office in 1967 was in part an attempt to enhance the role of the regional organisation. This change was not, however, completely successful, and in 1972 a new Regional and Small Firms Directorate was set up with 'a department to co-ordinate and improve communication between head office and the regional offices'.[24]

The twelve Regional Councils are seen as fulfilling two important functions within the organisation: they act as a sounding board for industrial opinion on local and national matters and they facilitate personal contact with members. Each region has a permanent secretariat which services the Regional Council and keeps head office in touch with local opinion. The twelve Regional Councils are elected by the members in each region; from time to time, there have been more candidates than seats available and ballots have been held. Member firms are likely to know something about the candidates when they come from their own area.

The Regional Councils regularly discuss national issues and the results of these discussions are reported to the CBI Council by their representatives so that regional problems can be taken into account in policy formation. The Regional Councils serve as a link between industry and the Economic Planning Councils, provide the machinery for consultation with local government and government offices in the region, and are frequently called upon to nominate the industrial representatives on official committees locally. It should be stressed, however, that relationships between the CBI's regional officials in England and civil servants in (to take the most important example) the regional offices of the Department of Industry are rather different from those between head office and civil servants in London. Contacts are rather less intensive and less concerned with detailed administrative questions. A more common pattern is a fairly regular general exchange of views, supplemented by more intense contacts when some local industrial crisis arises.

The CBI's regional offices in Scotland, Wales and Northern Ireland have a somewhat different role from those in England. Much of their work involves regular, informal contacts with the special ministries serving their regions. These contacts are often concerned with administrative problems (e.g. problems over the approval of a government grant to a CBI member firm) as well as with more general policy problems. Regional government departments like the Welsh Office and the Scottish Office may welcome effective pressure from the regional CBI because it may help them in putting a case to central government. Case material prepared by the regional CBI may be used in approaches to London. Certainly, the close relationships between the CBI in Cardiff and Glasgow and the regionally located government offices should be stressed. However, the CBI should not be seen as enjoying a 'special relationship' with the Scottish Office or the Welsh Office. The Scottish and Welsh political communities are characterised by a closer and more intensive pattern of relationships than generally obtains in London. The relatively small size of the political community in both countries makes it possible for every-one to know everyone else and form some estimate of their worth, thus facilitating close, informal relationships.

The CBI has over one thousand company members in Scotland and approximately six hundred in Wales, but only one hundred and fifty in Northern Ireland. The latest available figures indicate that these one hundred and fifty firms employ 64,000 people, which is only 36 per cent of the total labour force employed in manufacturing industry in the province.[25] Clearly, recruitment is somewhat difficult in the present situation.

The FBI never had an office in Belfast, although the NABM was active in the province. The CBI has only one senior official there and it took some time for close relationships to develop with the civil service. In a sense, the political problems of Northern Ireland have given the relation-ship a new impetus. There are now very close contacts, and the local view is that 'communication between the industrialists and civil servants is much closer than in Whitehall.'[26] Following the introduction of direct rule there were many meetings with the Secretary of State for Northern Ireland and his ministers; the Regional Council Chairman and Vice-Chairman met the Secretary of State each week as members of his Advisory Commission. The CBI is the kind of responsible organisation with which the British authorities in Belfast are only too pleased to have good contacts.

The CBI admits that the fact that it operates in Northern Ireland at all involves a presumption 'that it is part of the United Kingdom and that, by the implicit acceptance of the Union, by our presence here, we adopt the Unionist standpoint'.[27] The CBI has, however, been more willing than some people in Northern Ireland to develop contacts south of the border. It has had a series of meetings with the Confederation of Irish Industry in Dublin to discuss matters of common concern, although it has to be careful not to go too quickly to avoid offending the political susceptibilities of its Ulster members.

In some regions, there is a system of area committees below the Regional Council. Some of these area committees are remnants of the old district committee system of the NABM. The Wolverhampton and Dudley committee in the Midlands Region falls into this category. It is seen by its members as a 'chance for local firms to pressurise local councils to get things done'. In other regions, a system of area committees has been developed since the formation of the CBI to improve contacts with the membership and to provide a forum for the discussion of purely local problems. Such area committees may have a particularly important part to play in the work of the CBI in areas such as Wales where industry is thinly scattered and road and rail communications are poor. Among the industrialists we interviewed, the most lavish praise for the experiment came from those who were most involved in the area committees. For example, the chairman of one area committee assured us that it was 'where the real work went on'. Another less involved respondent commented: 'The area committee is a bunch of well-intentioned chaps who discuss road access to this area and call some junior member of British Rail before them to discuss train timetabling.' Our general impression was that the area committees achieved mixed results. Often, locally-based associations such as the North Devon Manufacturers' Association or the Mid-Wales Industrial Development Association were able to do more to tackle the specific problems of their areas. One advantage that an association like the Mid-Wales Industrial Development Association has over the CBI is that its permanent staff are located in the area. The CBI recognises the importance of this factor and has considered opening an office in Colwyn Bay to service the North Wales area.

Although the CBI has devoted a great deal of attention to refurbishing the regional organisation it inherited from the FBI, the Regional Offices are, like other sections of the organisation, competing for an annual budget of about £2.6 million a year, which may seem to be large but is not really adequate in relation to the tasks the CBI attempts to undertake. The staffs of Regional Offices are quite small – Birmingham, which is the most important regional headquarters outside London in terms of members served, has a senior staff of four – and much of the energy of these Regional Officers is devoted to the important but time-consuming tasks of 'cultivating' the CBI's existing membership and recruiting new members. More often than not, the staff of the CBI's Regional Office in a particular city will be smaller than that of the local chamber of commerce – a complete reversal of the national situation – or of a trade association serving a locally-based industry. The position of the London and South-Eastern Regional Council, which operates from Tothill Street, is rather different. Its membership includes directors of many large firms based in London and it would appear to be particularly influential within the CBI.

The Devlin Report passes some harsh judgements on the CBI's regional organisation. The report concluded, 'the CBI over-estimates its strength and effectiveness in the regions'.[28] As one might expect, those CBI members we interviewed who were most actively involved in the work of the Regional Councils tended to hold the most favourable views about their effectiveness. Nevertheless, even some of those respondents who were active members of a CBI Regional Council were critical of the work of the CBI's regional organisation. One respondent characterised regional councils as 'a placid offshoot of communication from the centre, they tend to come and tell us what they've done, to cloak it with amusing backstairs gossip that makes one appear to be in the centre of things, but it's all cut and dried by the time it comes back to the regions'. A respondent with long experience of the FBI and CBI commented: 'The Regional Councils are of relatively little value in the CBI organisation. They are largely attended by people who like attending meetings. There is no real communication between the Regional Council members and the ordinary CBI members in their immediate vicinity.' There was, however, a general consensus of opinion that the regional organisation of the CBI was more effective than that of the FBI. As one respondent commented, 'I certainly think that in the three years that I've been on the Regional Council, the members are taking a much greater interest in the CBI and firms are sending their senior people. They're not just saying, "Send old Sidney, he'll keep our seat warm." Industry is now taking the CBI seriously.'

Nevertheless, as one Regional Council chairman pointed out, 'Regional Councils meet only four or six times a year. You can't check or double-check everything.' All the Regional Council chairmen now have small groups of senior members whom they can consult for a speedy reaction to developing events. However, CBI staff admit that it is not always easy to obtain 'positive feedback' in the limited time often available. The value of the Regional Councils as sounding boards of grass roots opinion is further limited by the fact that, although the Regional Councils are generally representative in the 'microcosmic' sense, they may not necessarily reflect the spectrum of industrial opinion. This problem is accentuated by the lack of communication between Regional Council members and ordinary members. The CBI has tried to get round this problem by holding area meetings, but unless they are concerned with a controversial topic they are not always well attended.

Whether or not the CBI's Regional Councils reflect the balance of industrial opinion – and for much of the time they probably do – they certainly have influence within the CBI's decision-making structure. In 1967 the CBI strongly opposed the introduction of Regional Employment Premium. In 1973 they argued that it should be retained at least until 1978. In changing its mind about REP, the CBI was greatly influenced by the view of its members in development areas, as expressed through their Regional Councils, that the abolition of the premium would have serious repercussions on local industrial confidence. Indeed, regional development is an area in which the CBI's Regional Councils are generally influential.

The CBI and the smaller firm

In order to be effective, an interest group which claims to speak for a particular section of the community must organise as large a proportion as possible of its eligible membership. As the CBI has itself pointed out: 'There is . . . strength in numbers and the CBI's efforts will be strengthened as its small firm membership (which already comprises more than one-third of the total number of individual company members) increases. . . . The larger the number of members we have, the more authoritatively we can speak.'[29] The CBI has approximately 4,500 small firms in membership; it has been estimated that there are 820,000 small businesses in Britain.[30] More small businesses are in membership of the Smaller Businesses Association (which claims over 1,000 direct members, although this is said to represent substantially more firms) or the National Chamber of Trade than are in the CBI. Moreover, the Association of British Chambers of Commerce has recently been placing particular emphasis on its ability to look after the needs of smaller firms and has initiated negotiations with the National Chamber of Trade and the Smaller Businesses Association (now renamed the Association of Independent Businesses) to form a coordinated front on behalf of small firm interests.

The CBI has made a considerable effort to pay special attention to the problems of small firms. Up to 10 per cent of the central committee membership and 25 per cent of Regional Council membership is supposed to be representative of the small manufacturer. As we have noted, most of the key posts in the organisation tend to be held by directors of larger firms. However, small firms may not necessarily be unhappy about this situation. They may feel that they are unable to spare their managers for work which is not of immediate, direct benefit to the company and they may consider that in any case the directors of the larger firms have expertise which equips them to deal with problems of public policy affecting industry. In his study of the FBI, Finer quoted an informant who stated, ' "You come to the meeting, and there are all the big boys stuck up at the front." But this is to be understood, as he went on to make clear, only as part of the businessmen's general attitude that the bigger the firm, the bigger its stake and therefore its entitlement to "the big say". So long as the big boys make their points for them, the smaller firms are content to sit quiet at the back.'[31]

However, smaller firms do not always feel confident that an organisation in which larger firms are dominant will necessarily articulate their point of view. When the CBI was being formed, a number of smaller firms were apparently concerned that the new organisation would be too muted in its defence of private enterprise, that it would be too willing to enter into a cosy, corporate relationship with government. A number of smaller firms refused to join and set up the Society of Independent Manufacturers, later the Smaller Businesses Association, to represent their point of view. However, despite its claim of success in making representations to the Department of Trade and Industry, the Smaller Businesses Association's demand for the appointment of a senior minister with sole responsibility for privately owned business, with the full-time task of understanding and keeping the Cabinet informed of their problems, reflects a persistent feeling among smaller businessmen that they are not really listened to by government. This has led to some calls for militant action, leaders of small business organisations pointing to the success enjoyed by French organisations which have adopted militant tactics.[32]

Apart from guaranteeing them 10 per cent representation on its committees, the CBI has tried to retain the loyalty of small firms in two ways. First, it has made special arrangements within the organisation for the articulation of their point of view. Initially, it set up a Steering Group for Small Firms to ensure that their views were articulated systematically. This was subsequently upgraded into a full standing committee of the CBI, which has now acquired the special status of a Smaller Firms Council. The Council has generally been a loyal supporter of CBI policies, including the voluntary prices initiative, even though 'it was not generally to the advantage of small firms to be restricted in this way owing to the distortion which the policy created'.[33] A second way in which the CBI tries to help its small firm members is, of course, by providing a wide range of services which are particularly useful to the smaller firm which lacks expertise of its own in certain specialised areas.

The CBI's recruitment literature stresses that 'small firms really matter to the CBI', but some independent observers are not convinced that the CBI has successfully defended the interests of its small firm members. The Bolton Committee on Small Firms concluded that small businessmen had been 'extremely ineffective as a pressure group',[34] although the formation of the CBI's Smaller Firms Council had done something to improve matters. In part, the committee felt, this was because small businessmen were overwhelmingly Conservative in their politics and 'unqualified loyalty to one party may result in the small firm being taken for granted by one side and written off by the other'.[35] Moreover, 'small businessmen are often fiercely independent, very reluctant to join in group activities, and also heavily overworked so that even if they have the inclination for such activities it is very hard to find time for them'.[36]

Most of the industrialists we interviewed thought that the CBI had already done more than enough to look after the special interests of small firms. Indeed, among some large firms, there was a feeling that too much notice of smaller firms was taken by the CBI. One respondent remarked: 'There is more talk about small firms at national council and regional council than anything else. It's overdone, it's almost got neurotic, a nursemaid attitude.' Some small firm respondents, however, were not entirely satisfied. One member of the Smaller Firms Council told us:

> There is a big business grip on the CBI. In big firms people can take twelve months or two years off to participate in the CBI. The CBI administrators are very good, but they would be better off for having experienced some of the problems they are trying to solve. I can understand the difficulties that face a small firm, I can explain them, but you can never impart the feeling. Not enough administrators have experienced just what it means. You know that when you talk to some people at the CBI they don't know anything they haven't gleaned from reports.

The formation of a small firms division within the Department of Trade and Industry gave small firms their own point of access within government, but many people still take the view of David Mitchell, Conservative MP for Basingstoke, that the contribution and problems of small firms are not sufficiently recognised in 'the corridors of power'.[37] In

1973 Mitchell formed a Conservative backbench committee with thirty members to speak on behalf of small firms. Mitchell argues: 'There has been an enormous tendency for governments to go to the CBI as if it were the voice of all industry, whereas there are often quite differing interests for the smaller firms.'[38]

The Bolton Committee wanted to see the various representative bodies for small businessmen cooperate 'with the object of presenting a common front to government wherever possible'.[39] Although the ABCC initiative may achieve something in this direction, it is difficult to believe that agreement between the Smaller Firms Council of the CBI and the Smaller Businesses Association will be possible very often. The two bodies adopt fundamentally different strategies and tactics in attempting to influence government. The Smaller Firms Council follows the usual CBI line of maintaining a 'constructive dialogue' with government. The Smaller Businesses Association, although denying that it is in any sense Poujadiste, adopts more of a 'drum-beating' approach, vigorously articulating the demands of small businessmen whether or not they contrast strongly with current government thinking. The problem with the latter approach is that civil servants do not like the sound of drums, the problem with the former is that an organisation can be drawn into a deadly collectivist embrace which stifles its independence and vitality until it becomes a willing pawn in power struggles within government.

The CBI derives about 13 per cent of its income from firms with less than two hundred employees. It probably costs rather more than this income to provide these firms with the services they demand. However, there is more to the problem of small firm participation in the CBI than simple questions of income and expenditure. One of the major constraints on the CBI is that it can be labelled by its opponents as an organisation of 'big business'. This is a dangerous accusation, because neither Conservative nor Labour governments are anxious to appear to be in the pockets of big business. As long as the CBI has small firm members, it can at least counter that it also represents the small entrepreneur. It seems likely that the CBI will continue to offer a home to those small industrialists who prefer an organisation which can back up a constructive dialogue with government with staff resources far greater than those possessed by its rivals.

The nationalised industries
Industrialists might be expected to be hostile to state enterprise in any form. Certainly, individual firms have provided most of the funds for the

various 'defence organisations' which have endeavoured to present to the British public the claims of private enterprise. However, towards the end of the 1950s there were signs of a new attitude, at least on the part of the leaders of the employers' organisations, towards the nationalised industries. In 1960, the FBI held a conference at Brighton to consider various problems facing British industry, and the fact that representatives of the nationalised industries were present is evidence of the development of a closer relationship between the private and public sectors.

When the CBI was established in 1965, it was decided to admit the nationalised industries to membership as industrial associates. It was recognised that 'their membership of the CBI could create embarrassment when certain subjects are under discussion and arrangements were made to avoid this'.[40] However, it was felt that there were many areas in which the interests of the boards of nationalised industries as large employers of labour coincided with those of privately owned industry and that advantage would accrue to both from their common membership of the CBI. Representatives of the nationalised industries soon began to play an important part in the committee work of the new organisation, and in 1969 the category of associate membership was abolished and the nationalised industries were admitted to full membership.

Despite the CBI's opposition to the extension of state ownership, the relationship with the nationalised industries seems generally to have been a fruitful one, but tensions over divergences of opinion on policy problems have arisen from time to time, particularly when any extension or diminution of the size of the public sector has been the subject of debate. The CBI's opposition in 1966 to government proposals to extend the manufacturing powers of the nationalised industries does not seem to have placed a particular strain on relationships, but in 1971 'mounting disagreement' was reported within the CBI over the government's plans for selling parts of the public sector to private industry. The chairmen of the nationalised industries were anxious to protect their own concerns, whilst the heads of a number of major companies wanted to see the public sector severely pruned. It should be stressed that public and private industry were in agreement over a number of points, and there was certainly no likelihood of relations being broken off between the state industries and the CBI. However, it was necessary to arrive at a formula whereby the CBI indicated in its talks with the Department of Trade and Industry that nationalised industry members had expressed reservations about some of its proposals.

Nationalised industry membership of the CBI may have a moderating effect on both the organisation's outlook and policies. The pro-state enterprise Public Enterprise Group welcomed a CBI statement in 1971 as taking a 'remarkably undoctrinaire view of the nationalised industries' and commented 'the document as a whole may be quite a strong weapon for the public corporations as they continue their fight for existence under a Conservative government'.[41] Nevertheless, the existence of latent tension is indicated by the fact that the CBI has two committees dealing with the nationalised industries. The Committee on State Intervention in Private Industry performs a 'watchdog' role on the boundary between the public and private sectors, whereas the Committee on Private and Public Sector Relationships endeavours to create an atmosphere of understanding between public and private industry.

The nationalised industry members of the CBI we talked to seemed to value their membership of the organisation for two main reasons. First, it allowed them to keep in touch with industrial developments within their region and nationally. One respondent commented: 'The main advantage I get from the Regional Council is a review of the state of business. At each meeting we go round the table and everyone says how they are doing. It gives me a barometer of local business. This sort of information helps me in my forward budgeting. Also, I can go through the CBI briefs with our management team and I can say, "This is what the CBI is saying to government, what will happen to our business if it went through?" ' Second, it improves their range of customer contacts. This should not be interpreted as meaning that nationalised industry representatives attend Regional Council meetings to listen to a long list of all too familiar complaints. As a British Rail divisional manager commented: 'We don't get railway complaints in the parochial sense that if I went to a chamber of trade you might get the chairman complaining that he had a dirty seat when he went to Bristol.' Nor do nationalised industry representatives use the CBI as a way of getting new customers: 'I don't use the Regional Council as an opportunity to go round and tell everyone they should send their parcels by train. I do hope it causes people to say that rail management isn't as clapped out as we thought. It's a matter of creating a credibility, not buying someone a large gin and chatting him up.' One nationalised industry representative summarised the value of the CBI to him in the following terms, 'I don't know where I would find a sounding board with the same range of sounds.'

In general, any difficulties which may arise between the public and private sectors of industry within the CBI are far outweighed by the benefits of membership of a common organisation. However, it is likely that the nationalised industries will sometimes have interests which diverge from those of private sector companies, and the CBI may occasionally experience difficulty in reconciling such differences of opinion. Moreover, it is always possible that, as happened in Sweden, pressure from a left-wing party in government will force the nationalised industries to leave the CBI. Further nationalisation might also place the delicate relationship in jeopardy.

The resignation of the Post Office, the largest employer among the nationalised industries, from the CBI in 1975 was a damaging blow to the organisation's claim to act as a spokesman for the state employers. Even more serious was the formation in 1976 of an independent pressure group for the nationalised industries, the Nationalised Industries' Chairmen's Group (often referred to as the 'Group of 21' because it has twenty-one public undertakings in membership). Nearly all of the important nationalised corporations and public undertakings are members of the group (the major exception is the Central Electricity Generating Board which is to become a less independent body) which was formed in response to what the nationalised industry chairmen saw as increasing government interference in their activities. Although it was stressed that the new group was to be seen as complementary to the CBI, rather than as a substitute for nationalised industry membership of the CBI, the formation of the 'Group of 21' must complicate the CBI's endeavour to represent both privately and publicly owned industry.

The Industrial Policy Group

The success of any interest group is to a substantial extent dependent on the respect in which it is held in Whitehall. Such respect is most easily earned by adopting what is often referred to as a 'responsible' stance; that is to say, cooperating with the government in the implementation of its policies and presenting cases to ministers and civil servants which are not exaggerated or based on insufficient evidence, even if this sometimes means muting the views of members. However, it is not easy to draw a distinction between responsibility and collaboration. There are many industrialists who are suspicious of the close relationship which exists between government and industry today, and who sometimes share Enoch Powell's fear that 'the representatives of capitalism are often at heart halfway to being anti-capitalist themselves'.[42] These fears are likely to be accentuated when government policies with which the representative organs of industry have cooperated seem to be failing to attain their objectives.

Such a mood prevailed in the months after the Labour government had devalued the pound in November 1967. The CBI sent a critical letter about the government's policies to its members, but some leading members of the CBI considered that some further action was needed; one way of doing this was through an industrial Policy Group of some twenty senior industrialists which had been set up under the chairmanship of Sir Paul Chambers of ICI in October 1967 to examine the problems of the British economy. This development was regarded with some alarm by James Callaghan, then Chancellor of the Exchequer, who told the House of Commons: 'I regard as potentially sinister this new organisation which has been set up, with some rather dubious people heading it, who are claiming that it is impossible for this House of Commons and the country to solve the economic problems with which we are confronted.'[43]

The slightly fevered political atmosphere of the post-devaluation period was soon replaced by more normal conditions, and in an astute move John Davies ensured that the original Industrial Policy Group members, a number of whom were associated with the right-wing Institute of Directors, were joined by businessmen with more liberal views. The Industrial Policy Group became a kind of 'think-tank' within the CBI, producing tastefully designed pamphlets on contemporary economic problems.

A new problem arose in 1972, which, although it did not have the wider implications of the 1967 dispute, did nevertheless cause a certain amount of controversy within the CBI. The Industrial Policy Group drafted a pamphlet which argued that British economic recovery would be greatly facilitated if there were a wider recognition of the importance of higher profits as a stimulant to a faster rate of growth.[44] Sir John Partridge, then President of the CBI, and Campbell Adamson found themselves unable to agree with all the views expressed in the paper. When the pamphlet was eventually published, it contained a note of reservation dissociating the CBI's President and Director General from the document as a whole and arguing that the paper did not sufficiently stress the importance of investment as a key to competitiveness. After this public rebuff, the Industrial Policy Group went into a prolonged sulk and confined itself to the circulation of private views and papers on various issues. It was eventually disbanded early in 1974.

The Industrial Policy Group may in some ways have acted as a 'safety valve' which allowed businessmen to affirm their faith in the fundamental tenets of private enterprise. Certainly, internal tensions between 'progressives' and 'traditionalists' (as the 'backwoodsmen' are now usually called) in the CBI have been sufficiently serious at times to require some kind of 'safety valve'. The existence of some tensions about policy within the CBI was emphasised when the Director General, Campbell Adamson, asked the Economic Director, Dr Barry Bracewell-Milnes, to leave in January 1973. The request was made following 'differences of opinion about certain aspects of the CBI's affairs'. Dr Bracewell-Milnes was known to take a classical view of private enterprise and market economics which was not entirely in sympathy with the corporatist orientation which the CBI had developed.

One interpretation of the CBI's willingness to acquiesce in a compulsory prices and incomes policy and to cooperate generally with the policies of the Heath government – in contrast to its somewhat tempestuous relationship with the 1966 Labour government in its later years of office – has been that the organisation was dominated by a 'progressive coalition' headed by Campbell Adamson. Such an argument, however, represents a simplistic distortion of the internal decision-making structure of the CBI. The CBI is not an oligarchy. The leading permanent officials and committee chairmen certainly have a great deal of influence over the course taken by the organisation, but their freedom of manoeuvre is limited by the fact that they must pursue policies broadly acceptable to the majority of CBI members. Loyalty to the organisation allows them a certain amount of leeway, but not too much.

Certainly, there is a recurring tension between those who would like to see the organisation become more vigorous and outspoken in relation to the issues of the day and those who prefer a strategy which offers cooperation with the government in exchange for negotiated concessions. The row over Campbell Adamson's speech to the Industrial Society served to crystallise some of the discontent which had been building up within the organisation over a period of time. Subsequently, the CBI leadership made a number of forceful and wide-ranging attacks on the policy of the new Labour government. Moreover, they agreed to suggestions that a special high-level committee should be set up to advise the CBI President on policy. As initially set up, the committee contained a number of leading businessmen who had been critical of the way in which the CBI had conducted some aspects of its operations. Among them were Sir

Raymond Brookes, chairman of Guest Keen and Nettlefolds; Lord Robens, chairman of Vickers; Lord Plowden, chairman of Tube Investments; Sir Arnold Hall, chairman of Hawker Siddeley; and Sir John Clark, chairman of Plessey. The committee also included such leading industrialists as Sir Jack Callard, chairman of ICI; Viscount Watkinson, chairman of Cadbury-Schweppes; Sir Derek Ezra, chairman of the National Coal Board; and Mr Richard Marsh, chairman of British Rail. Six members of the committee as first established were formerly members of the Industrial Policy Group. The proponents of the advisory committee idea argued that, although the committee would not have executive powers, by attracting members of high standing it would create a strong caucus within the CBI which no President or Director General could ignore. Developments of this kind may appease those who think, rightly or wrongly, that the organisation has lost touch with its grass roots membership, but they may also make the internal decision-making process more cumbersome and thus hinder the organisation's ability to respond quickly to developing political events.

Interest group theorists have stressed the relationship between an organisation's internal structure and its ability to influence public bodies. As an organisation's span of membership widens, the risk of damaging internal conflicts that may adversely affect its credibility grows. There is always a risk that an interest group may attempt to sidestep such problems by 'sitting on the fence' and issuing policy statements that are so innocuous as to be totally ineffective as 'messages' directed at policy-makers. It is a trap into which the old FBI sometimes fell. The CBI has been much more willing to take risks and to make statements which may offend some of its members. As a result, some of its internal disputes have become public knowledge. The CBI often seems to be more coy about this than it needs to be. Just as there are disagreements within wide-ranging political parties, one may expect disagreements to occur within wide-ranging interest groups.

Clearly, there are certain key figures within the CBI who have a considerable influence over the organisation's policies and pronouncements. However, this does not mean that the CBI is an oligarchy. The leadership's exercise of its freedom to manoeuvre is always conditioned by its need on the one hand to retain the confidence of the membership and on the other to retain the confidence of government.

Notes and References

1 A. H. Hanson and M. Walles, *Governing Britain* (London: Fontana, 1970), p. 162.

2 Alan Day, *The Observer*, 13 May 1973.

3 *A Pocket Guide to the CBI*, CBI publication, undated.

4 The Devlin Report called the CBI Council 'a constitutional lawyers' nightmare', pointing out that the industrial and commercial associations have over 40 per cent of the seats but contribute only 12 per cent of the CBI's revenue. Devlin Report, op. cit., p. 11.

5 Sir N. Kipping, *Summing Up* (London: Hutchinson, 1972), p. 48.

6 Devlin Report, op. cit., p. 58.

7 *The Policy Work of the CBI*, CBI publication, 1972.

8 S. E. Finer, 'The Federation of British Industries', *Political Studies*, **4** (1956), pp. 61–84, p. 74.

9 Wigham, *The Power to Manage* (London: Macmillan, 1973), p. 226.

10 ibid., p. 235.

11 ibid., p. 254.

12 1973–74 figures.

13 Political and Economic Planning, *Industrial Trade Associations: Activities and Organization* (London: Allen and Unwin, 1957), p. 178.

14 *CBI Annual Report*, 1965, p. 3.

15 *Daily Telegraph*, 20 March 1973.

16 G. Turner, *Business in Britain* (London: Eyre and Spottiswoode, 1969), p. 87.

17 From transcripts supplied by CBI.

18 *Birmingham Post*, 28 February 1974.

19 ibid.

20 *Daily Telegraph*, 22 January 1974.

21 J. P. Nettl, 'Consensus or elite domination: the case of business', *Political Studies*, **13** (1965), pp. 22–44.

22 ibid., p. 33.

23 ibid., p. 23.

24 *CBI Annual Report*, 1972, p. 27.

25 *Commission on the Constitution, Minutes of Evidence, Northern Ireland*, memorandum submitted by the Northern Ireland Council of the Confederation of British Industry, p. 147.

26 Evidence by R. D. Rolston to the *Commission on the Constitution*, ibid., p. 147.

27 Evidence by Lt-Col. J. Sleator, Regional Secretary, CBI Northern Ireland, to the *Commission on the Constitution*, ibid., pp. 156–7.

28 Devlin Report, op. cit., p. 12.

29 *Britain's Small Firms: Their Vital Role in the Economy* (London: Confederation of British Industry, 1970), p. 2.

30 *Report of the Committee of Inquiry on Small Firms (Bolton)*, Cmnd. 4811 (London: HMSO, 1971), p. 33.

31 Finer, op. cit., p. 71.

32 For example, by the National Chamber of Trade.
33 *CBI Annual Report, 1972*, p. 26.
34 Bolton Committee Report, op. cit., p. 93.
35 ibid.
36 ibid.
37 Interview in *Industrial Management*, April 1973.
38 ibid.
39 *Bolton Committee Report*, op. cit., p. 94.
40 *CBI Annual Report, 1965*, p. 7.
41 *Public Enterprise*, No. 1, p. 1.
42 E. Powell, 'Capitalist Spokesmen and Socialist Government', *The Director*, February 1965, pp. 244–7, p. 247.
43 *H. C. Debs.*, Vol. 754, c. 1441–2.
44 Industrial Policy Group, *Economic Growth, Profits and Investment* (London, 1972).

6

Channels of access

Before an interest group can influence policy it must have access to decision-makers. In this chapter we shall consider the CBI's access to various levels of decision-making. Our main concern is to deal with channels of access within British government, but the final section in this chapter will deal with the CBI's access to the EEC Commission.

Before we can deal with the CBI's access to decision-making it is necessary to state what we understand to be the meaning of some key terms which will be used in this chapter and throughout the rest of the book. There has been a long debate among students of public administration about the utility of the distinction between policy and administration.[1] There is no consensus about the meaning of these terms, and Keeling goes so far as to dispense with the term 'policy' altogether.[2] However, we consider that it is possible to arrange the activities of government along a 'policy–administration continuum'. Policy (despite the objections advanced by Vickers[3]) can be seen as the formulation of goals and objectives and of an interrelated set of general proposals for the attainment of those goals. These are then usually embodied in legislation which includes detailed provisions for the attainment of the specified goals. In most cases, this legislation will be in part brought into effect and often amplified by subsequent delegated legislation or by circulars issued by government departments. This kind of activity is located towards the 'administration' end of the continuum. 'Administration' as such is seen as the application of established rules to particular cases. It is characterised by an attempt, rarely successful, to contain discretion on the part of the administrator within specified limits. The distinction we have drawn between general policy, the detailed implementation of policy in the clauses of a bill and in subsequent delegated legislation, and the activity of administration may be illustrated by an example. The Clean Air Act of 1968 (discussed in a later chapter) was intended to bring about 'the further abatement of the pollution of the air'. The Act embodied a number of general provisions designed to promote this objective, such as empowering the minister to prescribe limits on emissions from furnaces. These provisions were amplified in detail in the clauses of the bill and implemented by subsequent delegated legislation.

We can identify three major channels of access to British government used by interest groups: the administration, both civil servants and ministers; the legislature, both Commons and Lords; and the political parties, both within and outside Parliament. In addition, and in a rather different sense, one might also consider the mass media – and through it public opinion – as a channel of access, since interest groups can and do use publicity as a means of influencing policy.

(i) THE ADMINISTRATION

It is one of the better documented generalisations involved in the study of interest groups in the British political system that the more important pressure groups have, and wish to keep, the majority of their contacts with Whitehall rather than with Westminster. The CBI is no exception. It devotes the majority of its efforts to attempting to influence ministers and civil servants rather than to briefing MPs or attempting large-scale publicity campaigns. In fact, the CBI has extensive formal and informal contacts with both ministers and civil servants in a large number of government departments, although, of course, the majority of its contacts are with the Department of Trade and the Department of Industry (previously the Department of Trade and Industry – DTI) and to a lesser extent with the Department of Employment.

There have always been such contacts between industry and government departments, but their frequency and scope have increased gradually throughout this century. Of course, consultation with many other interest groups has also increased, for as government has become more complex the advice of experts has been increasingly sought.[4] Such experts give government information as well as advice and can make the process of governing and particularly administering a great deal easier. As one observer said after emphasising the gathering tide of consultation: 'Of all the components of the political system it is the administration which has contributed most to the development of the politics of consultation and which has undoubtedly drawn greatest advantages from it.'[5] Such consultation is a feature of modern government in Western democracies, and within this pattern industry has always played a central role. At the same time it must be acknowledged that government itself has developed, within the civil service, considerable expertise so that in most cases interest groups no longer enjoy a 'near monopoly of specialist technical knowledge'.[6]

Why does industry in general, and the CBI in particular, have such good contacts with government? The nature and scope of the contacts which any interest group has with government depend to a large extent on the credibility which the group can establish with government. The basic credibility which industrialists, and the CBI as a body representing industrialists, have results from the crucial role which industry plays in the economy. Even in an economy where there is a substantial state sector, decisions taken by private industry about investment, expansion and employment are likely to be of major importance in determining the state of that economy. In addition, the success or failure of the government in the economic sphere has a substantial impact upon that government's electoral chances. So decisions taken by key industrialists influence the fate of a government, and such decisions are taken in the light of the government's performance in relation to industry.

However, policy-making and legislation are only one aspect of government, for legislation has subsequently to be administered. If a government can ensure the cooperation of those people to whom a policy decision applies it can ease the problems of administration. This can give any interest group concerned considerable influence over the details of legislation and over the way in which it is administered. Administration in the industrial sphere intimately concerns the membership of the CBI and the various trade associations and this fact tends to ensure that these organisations have access to government.

At the same time, industrialists, administrators and senior politicians tend to share common backgrounds and experiences and this too helps to ensure industry's credibility with government. Most of the key people in British industry and within the CBI come from similar social and educational backgrounds to those of senior civil servants and ministers (see Table 7).

We are not implying that industrialists, ministers and civil servants must all think alike, but merely that their shared background makes trust and credibility between administrators and interest group officials easier to

Group	% with public school education	% from top public schools	% with Oxbridge education	% with university education
Labour cabinet ministers,[1] 1970	29	14[4]	52[5]	86
Labour government ministers,[1] 1970	24	8[4]	32	64
Conservative cabinet ministers,[1] 1970	78	55[4]	83[6]	83
Conservative government ministers,[1] 1970	85	53[4]	69	79
Senior civil servants[2]	69	16[7]	84	94
Directors of top City institutions[3]	82	56[7]	59	63
Directors of leading companies[3]	66	23[7]	13	53
CBI Committee Chairmen, 1965–73	78	15[7]	41	73

TABLE 7: AN ANALYSIS OF THE EDUCATIONAL BACKGROUND OF
VARIOUS ELITE GROUPS

[1] Source: R. M. Punnett, *British Government and Politics* (London: Heinemann, second edition, 1971).

[2] Source: We assembled these figures ourselves by tracing in *Who's Who* all Permanent Secretaries and their Deputies.

[3] Source: R. Whiteley, 'The City and industry', in P. Stanworth and A. Giddens, *Elites and Power in British Society* (London: Cambridge University Press, 1974), pp. 65–80, see Tables on pp. 70–1.

[4] 'Top schools' refers to the nine Clarendon Schools.

[5] Ten times as many Labour Cabinet Ministers came from Oxford as compared with Cambridge.

[6] Twice as many Conservative Cabinet Ministers came from Oxford as compared with Cambridge.

[7] Here 'Top public schools' refers to Eton, Harrow, Winchester, Rugby, Charterhouse and Marlborough only. Thus care must be taken in comparing figures in this column.

establish. This credibility and trust is reinforced by the fact that it is fairly common for industrialists to become involved in politics and administration and for politicians and administrators to become involved in industry. The CBI provides us with an apt and excellent example of this process of cross-fertilisation. In 1969, John Davies, then Director General of the Confederation, left to become a Conservative MP. He quickly rose to the position of Secretary of State for Trade and Industry. His replacement as Director General of the Confederation was Campbell Adamson who was previously for a short time Deputy Under-Secretary of State and Coordinator of Industrial Advisors in the Department of Economic Affairs. In addition, soon after Campbell Adamson became Director General, two other former civil servants became heads of crucial CBI committees.[7] In a more general way it is significant that 67 per cent of the forty-one committee chairmen whose biographies we could trace had held public office.[8] This public work often took the form of service on government advisory bodies where they mingled with high level civil servants. Contacts of this sort together with a certain amount of cross-fertilisation ensures that each side appreciates the other's difficulties. Familiarity breeds not contempt but contact and trust, provided of course that this trust is not abused.

It is not difficult therefore to understand why contacts between government and industry are extensive. At the same time, these contacts have multiplied as government has intervened increasingly in the industrial sphere and as economic problems have come to dominate the lives of successive governments. However, many of these contacts are between individual firms, or industrialists within these firms, and government. The CBI, although it is the peak organisation of industrial representation, does not carry on the dialogue between government and industry single-handedly. It has had to establish itself – and is still establishing itself – as a body which at least can speak for all manufacturing industry. How has this organisation, as distinct from industry in general, established its credibility?

The fact that the CBI can claim to be a peak organisation speaking for industry ensures it access to the administration if only because its existence considerably reduces for government the complexities of consultation. Indeed, George Brown encouraged the formation of the CBI for this very reason. If the CBI is consulted as the representative of industry, this speeds up, although it does not necessarily improve, the whole process of consultation in industrial policy-making. In fact some more cynical industrialists see the CBI as the government's token voice of industry. This is rather unfair, for unless the CBI had other claims to credibility the government would not be able to escape so often with consulting it exclusively.

The CBI can claim with some validity to have the vast majority of Britain's major manufacturing firms in membership. This strengthens its credibility with government and the credibility of the government's claim that it is talking to 'manufacturing industry' when it consults with the CBI. However, numbers alone prove little. If the membership were totally lacking in cohesion, and the officials unable to speak for their members, access would be likely to be limited. In this light, there is little doubt that the CBI's ability to instigate and coordinate the 5 per cent voluntary price restraint among its members in 1971–72 was of great importance. The CBI showed that it could speak for its members and, in government terms, act responsibly. The success of this price-restraint policy considerably increased the CBI's credibility with government and within industry. In contrast the conflicts within the organisation early in 1974 inevitably weakened the CBI's credibility with government. Thus credibility fluctuates with performance.

Thus the CBI has extensive contacts with the administration. These contacts, as we shall see later, can vary between grand talks on the economy at Downing Street or Chequers and more ordinary discussions over details of legislation in Whitehall ministries. However, there is little doubt that the CBI is one of the interest groups enjoying the most frequent and wide-ranging contacts with Whitehall. These contacts are increasing and will continue to increase further as governments continue to search for voluntary agreements in the economic sphere for as long as government views the CBI as an effective spokesman for industry.

(ii) THE LEGISLATURE

As the influence of Parliament has decreased, so the major interest groups in Britain have expended less effort on trying to influence its decisions. There are few occasions, even on the minor details of a bill, on which Parliament can successfully amend legislation in a way which is not acceptable to the government.[9] The CBI, like other interest groups, is well aware of this simple fact of political life. So while the smaller individual firms may approach MPs, usually the local MP for the constituency in which the firm is based, the CBI does so infrequently. Each MP may on occasion receive material from the CBI, but this is most likely to consist of handouts of speeches by the President or the Director General rather than detailed arguments concerning particular legislation.

There are of course, numerous exceptions to this general pattern. Thus, in 1969, when the Labour government refused to make changes in its earnings-related Social Security proposals contained in the National Superannuation and Social Insurance Bill, the CBI asked members of the Opposition to press its views at the Second Reading stage. The briefing it supplies on these occasions can help considerably to supplement the limited sources available to back-benchers.[10] However, in this case the amendments were unsuccessful, as tend to be any attempts to make major, or even minor, changes in government legislation once it has reached the House.[11] The CBI, realising this fact, is not anxious to waste its limited resources on projects doomed to failure.

However, in so far as the CBI does brief MPs, it relies almost exclusively on the Conservatives. In talking to a number of prominent Labour party back-benchers we could find little evidence of the CBI providing them with information for use in debate. Even though the CBI has increasingly attempted to appear apolitical, its contacts with Conservative back-benchers are better than with their Labour counterparts. The reasons for this are obvious. Historically, business has had close connections with the Conservative rather than the Labour party.[12] Conservative MPs and leading industrialists tend to share similar social and educational back-grounds. Finally, the Conservative party ideologically has been, and is, more committed to the capitalist system favoured by industrialists than the Labour party.

Nevertheless, this does not mean that the CBI has very close contacts with Conservative back-benchers, providing them with extensive information and elaborate briefs. Indeed, many backbench Conservative MPs have complained strongly that the CBI takes little notice of them and provides them with little information and that it has rigorously attempted to disassociate itself from the Conservative party. The depth of the problem was indicated when in March 1973 Michael Clapham, then President of the CBI, was invited to an informal meeting of forty Conservative back-benchers to explain the CBI's reluctance to associate itself with the Conservative party. The meeting was fairly heated, the back-benchers complaining that the CBI was cutting its links with its natural spokesmen in Parliament. This move forms part of the CBI's attempts to appear apolitical, but it also illustrates how unimportant it considers Parliament to be as a channel of access in influencing policy.

Even when the CBI attempts to obtain detailed amendments to government legislation, it is often likely to view the House of Lords as a more useful place in which to press for such amendments. Although the few amendments obtained in the Lords may seem to be esoteric, they can nevertheless be of considerable importance to particular industries. Indeed, when the Labour government of 1966–70 proposed to reduce the powers of the House of Lords and eliminate its hereditary basis, the CBI noted: 'The procedure of the House of Lords and the comparative independence of its members have proved helpful in ensuring the presentation of the views of industry in amending legislation . . . the CBI (intends) to take any opportunity of advocating the retention of arrangements which would preserve the advantages industry has enjoyed under the present system.'[13]

Despite this, it is true to say that in general Westminster is not a channel which is assiduously used by the CBI. The CBI aims to achieve certain detailed amendments by briefing Conservative back-benchers, notably those back-benchers who are serving on the Standing Committee taking the Committee Stage of the bill, or Lords. However, it has very little real hope of success. Indeed, it is the smaller groups, particularly the weaker trade associations and groups like the Smaller Businesses Association, which actively court MPs. These groups and certain smaller individual firms approach MPs largely because they have no contacts, or poor contacts,[14] with Whitehall.

As far as the Parliamentary arena is concerned, the CBI is probably most interested in the myriad of private bills deposited in Parliament by local authorities and other organisations. In this field, the CBI's Environmental and Technical Legislation Committee examines all private members' bills and has been remarkably successful in getting many of those affecting industry amended or in having clauses in them withdrawn. In 1969 for example, among clauses withdrawn from private bills as a result of CBI representations were provisions dealing with dark smoke, mobile shops, polythene bags, chimney heights, patent rights as they affect sewage and tyre air-pressure gauges.

(iii) THE POLITICAL PARTIES

An outline of a government's likely policy is contained in the party manifesto drawn up in part as a result of discussions within the party machines. Both political parties, particularly when they are in opposition, establish a number of specialised committees to advise on policy, responsible to Transport House, in the case of the Labour Party, or Conservative

Central Office. These committees consider certain policy areas and are composed of experts in those fields who are also supporters of the party. The job of the committee is to prepare discussion documents and policy papers which are then exposed to scrutiny and debate within the party. Often the proposals of these committees fade into oblivion, but sometimes they are incorporated into the policy statements issued by the party and ultimately into the manifesto. Thus important decisions which may limit the future Cabinet's range of policy choices can be made outside Westminster or Whitehall within the political parties. It is not surprising that a group like the CBI is aware of these deliberations and anxious to attempt to influence them.

Once again, however, it must be said that the CBI has few, if any, contacts with the policy committees of the Labour party or with Transport House. Indeed, Labour leaders have always been wary of organisations of industrial representation. At the same time, they have been aware of the need for advice in this sphere, and the result has been a series of more or less formal committees of pro-Labour industrialists set up by Labour leaders to inform and advise them on policy in the industrial and economic sphere. The first such committee was the 1944 Committee established by Clement Attlee in that year. This however appears to have been mainly an excuse for dining-parties, and it proved of little use to Labour leaders. However, Hugh Gaitskell resurrected the idea and established a secret committee of industrialists with a long history of support for the Labour party. Advice was sought from this Committee on matters of economic and industrial policy, and it played a role in the drafting of the 1959 election manifesto. This Committee again tended to work well in opposition, but when the Labour government came to power in 1964 the picture began to change. Once again the Committee became a medium of advancement, membership being used by certain industrialists as a way of becoming socially acquainted with ministers in the hope of political, or perhaps even economic, preferment. The result was that Harold Wilson and other senior Labour ministers stopped using it as a source of advice on economic policy and resumed more informal *ad hoc* contacts with individual industrialists whom they trusted. Nevertheless, the Labour party leader decided to experiment again with a more formal committee, and after discussions with notable pro-Labour industrialists – especially Joseph Kagan and Lord Wilfrid Brown – the 1972 Committee was launched under the latter's chairmanship.

The membership of the 1972 Committee is more firmly controlled than that of its predecessors. All potential members are fairly well screened before they are approached. No one without a long background in the Labour movement is accepted into membership. The Committee is at present dominated by ex-MPs and by people involved in commerce and trade rather than in manufacturing. However, efforts are being made to expand the membership by attracting more industrialists and more people from the regions. The initial aim of the Committee was to provide advice for the Shadow Cabinet and for Transport House when it was requested. At the outset Transport House was a trifle suspicious, but the Committee was consulted more and more, particularly on technical matters, by Parliamentary spokesmen while the party was in opposition. The Committee continued during the minority Labour government of March to October 1974, and its contacts with Transport House seem to have improved. This has been aided by the fact that many of the 1972 Committee's members are also represented on certain of the policy advisory committees of Transport House. Overall the Committee seems to be filling an important need, for the Party's contacts with industry are generally not good and the CBI itself had little or no contact with the Labour party in opposition. Before the Committee came into being, contact with industrialists tended to be informal and *ad hoc*; its existence means that advice on industrial and economic matters is more easily, and perhaps more extensively, available than would otherwise be the case.

The CBI has much better contacts with the Conservative Central Office. There are CBI councillors on many of the committees established within the Conservative party machine to consider various policy areas, although they are not there as formal representatives of the CBI. Industry's and the CBI's views are articulated within the Conservative party at a much earlier stage than they are in the Labour party. This does not necessarily mean that they have more influence over Conservative policy formation, but they are in on the ground floor when outline policy, to be incorporated in policy documents or in the manifesto, is being formulated.

In certain circumstances, the research departments of the two parties can also provide a channel of access.[15] These departments fulfil a variety of functions, but certainly within recent years some research officers in the Conservative party have increasingly seen their role as keeping their party leaders in touch with the views of leading representative organisations. Thus, under Heath's government, this became a limited channel of access. In particular, a number of individual companies, although not the CBI, used this means of approaching ministers directly.

The Parliamentary parties also represent possible channels of access for interest groups. The Parliamentary Labour Party (PLP) and the Conservative 1922 Committee each have a wide range of back-bench committees. However, once again the CBI's contacts are almost exclusively with Conservative committees, although even these contacts are neither extensive nor intensive. Each back-bencher in both parties is a member of all committees of his own party, but the attendance at committee meetings varies widely, and each committee has a hard-core of activists. So if the CBI approaches a Conservative back-bench committee, as it sometimes does, and if it can convince the activists involved about a certain amendment, then these amendments will be introduced by those Conservative back-benchers who are most involved in that policy area. However, even if the CBI can convince the activists to introduce amendments in the Standing Committee they have little chance of success even with a Conservative government. So once again the rewards connected with this channel are not high, and the CBI expends little effort in this sphere.[16]

(iv) THE MASS MEDIA AND PUBLICITY

Mass media coverage and publicity is not a channel of access in the same sense as the others we have discussed. It represents an indirect rather than direct way of influencing policy-decisions. In fact publicity may be used by an interest group as a way of influencing the legislative process or as a way of influencing its own membership. An interest group which has good contacts in Whitehall is reluctant to use publicity as a stick with which to beat the government. Such action would make little sense in a system in which influence depends to a considerable extent on access to key decision-makers, and access on credibility. Only groups with little access to the administration attempt to use publicity as a weapon in a crude sense. Often the CBI's main aim in attracting publicity seems to be to improve its own image, rather than to defend industry from government intervention or to push for specific policies. The CBI's aim is to be viewed by the 'informed' public and government as representative of industry and responsible in its attitudes so that its credibility with government is increased. Obviously the furtherance of this aim is considerably aided by the fact that most newspapers in this country tend to support the capitalist economic system in Britain.[17]

Despite all this, on occasions CBI officials do launch violent attacks on government policy, as did John Davies against the Labour government's Industrial Expansion Bill in 1968, Michael Clapham against the Conservative government's Industry Bill in 1972, and Ralph Bateman's on the government's general economic strategy in 1974–75. Such outbursts, however, are unusual and occur only when relations with government are strained and on issues which the CBI view as fundamental. Indeed even when such outbursts do take place they serve a dual purpose. They not only make government aware of the strength of the organisation's feelings but they also make it obvious to the membership that the CBI is taking decisive action. This is an important point because the CBI is always subject to the criticism, from an element of its membership, that it is too identified with government. Occasional outbursts in defence of free enterprise and against government intervention can stem such fears. A very good illustration of this point occurred in the spring of 1974, when the CBI leadership, particularly Sir Michael Clapham, under sustained criticism from many members, launched a series of strong attacks on the new Labour government.

The CBI's contacts with the press are generally good and they have achieved considerable and growing exposure, as can be seen from Table 8. This ensures that when the CBI wishes to gain publicity for a case or an argument outlets are readily available.

Year	No. of references January/February	No. of references July/August	Total
1960	12	8	20
1961	21	16	37
1962	14	13	27
1963	39	13	52
1964	29	18	47
1965	15	13	28
1966	18	16	34
1967	18	9	27
1968	24	14	38
1969	15	17	32
1970	29	18	47
1971	20	10	30
1972	23	40	63

TABLE 8: AN ANALYSIS OF THE 'EXPOSURE' OF THE CBI AND ITS PREDECESSORS IN *The Times*, 1960–72[18]

If one looks at the CBI's use of the various channels of access, there is no doubt that it concentrates almost exclusively on attempts to influence the administration. In the British political system power lies at this level and decisions are taken there, and so this is where any major interest group must concentrate its efforts. The CBI is well established enough to have ready access to the administration. This does not mean that it has influence, but it does mean that if it fails to convince ministers and civil servants of the merits of its position prior to the drafting and presentation of legislation it has little chance of subsequently changing their minds, even if it can persuade a number of MPs or journalists to take up its cause. However, if and when the CBI does use the political parties or Westminster as a channel, it concentrates almost exclusively on Conservative party committees. Its contacts with the Labour party in opposition, with the party machine and with Labour back-benchers in power and in opposition are minimal.

Levels of access
We have emphasised the way in which the CBI concentrates upon access to the administration, but at what level are those contacts made? In one of the more interesting books published in recent years on British interest groups, R. D. Coates argued that, because power within British government is shifting from the departments towards the Treasury and the Cabinet Office, the successful pressure group will be that which has access at this level as well as at the departmental level. Indeed, Coates shows that throughout the 1960s the educational pressure groups he studied were mainly concerned to establish contacts at this level but were largely unsuccessful in doing so because access at this level was largely confined to the peak organisations representing both sides of industry.[19]

There is no doubt that many decisions which are crucial both to educational pressure groups and, in other spheres, to the CBI are taken by the Cabinet and are strongly influenced by the concerns of the Treasury. Thus if public expenditure is increased in one area, this means either an increase in taxation or a cut in expenditure elsewhere. It is possible that Coates has overestimated the trend in this direction, for such decisions have always involved other than purely departmental interests. Nevertheless there is no denying that if an interest group has access to the Cabinet and the Treasury, it seems likely to be at a considerable advantage. In its short life the CBI has fairly consistently had access at this level in a way that few other groups have had and on a scale which previous employers' organisations could not match.

The access the CBI has at this level results largely from the desire of successive governments to establish voluntary agreements in the field of pay and prices. So senior CBI officials, usually the President and Director General, have had extensive talks with Harold Wilson and his senior Cabinet ministers over the Labour government's pay and productivity policy between 1964 and 1970, while later they were involved in a number of discussions with Edward Heath and his senior Cabinet colleagues. At the same time, the National Economic Development Council (NEDC) has provided a forum in which senior CBI and TUC officials meet several times a year with senior ministers and civil servants. There is no doubt then that the CBI has frequent access to the Cabinet and even to the Prime Minister. There is equally no doubt that the nature and form of this access is very different from the contact it has with the Department of Trade, the Department of Industry, or the Department of Employment. The meetings which the CBI have with a Prime Minister and his senior colleagues are relatively infrequent, are fairly formal, are called by the government and are not usually called to discuss individual pieces of legislation. In effect then, these meetings are very different from the negotiating sessions that the CBI officials hold with officials of the Departments of Trade and Industry which are much less formal, are often instigated by the CBI, and concentrate on the discussion of detailed aspects of individual legislative proposals.

If one follows Coates' argument, one would expect the CBI's contacts with the Cabinet to be more important to the organisation than its contacts with the individual departments. However, this does not at present appear to us to be so, although the picture may change. In the future, it is possible that meetings between government, CBI and TUC will play a crucial role in the determination of policy in the economic and industrial sphere. They did not do so during the period of the Heath government, largely because no basis of consensus, around which negotiations might have taken place, existed between the TUC and the Conservative government. This meant that in discussions over the various phases of the Heath government's prices and incomes policy, the government could make little real acknowledgment of the CBI-initiated price-restraint policy to which large sections of manufacturing industry voluntarily agreed in 1971–72.

The return of the Labour Government after the General Election of

February 1974 did nothing initially to improve the CBI's position in talks with the Cabinet, nor to encourage those observers who saw tripartism as a solution to Britain's economic problems. Certainly, there were much closer contacts between the new government and the TUC. This resulted, amongst other things, in the establishment of a voluntary wage policy as an outcome of the Social Contract developed between the TUC and the Labour Party while in opposition. The CBI had no influence here, nor were they able to exert much influence over the shape of the £6 wage limit in 1975/76, or the subsequent 4½ per cent wage norm agreed in April 1976 between the Chancellor and the General Council of the TUC. Again these reflected the good access the TUC enjoyed to the Labour Cabinet in the field of prices and incomes policy. However, the worsening economic position caused the government to respond more favourably to pressure from industry and the CBI, particularly in the area of price controls and taxation.

Thus by spring 1976 it is possible to argue that while the TUC enjoys better access to the Labour Cabinet than it has previously had to any other Cabinet, there are also signs that the CBI and industry are increasingly being consulted on economic policy. Nevertheless, there is still no real sign of active cooperation between the TUC, the CBI and the government in developing a coherent economic policy. At present it seems to us that it is in the everyday negotiations with the individual government departments where the CBI's influence is most evident. Access at this level is not so dramatic, but at present it is likely to be more productive.

The form of access

A considerable amount has been written on the form of the access interest groups have within our political system, and a number of typologies have been used. The most usual distinction is between informal and formal contacts involving interest groups and government. When researchers refer to formal contact they are usually confining themselves to the interest group's contact with the administration through the medium of government advisory bodies. However, it must be remembered that the term 'advisory body' describes a wide variety of different types of groups.

Dion, in a recent contribution to the literature on the comparative study of interest groups, identifies three different criteria which could be used to classify consultative bodies:[20] according to the amount of publicity their deliberations receive – do they deliberate in public or private, and are their recommendations published?; according to their official status –

are they official, semi-official or unofficial?; and, perhaps most crucially, according to their status and power – does government have to consult them or is consultation optional, and are their decisions in any way binding on government? In the pattern of advisory bodies in this country we have consultative committees which fit into most of Dion's categories, although it must be said that Britain has few consultative bodies with executive powers. Certainly, to talk baldly of 'formal contacts' is to oversimplify the picture.

The pattern of informal contacts is even more complex. The tendency is to classify as informal all contacts which are not through advisory bodies. Yet such contacts vary so much in form that a much fuller typology is needed. These contacts may involve: one group, or more than one group, talking to government; or they may involve a conversation over the phone, or a meeting with an agenda and minutes. Any full typology needs to be more sophisticated to cope with these differences.

We have developed our typology as a result of a considerable number of talks with civil servants and with officials of a large number of interest groups. It seems to us to provide a more adequate typology of the range of 'forms of access' which exist in British government. The basic distinctions we have made are: 1 a distinction between bipartite and multipartite contacts; 2 a distinction between contacts inside and those outside advisory bodies; 3 a distinction between contacts which involve ministers and civil servants and those which involve only civil servants; and 4 a distinction between contacts when the principles of legislation are discussed and those when the details of legislation are discussed.

The most important distinction is that between bipartite and multipartite contacts. Bipartite contacts involve meetings between representatives of one interest group and members of the administration. Bipartite discussions obviously take place outside advisory bodies, which of their nature are multipartite since they include representatives of various interest groups and 'independent' members, though not all multipartite discussions take place within advisory bodies. At the same time, meetings outside advisory bodies, between interest group representatives and members of the administration, whether they be multipartite or bipartite, can involve officials of different levels of seniority on both sides. If the matter under discussion is a crucial, wide-ranging policy decision (like the shape of phase III of the Heath government's pay and prices policy) then top level interest group officials and ministers will be involved. However, if the outline of a more specific piece of legislation is being discussed, senior interest group representatives will usually talk to junior ministers and high level civil servants.

In the case of discussions on the details of legislation, contact will usually be between middle level civil servants (Assistant Secretary or Under-Secretary) and middle-level interest group officials (Deputy Director level). All such contacts outside advisory bodies can be more or less formal. In relatively few instances do meetings have an agenda and some form of minutes, and outline discussions may be carried out on a much more informal basis, by letter or telephone, or in more pleasant circumstances, over lunch or dinner. The nature of such contacts will depend upon the relationship which exists between the ministers/ civil servants and the officials of the interest group involved, and upon the department in question. However, the most usual pattern is for discussions to be informal and often *ad hoc* but to be held inside the government department rather than over the telephone or over lunch. At lunches or dinners the people involved are merely doing groundwork, detailed discussions taking place elsewhere. In classifying multipartite contacts within advisory bodies we have adopted the most important of Dion's distinctions and classified them according to their official status.

What forms do the CBI's access most often take? Which type of meeting does the CBI regard as most important and productive? Most studies of interest groups emphasise the importance of 'informal' or more accurately 'bipartite' contacts. In this vein Finer argues: 'The official channels do not nearly suffice to convey the swelling tide of the Lobby's problems, notions and grievances. Beyond and around them flows a veritable Atlantic of informal to-ings and fro-ings. This contact is close, pervasive and continuous.'[21] Indeed, it is easy on reading most such studies, and particularly that of Eckstein on the British Medical Association,[22] to receive the impression that most contact takes place over the telephone, in a club over dinner and drinks, or more generally in darkened backrooms.

In contrast, Dion has argued that within Western democracies consultative committees or advisory bodies are becoming increasingly important in the decision-making process. His argument is that, as government grows more complex, political parties and interest groups are no longer sufficient to channel interests, so that formal consultative bodies become inevitable. Thus, interest groups will increasingly make contact with government within such bodies, in which access is multipartite in nature and formality replaces informality as the norm. Which of these two distinct views is the more accurate?

The CBI has wide and varied contacts with government which correspond in form to all the different categories in our typology. However, there seems little doubt at present that it is the bipartite talks which the CBI, like other major interest groups, regards as most important. The majority of contacts between CBI and government consist of talks on the details of proposed legislation between the director, assistant director or technical advisor of the relevant CBI directorates and the civil servant responsible for drafting that particular policy. Telephone conversations or letters may help to clarify certain points or to arrange meetings, but it is the more formal discussions that are most important. These meetings are usually concerned with discussing individual clauses and their interpretation and changes or amendments suggested by the interest group. The leading CBI officials do have talks with Cabinet ministers over general economic policy. They also discuss the principles of individual pieces of legislation with the government minister and senior civil servants responsible, but it is the meetings at a lower level on these details of legislation that are most important. We have already touched on the reasons for this pattern, and we shall develop them at length later. Tripartism as yet is a description of a possible future development for at present talks on the general economic climate between government, TUC and CBI are largely unproductive. Government is much more ready to change the details of individual pieces of legislation than it is to change the principles behind a policy. This means that it is in detailed discussions between middle grade civil servants and CBI officials that real results can be gained.

All this does not mean that the CBI ignores multipartite contacts inside and outside advisory bodies. However, if other interests are represented, the CBI is in a sense competing both with government and with the other group. In such circumstances, interest groups tend to feel that they can be 'played off' against other interests by government.

The most important multipartite contacts definitely take place within advisory bodies. As the number of permanent advisory bodies in government has grown, so has the representation which industry has on those committees. The PEP report on advisory bodies found that the three industrial organisations, the Federation of British Industries, the National Association of Manufacturers and the British Employers' Confederation, were represented in 1958 on thirty-two separate advisory bodies.[23] In

1966, when the CBI last published full figures, the number stood at fifty-seven, and representation has increased still further since then. For the most part, this representation is in the area of industry and trade, and it is here too that the main increase has occurred.[24]

It is evident not only that the CBI has increased its representation but also that it increasingly regards the permanent advisory committees as an important arena for contacts with the government and other interest groups. There have even been occasions when the Confederation has suggested to government that certain advisory bodies be established. Indeed, in the CBI's annual reports one can read passages such as these: 'The NJAC Committee on Methods of Payment of Wages was set up at the end of 1968 at the request of the CBI',[25] or 'The CBI had meetings with the Community Relations Commission [of the Home Office] which led to the formation of a committee to advise the chairman of the Commission of problems arising in the employment field.'[26]

CBI literature is full of references to the various advisory bodies on which it is represented. Statements implying the importance of these bodies can often be found: 'The NEDC continued as a valuable forum at which the CBI management members can impress upon senior Ministers at first hand industry's views on the economic aspects of Government policies.'[27]

However, the CBI certainly do not see the advisory body as the most important channel of access to government. This is partly because, as we have said, in such meetings the CBI's views are not heard alone but in competition with the views of other groups. At the same time, the advisory bodies are often regarded by interest groups, and even by government, as arenas in which the government makes 'a ritual sacrifice at the altar of consultation'. There is certainly evidence that this impression is correct. Even a fairly conspicuous and important advisory body such as NEDC has often been treated very cursorily by government. A good example was provided in 1965 when the Labour party introduced its National Plan. George Brown only presented it to NEDC on a Thursday, asking for its approval by the following Wednesday. Governments, as well as interest groups, seem to prefer less formal meetings outside advisory bodies.[28]

However, such advisory bodies would be more important to, and more highly regarded by, interest groups if they had executive powers. Almost without exception, advisory bodies in British politics have only a consultative role, and in most instances the government is not even bound to consult them. This means that advisory bodies have little chance of influencing government to move in a direction which it does not wish. Thus it is not surprising that interest groups with extensive bi-partite contacts with government are sometimes disparaging of advisory bodies. Of course advisory bodies may still play an important role, but their decisions are in no way binding on government. Their advice is much more likely to carry weight in less political, more technical areas, such as industrial safety or training, than in main-line political policy areas. Indeed, there is an interesting current development in two of these technical, less political, fields which suggests that advisory bodies in these areas may increasingly be given executive powers. We shall deal with this important development at length in a later chapter.[29]

In general, however, the CBI most values its bipartite talks with government. The most important, or at least the most productive, talks as far as the CBI is concerned seem to be between civil servants and CBI officials on the details of individual policy proposals. At what stages in the evolution and preparation of legislation do these contacts occur?

The timing of access

Unless an interest group has access to the government decision-making process while a bill is being evolved and drafted, it is unlikely to have influence. The CBI, as we have said, makes most of its important representations at this stage. Before a Green Paper or a White Paper is published there will be ongoing talks about proposed legislation between CBI officials and ministers and civil servants. These will usually be bipartite, high-level and informal in nature, the Director General and President of the CBI often lunching with a government minister or minister of state. In many cases a committee of the CBI will have prepared a document on the particular policy area within which legislation is planned, and members of this committee, with senior CBI officials, may also meet ministers and civil servants in the more formal atmosphere of Whitehall. This process ensures that the views of the CBI are well known to the ministers and civil servants drafting the White Paper.

After the publication of the White Paper, the government minister concerned will usually meet senior CBI officials for discussions on any points of principle involved in the bill. Such talks are likely to be informative but not very fruitful for the CBI. The next stage involves detailed talks on individual clauses of the bill between civil servants and CBI officials from the relevant directorate. It is at these talks that the government makes those concessions it is willing to give. The number and scope of these discussions at staff level depend more on the importance of the proposed legislation and the speed with which it is to be introduced than on the number of objections the CBI puts forward. If the legislation is hurried, consultation is minimal and the CBI's chances of influencing the legislation poor.

Once the bill itself is drafted, the CBI still has contacts with both ministers and civil servants but is very unlikely to obtain major concessions from government. If the bill is presented to Parliament, major concessions are unlikely because a government is unwilling to be seen to be conceding to an interest group. Ministers are jealous of any encroachment on their policy-making role, and they are even more wary if such encroachment takes place in the full glare of publicity. Indeed, it is only after the bill is drafted that the CBI again fulfils an important role. At this stage CBI officials are constantly clarifying with government how certain provisions or clauses will be interpreted in practice. Such talks are particularly important if legislation involves a good deal of executive discretion. Increasingly legislation is amplified or brought into force by subsequent delegated legislation. It is often at this stage that the CBI can influence the details of legislation in a way which benefits its members.

Thus CBI's main access comes between the preparation of the White Paper, or other form of consultative document, and the preparation of the proposed bill for presentation to Parliament, and after the passage of the legislation. Does the CBI have greater access, at these and other times, to the executive when there is a Conservative government?

Access under Labour and Conservative Governments

We have already noted that the CBI's contacts with the Labour party and its MPs are minimal. However, this does not necessarily mean that the CBI has less access to the administration when there is a Labour government. Indeed, since civil servants retain their jobs under both Labour and Conservative governments, there is a great deal of continuity in contacts. Even if the ministers with whom CBI officials have to deal change, the credibility these officials have built up with civil servants ensures access, providing the civil servants are not themselves moved. In addition, a Labour government, as much as a Conservative one, relies upon the CBI to provide it with information about industries' views and to cooperate in the administration of certain industrial policies. All these factors ensure the CBI continuing access. However, it is true that Labour ministers have fewer personal contacts with industrialists and CBI officials. It is also true that the Labour party has always been wary of organisations of industrial representation and has preferred in most instances to seek information and advice more informally from pro-Labour industrialists. At the same time access does not ensure influence, and the CBI is likely to find itself more often at odds with the ideological views of Labour ministers than with their Conservative counterparts. So, while the amount of contact the CBI has with civil servants is probably similar under both Conservative and Labour governments, the extent of its contacts with ministers is probably less under a Labour government, although this can vary according to the personality and views of the minister.

Indeed, the personality and views of a given minister can considerably influence how much contact the CBI has with him. Thus, if a minister is very conscious of any encroachment on his policy-making role he is likely to be difficult to approach. At the same time, some Conservative ministers with experience in industry often feel that they know better than the CBI what industry thinks, so ensuring friction with the CBI. Indeed, the classic case occurred in the first year of John Davies' term as Secretary of State for Trade and Industry in 1970. Since he had previously been Director General of the CBI he seemed to be less willing to ask the CBI for its views, assuming that he knew what it would say. The CBI did not always find that having an ex-Director General in such a key government position was an advantage.

The overall picture, industries' contacts with government and the CBI's role
We have dealt extensively with the CBI's contacts with government. It must be realised that individual member companies (and companies who are not members), individual trade associations and individual industrialists also have contacts with government. When general issues are concerned, however, even the largest firms tend to use the CBI. So Arthur Knight says of his experiences with Courtaulds: 'In dealing with the general issues there is a more obvious choice to be made between direct representation to government and participation in the work of the appropriate representative body, usually the CBI. In formulating views about the EEC for example, there was never any doubt that the CBI was the most effective channel.'[30] Later he continues: 'Similarly in general taxation matters the company looked to the CBI Taxation Panel.'[31]

Of course, if a large company disagrees with the policy line taken by the CBI it may approach government directly. Thus one large firm we talked to was strongly in favour of the introduction of a two-tier system of VAT, when that tax was first introduced into Britain. The CBI favoured one basic rate, so this firm approached ministers and civil servants directly. Knight gives another example:

> The CBI sometimes finds it difficult to reconcile the interests of big companies, as in its representations in 1972 about proposed changes in Corporation tax where, faced by the Parliamentary Select Committee with [a choice] between the interest of companies with primarily overseas earnings and those with primarily UK earnings, the Chairman of the CBI Taxation Panel and the CBI official appeared in their answers to lean towards the interests of those with overseas earnings. In such circumstances Courtaulds decided to make their own direct representations to the Minister keeping the CBI informed.[32]

In addition the large firms are in constant touch with civil servants in that section of government which deals with their industry. Thus ICI has close connections with the chemical section of the Department of Industry, providing it with information about the industry, offering advice and asking for clarification of many of the provisions involved in legislation. Smaller firms may also have some contacts, though they are likely to be less frequent and less close.

In summary, it would seem fair to conclude that individual firms do not approach government direct with much hope of changing the principles of a government's policy. However, on the details of policy and particularly of its implementation, large firms can be extremely influential.

Individual industrialists however may have more influence in many ways than firms as such, for ministers are more willing to talk privately to industrialists whom they know than to negotiate with individual firms in a way which might become public. Indeed, as one senior industrialist told us:

> Government ministers are particularly interested in talking to individual industrialists because by doing this they can check on the views being presented to them by the CBI and particularly by their own civil servants. However, such contacts only work if they are informal and based upon trust. This means two things: first that ministers tend to contact people they have known for a long time and can trust, that is people they went to school with, were in the army with, were in business with, or belong to the same club (friends in other words);

secondly, it means that the industrialist must be careful and moderate in his views otherwise this delicate balance of trust breaks down. Different ministers have different personal contacts. I personally know two cabinet ministers very well. However, the situation changes when a Labour government comes to power; this does not mean that industrialists are less consulted then, but it means that different industrialists are consulted.

Certain industrialists have access because of their well established personal contacts with ministers. These individuals tend to be concentrated in the bigger firms because the more active and influential industrialists gravitate towards such firms. However, if they argue too strongly their own firm's point of view, a minister is likely to be wary. If he is seen to favour one firm too strongly, his political career may be in danger. Thus while it is obvious that individual large firms have considerable effect on the detailed application of policy and are in constant touch with the relevant civil servants, certain individual industrialists who are particularly trusted by ministers may have a much wider access, being heard on matters of policy as well as of detail. Harold Macmillan is reported to have paid particular attention to the views of Lord Mills on matters affecting industry,[33] and George Brown 'worked closely' at the DEA with Lord Kearton of Courtaulds.[34] Brown started a system of monthly dinners at which 'highly detailed discussions'[35] were held with a select group of leading industrialists. He recalls that 'this unpublicised body of industrial advisors had an enormous influence on the apparatus we set up'.[36] Certainly the CBI is far from being the only, or even the most important, organ of industrial representation.

Thus the overall picture shows that the CBI has extensive access at all levels of government which it regards as highly important. Access does not necessarily mean influence, but it is impossible to influence without access and the CBI thus has great potential influence. However, it would be wrong to give the impression that all industry's access to government is channelled through the CBI.

Access at the international level
Although the greater part of the CBI's activities is concerned with what is conventionally referred to as 'domestic policy', one of the organisation's eight directorates is exclusively concerned with overseas matters, and each of the other seven specialist directorates is involved in international

matters that impinge on its specialist interests. The activities of the
Overseas Directorate range from organising trade and investment missions
to consultations with the British government on a wide range of policy
issues, from EEC affairs and export credit to more routine subjects such
as changes in tariff regulations and customs procedures. For instance, the
Overseas Committee has taken a particular interest in attempts by
Britain's major trading partners to apply protectionist measures or other
trade barriers. In particular, the CBI has devoted considerable attention to
attempting to persuade Japanese political and business circles to adopt
more liberal trade and inward investment policies. The Overseas Investment Committee plays a similar role in trying to create a favourable
climate for British investors overseas, for instance by trying to change
restrictive foreign investment legislation.

The CBI has made a particular effort to develop relations with what it
terms the 'state-trading nations'. In February 1967 the CBI gave a
luncheon for Mr Kosygin of the Soviet Union during his visit to London
and in the following November a top-level CBI team had a two-day
conference in Moscow with a delegation of Soviet industrialists. As a
result, a number of working parties were established to examine the
possibilities for technical cooperation. Before the United Kingdom
established relations with the German Democratic Republic, the CBI was
responsible for many years for the negotiation of an annual trade agreement
with the East German Chamber of Foreign Trade. The CBI maintains a
close working liaison with 'country associations' such as the India,
Pakistan, Bangladesh, East Africa and Mauritius Associations as well as
the West India Committee and the similar body for West Africa. Staff
members are on the executives of these bodies, thus enabling appropriate
interests to speak with a common voice on affairs affecting British
industry in specific countries.

The Overseas Directorate has also been responsible for an *ad hoc* Committee on Rhodesia, not confined to CBI members, which has endeavoured
to represent the interests of 'those in British industry and commerce with
investment interests in Rhodesia'.[37] The Committee was consulted 'on the
implications for industry of Government measures, particularly those
taken to implement the sanctions policy'.[38] On a global level, the CBI is
a member of the Business and Industry Advisory Committee to the
Organization for Economic Cooperation and Development, in which the
industrial federations of the three main international trading entities, the
US, the EEC and Japan, play a leading part. Thus the CBI is involved in

a wide range of activities at an international level, although the external interests of British businessmen are also safeguarded by the British National Committee of the International Chamber of Commerce, of which the CBI is a member.

However, the main thrust of the overseas activities of the CBI as a whole is directed towards the mainland of Europe and concentrates on both internal and external aspects of the EEC's affairs. The Overseas Directorate has only a residual coordinating role in relation to European Community matters, as the CBI has followed a policy of treating European affairs as an integral part of the work of its specialist departments. Perhaps one of the main impacts of British membership of the Community on the CBI has been to increase the already considerable strain on the organisation's limited resources. The increased staffing and subscription costs resulting from the organisation's enlarged European activities were among the factors bringing about an increase in CBI membership dues in 1973.[39]

In endeavouring to exert influence on the development of Community policy, there are three separate (although not mutually exclusive) channels of access available to the CBI: it can work through Whitehall; it can operate through the European employers' organisation, Union des Industries de la Communauté Européene (UNICE), or it can use its own Brussels office to make a direct approach to the Commission. The first of these strategies has obvious attractions, and the CBI has made extensive use of its existing contacts with government departments in London. If the government can be persuaded to adopt CBI policy as British policy, then there is a reasonable chance that the eventual decision of the Council of Ministers, even if it is not exactly what the CBI wants, will at least not be injurious to British industrial interests.

The second strategy, using UNICE, also has its attractions. The Commission has encouraged industrial and other interests to form European organisations so that it can be presented with one common European view for each interest instead of nine national views. However, like all the 'umbrella' European interest groups, UNICE has to face the problem of reconciling the often divergent interests of its members in such a way as to produce a policy which is something more than a 'lowest common denominator' of the views of the national federations. It has been hampered in this task by its limited resources. Even after the recent appointment of two more senior staff members, it still has only ten administrative-level employees.

The CBI joined UNICE in February 1972 and has taken a leading role in the major reorganisation of UNICE which was approved by its Council of Presidents in September 1973. The reorganisation was intended to ensure a more continuous dialogue with the Commission and that the views of industry were heeded by the Commission at an earlier stage in policy formation. The committee structure was rationalised with the objective of identifying European industry's priorities and then concentrating on stressing these key issues to the Commission and member governments. A new Secretary-General, Bernard Sassen, was appointed: he comes from a Dutch industrial background and has had experience of European representational work as Vice-President of ORGALIME, the widely respected organisation covering the European mechanical, metalworking, electrical and electronic engineering industries. These changes should enhance UNICE's effectiveness, although the CBI has warned that 'we shall be keeping under close scrutiny the question whether the benefits to our membership we receive from UNICE are commensurate with the outlay involved'.[40]

The Brussels office of the CBI has two main functions: liaison with UNICE and serving as a 'listening post'. As far as the first of these is concerned, the head of the office attends a weekly meeting of the Brussels representatives of the various national industrial organisations under the chairmanship of the Secretary-General of UNICE. This committee works on general policy issues between meetings of the Council of Presidents and the Executive Committee. The Brussels office is also represented on a number of UNICE committees which are not attended by industrialists or head office staff. As far as acting as a 'listening post' is concerned, this involves passing back 'intelligence material' to London in terms of 'what people are saying, how they are reacting to developments'. The Brussels office does have links with the UK Permanent Delegation and the CBI still has a considerable amount of direct contact with Commission officials, largely a residue of the close links forged during the entry negotiations. However, the CBI regards a direct approach to the Commission as a 'fall-back', something that it does not use frequently. Normally it works through Whitehall and UNICE, 'using as many channels as we feel are open to us in getting our views across', as one CBI official put it.

Notes and References

1 One of the most recent discussions is to be found in A. Dunsire, *Administration: The Word and the Science* (London: Martin Robertson, 1973), especially Chapter 9.

2 D. Keeling, *Management in Government* (London: Allen and Unwin, 1972), p. 36.

3 Vickers argues that 'great confusion results from the common assumption that all course holding can be reduced to the pursuit of an endless succession of goals'. Sir G. Vickers, *The Art of Judgement: A Study of Policy Making* (London: Chapman and Hall, 1965), p. 98.

4 See R. N. Vernon and N. S. Mansergh, *Advisory Bodies* (London: Allen and Unwin, 1940), especially pp. 20–1, and Political and Economic Planning, *Advisory Bodies in British Government* (London: Allen and Unwin, 1960). For a useful summary of this process see J. Kingdom 'Advice in government', *South-Western Review of Public Administration* (1973), pp. 20–35.

5 L. Dion, 'The politics of consultation', *Government and Opposition*, **8** (1973), pp. 332–53.

6 W. Plowden, *The Motor Car and Politics in Britain* (Harmondsworth: Penguin, 1973), p. 391.

7 Alex Jarratt, formerly Chairman of CBI Economic Policy Committee, was a career civil servant before joining the International Publishing Corporation. Richard O'Brien, formerly Chairman of the CBI Employment Policy Committee, was an adviser at the Department of Economic Affairs from 1966 to 1968.

8 Our definition of 'public office' includes service on quasi-governmental committees, public corporations, Royal Commissions and departmental committees of enquiry but excludes local government and the governing bodies of universities.

9 See R. Leonard and V. Herman, *The Backbencher and Parliament* (London: Macmillan, 1972).

10 A more detailed example of the CBI's use of back-benchers is given in our study of the Industry Act (1972). See below, pp. 161–3.

11 The situation is obviously vastly different when there is no party with an overall majority in Parliament.

12 See A. Roth, 'The business background of MPs' in J. Urry and J. Wakeford (eds), *Power in Britain* (London: Heinemann, 1973), pp. 131–5.

13 *CBI Annual Report*, 1967, p. 22. The CBI clearly values its contacts in the House of Lords. In contrast, Vincent argues: 'The overwhelming majority of opposition amendments of a "constructive" and substantial character were refused and withdrawn without being put to a division . . . the amendments that get carried . . . [are] of little practical significance.' J. R. Vincent, 'The House of Lords', *Parliamentary Affairs*, **19** (1966), pp. 475–85, p. 483. See also J. R. Vincent, 'Legislation in the House of Lords: A correction and recommendation', *Parliamentary Affairs*, **20** (1967), pp. 178–80. It may be of course that the role of the Lords as amending chamber has increased since Vincent's study as a result of the increased importance and activity of life peers. In addition, opposition to Lords amendments is likely to be more successful when there is a Labour government, given the Lords' in-built Conservative majority, and when there is a minority government.

14 The Smaller Businesses Association is an interesting case, in that it was set up specifically to canvass for support in *Parliament* and not in Whitehall.

15 This is really an under-researched area, but see A. Beichman, 'The Conservative Research Department: The care and feeding of future British political elites', *Journal of British Studies*, **13** and **14** (1974), pp. 92–113.

16 Once again this point is well illustrated in our case-study of the Industry Act (1972), pp. 161–3.

17 The CBI does not define very accurately what it means by 'informed opinion'. However, it seems most anxious to get a good press in the *Daily Telegraph*, the *Financial Times* and *The Economist*.

18 *The Times* index provides an informative guide to the coverage that a group or individual receives. We have examined the entries in the index for the months January/February and July/August. These two periods were chosen arbitrarily, and the entries in the index for those months in the years 1960–72 were counted. This procedure has been used in a similar way by R. M. Punnett, *Front Bench Opposition* (London: Heinemann, 1973), see pp. 481–3.

19 R. D. Coates, *Teachers' Unions and Interest Group Politics* (London: Cambridge University Press, 1972).

20 L. Dion, op. cit.

21 S. E. Finer, *Anonymous Empire* (London: Pall Mall Press, 1966), p. 34.

22 H. Eckstein, *Pressure Group Politics* (London: Allen and Unwin, 1960).

23 PEP, op. cit., pp. 194–5. Often more than one of these organisations was represented on a single committee.

24 See *CBI Annual Report*, 1966, p. 66. The CBI still publishes annually the names of over fifty government bodies on which it is represented, but these are no longer full figures. Representation of the TUC has increased and it is now represented on more than fifty advisory bodies: see *ABC of the TUC* (London: TUC, 1971), pp. 31–2. This figure may be compared with one of thirty recorded in the PEP report of 1960.

25 *CBI Annual Report*, 1969, p. 35.

26 ibid., p. 36.

27 ibid., p. 17.

28 See G. Turner, *Business in Britain* (London: Eyre and Spottiswoode, 1969), especially pp. 75–91.

29 See below, pp. 141–5.

30 A. Knight, *Private Enterprise and Public Intervention: The Courtaulds Experience* (London: Allen and Unwin, 1974), p. 172.

31 ibid.

32 ibid., p. 173.

33 A. Sampson, *Macmillan: A study in ambiguity* (London: Allen Lane, 1967), p. 173.

34 Lord George-Brown, *In My Way* (London: Gollancz, 1971), p. 195.

35 ibid., p. 94.

36 ibid., p. 94.

37 *The Policy Work of the CBI*, CBI publication, 1972, p. 13.

38 ibid.

39 For a fuller discussion of this point see W. P. Grant, 'British employers' associations and the enlarged community', *Journal of Common Market Studies*, **11** (1973), pp. 276–86.

40 *CBI Annual Report*, 1973, p. 33.

7

Tripartism:
a constitutional trinity?

IN THE LAST CHAPTER, WE ANALYSED THE NATURE AND FORM OF THE CBI's relationships with government. However, these relationships are clearly affected by the priorities and outlook of each new administration. Clearly, any modern government, unless it subscribes wholeheartedly to 'free market' principles, will have extensive contacts with the CBI. Nevertheless, administrations – or phases of administrations – tend to be characterised by styles of decision-making. For example, the minority Labour government between March and October 1974 tended to place rather less emphasis on top-level contacts with the CBI than the previous Conservative administration, although subsequently the pattern has somewhat changed. However, it should be remembered that the CBI has always valued its continuing contacts with civil servants rather more than meetings on specific subjects with ministers, believing that since the former remain while politicians come and go it is the civil servants who should be influenced on a long-term basis. At the stage when the CBI is having meetings with Ministers, it is probably fighting openly stated policies rather than influencing the long-term development of those policies.

In this chapter, we are particularly concerned with the notion of 'tripartism' that was publicly adopted by the Heath government after the summer of 1972. The Conservatives came to power in 1970 espousing a philosophy of 'non-interventionism' or 'disengagement'. The Industry Act of 1972 marked the burial of this doctrine as a guiding political principle, although the failure of an incomes policy based on the concept of non-interventionism and the need to replace it by something more tangible (particularly in the light of the first miners' strike) was perhaps more significant than the Act in bringing about the demise of 'disengagement'.

In a search for an alternative doctrine, the Conservatives turned to 'tripartism', an attempt to manage the economy by the government, the CBI and the TUC. Similarly, the talks held at Chequers in November 1975 on the Labour government's New Industrial Strategy represented another attempt to explore the possibilities of a tripartite agreement on an economic strategy.

Much of the analysis of these developments has centred on the high-level discussions on economic policy between the government, the CBI and the TUC. It is these discussions that are usually referred to when Mr Heath is accused by his critics of having attempted to set up a 'corporate state'. Rather less attention has been paid to the close involvement of the CBI and TUC in new 'hived-off' agencies such as the Manpower Services Commission and the Health and Safety Commission. However, the close involvement of the CBI and TUC in the operation of important public agencies may have significant long-term implications for the decision-making process.

One of the difficulties of discussing these developments is the vague and emotive nature of many of the key terms. 'Corporatism' is largely a pejorative word; as Harris has pointed out, it certainly does not represent a single unified doctrine.[1] It has been embraced by both the left and the right in its different versions and there has been no 'single, political movement to stamp upon the diversity a single pattern'.[2] Even the distinction made by Harris between '*étatiste* corporatism', whose advocates accept that the state should have a major role in economic reorganisation, and 'pluralist corporatism', whose proponents see businessmen guiding a more conservative economic strategy, does not refine the term sufficiently to permit it to be used in this particular analysis. In its weaker sense, it means little more than a belief in the desirability of some form of functional representation. Relatively few writers today are prepared to attack the role of interest groups in politics as 'pernicious'[3] but this does not mean that there is not some resistance among the general public to the spectacle of 'deals' between the government and the major producer interest groups. Mr Heath felt it necessary to reassure his supporters at the 1973 Conservative conference that, 'We have not been thinking just of the TUC and the CBI. . . . We have been thinking of those not represented by a big organisation.'[4]

What we are concerned with here is not so much 'corporatism' as 'tripartism'. We see the key feature of tripartism as a belief that the peak organisations representing management and the trade unions are of special importance among all producer groups, that negotiations should take place with these peak organisations on the major issues of economic policy, and that agreement with these groups will provide a basis for the successful implementation of the government's economic policy. Tripartism thus implies a hierarchy of interest groups. As Coates has pointed out, the government structure is not open to all associations at all points all the time.[5] Groups such as the teachers' associations do not enjoy the access to the Treasury, the Cabinet and the Prime Minister which is available to the CBI and the TUC. If one assumes that access to these central points in the decision-making structure confers bargaining advantages, then clearly a tripartite style of government has implications for the relative influence of different interest groups and thus for the political process as a whole.

In particular, it is difficult to reconcile tripartism with a strong belief in the importance of Parliament in the political process. Members of Parliament are naturally reluctant to lose their powers to outside organisations, but despite their unique law-making function outsiders often feel that MPs do not have the time, expertise or direct knowledge to comment authoritatively on draft proposals that are still at the formative stage. Not surprisingly they have become increasingly restive about the diminution of their role.

It should be stressed that tripartism did not emerge for the first time as a feature of the decision-making process in the summer of 1972. The wage restraint bargain of 1948 may be seen as a historical precedent. Beer stresses that the bargain 'was remarkable as much for the way in which it was reached as for its content and results. The principal negotiators were three – the Government, organised labour and organised capital.'[6] However, by the summer of 1949, Cripps' 'experiment in tripartite consultation on long-term economic planning was collapsing'.[7] Apart from the quarterly meetings of the National Joint Advisory Council to the Ministry of Labour, tripartism lapsed until the formation of the National Economic Development Council in 1962.

It is not our intention to chart the history of the National Economic Development Council; this has been done more than adequately elsewhere.[8] Rather our concern is with the contention of Berry et al that when the NEDC was formed 'the major theme of contemporary public discussion was the need for indicative planning and more expert economic advice, and the minor theme was tripartism'.[9] Was this in fact the case and did tripartism at any point become a major theme? In answering this question one must also consider the role of the Economic Development Committees first set up in 1964; these attempt to tackle the problems of individual industries on a tripartite basis.[10]

The very existence of the NEDC and the EDCs is itself a declaration of faith that tripartite consultations are important and useful. However, it would be wrong to suggest that when the NEDC was set up there was any emphasis on the general desirability of creating tripartite institutions. In the short term the formation of the NEDC was a response to the sterling crisis of July 1961 and a means for the government to demonstrate that it had some kind of economic strategy that transcended the limitations of the much criticised 'stop-go' policy.[11] It also reflected a new interest within industry in the possibility of tackling the difficulties of the British economy (particularly its poor rate of growth) by a form of planning based on what was seen as the success of the French *Commissariat au Plan*.[12] All these developments in industrial and government thinking were of considerable importance, but none of them rested on the belief that the peak organisations of management and labour should be brought into a decision-making partnership with government.

One problem was, of course, that the employers were still represented by three distinct organisations. Indeed, until 1965 the employers were represented on NEDC by independent members, although this 'independence' was nominal in the sense that the views of the employers' organisations were sought on the merits of potential employer members of the Council. However, this reluctance to be directly represented on NEDC did reflect a somewhat cautious attitude on the part of employers' organisations towards the whole idea of tripartite bodies. The employers welcomed NEDC as an additional channel of access to government and as an attempt to tackle the country's economic problems with which they were basically in sympathy, but 'they would not accept the notion that the NEDC would (provide) the setting for binding deals between the industrial interests'.[13]

In 1964 the majority of the staff in the National Economic Development Office were transferred to the new Labour government's Department of Economic Affairs. NEDC was closely involved in the preparation of the National Plan and Lord George-Brown stresses in his memoirs that he regarded the final consent of the Council as of crucial importance to the success of the plan,[14] although he did not give them much time to consider it. As long as the commitment to growth remained, the Council had a definite function to perform, even if it was somewhat overshadowed by the Department of Economic Affairs. However, the collapse of the National Plan in July 1966 'once again gave rise to doubts'[15] at the CBI about the usefulness of the Council. The CBI's view is that meetings of the Council are useful because 'it is a valuable forum at which CBI management members can impress upon senior ministers at first hand industry's views on the economic aspects of government policy'.[16] It is primarily seen as an additional channel of access to government.

After the collapse of the National Plan in 1966, NEDC placed increasing emphasis on the work of the individual Economic Development Committees. As Berry *et al* have pointed out, 'the EDCs varied in their capacity and willingness to tackle problems on a tripartite basis'.[17] Some of the EDCs have had to be disbanded because it was thought that there was little more they could achieve, but in general they have performed 'a great deal of useful, though unspectacular, work'.[18] Vaughan argues that the association of management, unions and government in the EDCs could 'result in the development of a corporatist attitude'.[19] but one should not exaggerate the influence of the experience of EDC work on the committee members.

The NEDC has survived three changes of government and has established a permanent niche for itself in the machinery of economic policy-making. Nevertheless, its record has not been one of continuous progress towards regular tripartite discussions on the most pressing economic issues of the day. It has provided the locale for much of the tripartite contact that has taken place, but it has not evolved from a useful framework for the exchange of differing views into a forum in which economic concordats can be concluded and promulgated. The NEDC has probably helped both sides of industry to become accustomed to tripartite discussions, but as Berry *et al* have pointed out: 'The operative question is whether tripartism can acquire a real meaning outside the National Economic Development Council as well as within it.'[20]

Mr Heath's government apparently thought that tripartism need not be confined to high-level discussions on economic policy between ministers, the CBI and TUC. Indeed, the application of the notion of tripartism to the executive operations of government may be of more significance in the long run than the dramatic talks at Downing Street and Chequers. Since 1974 the Labour government has continued with the development of tripartite executive agencies initiated by the Heath government.

The Manpower Services Commission may be regarded as the first of the new tripartite agencies.[21] In many respects, the Commission is similar to other new agencies which have been 'hived off' from government departments in recent years. However, Mr Maurice Macmillan, speaking as

Secretary of State for Employment, stressed that the Commission 'is a new concept, a new kind of organization'.[22] Of the Commission's ten members, three were nominated by the CBI, three were drawn from the trade union movement, two were appointed after consultation with local authority associations and one after consultation with professional and educational interests. Thus, the majority of the Commission's membership is drawn from the two main groups representing producers. The Commission's task will be to supervise the operation of the job placement and training services hitherto run by the Department of Employment. The Commission's annual budget and programme has to be approved by the Secretary of State for Employment, and most of the executive work is carried out by two agencies reporting to the Commission, the Training Services Agency and the Employment Services Agency. Although the Commission's staff is small, it is responsible for expenditure in excess of £100 million a year[23] and has a considerable say in the formulation of manpower policy.

The creation of the Commission was explicitly linked by the then Secretary of State for Employment to a philosophy of tripartism. Although pointing out that the Commission was not exclusively tripartite, Mr Macmillan emphasised that 'the government attach great importance to what has become known as the tripartite approach . . . as is shown by the proposed membership'.[24] Mr Macmillan stressed the way in which the Commission differed from any existing body. There were plenty of advisory bodies made up of interest group representatives, but these did not operate any particular organisation. The Commission should also be distinguished from 'committees and boards which run important activities on which industrialists and trade unionists sit, but in a purely personal capacity'.[25] Although the members of the Commission were not to be regarded as delegates of the interest groups, it was hoped that they would remain responsible to 'those bodies which proposed them'.[26] Although not required to refer back to their organisations on every major point, the members of the Commission 'in forming judgements about what policy to follow . . . must keep in mind the general views and interests of those who helped to put them there'.[27] In other words, representatives of the CBI and TUC sit on the Manpower Services Commission and run an important part of the government's operations in the light of their own 'views and interests'.

It must be remembered, of course, that the Commission includes three members nominated by interests other than the CBI and the TUC, as well as an independent chairman (a former senior civil servant). The presence of these other members, and the absence of any formal government representation, does dilute the tripartite content of the Commission. After all, tripartism means the TUC and CBI talking directly to one another and to government.

In presenting his proposals Mr Macmillan was at pains to stress that there would be a simple chain of command stretching back from the executive agencies to Parliament: 'The agencies will be the executive agents in charge and will be responsible to the Commission for the money they spend, the Commission will be responsible to me, and I shall be responsible to Parliament.'[28] However, Mr Macmillan also pointed out that 'a body which has sufficient freedom of action to be really effective in this sphere should not be subject to day-to-day Parliamentary questions',[29] although he did foresee that the Select Committee on Expenditure would carry out long-term reviews of its activities. Parliament may, of course, assert greater control over the Commission than was originally intended. It is somewhat perturbing, however, that there was very little discussion in Parliament about the general merits of tripartite institutions of this kind. Some worries were expressed about the relationship of the industrial training boards to the new structure and there was an attempt to secure representation for the Retail Consortium on the Commission on the grounds that the CBI did not represent the interests of retailers.[30] However, the general response of the Labour party to the proposals was expressed by Mr Reg Prentice, who commented: 'This is an idea which has been put forward for many years by the Labour Party and the TUC.'[31]

A similar agency dealing with safety and health at work has been established by the government in line with the recommendations of the Robens report, which argued that 'the "user interests" (must be) able to play an effective part in the management of the new institution'.[32] The report criticised representative advisory bodies because they 'have no way of ensuring that their advice really affects what the Government actually does, and consequently the interests represented on them are unlikely to feel any sense of direct participation in, or commitment to, the eventual decisions made. What is needed is participation in the actual machinery of taking decisions, both at technical level and also in the overall management of the system, at the level where policy is determined.'[33] The Conservative government subsequently indicated that a suitable structure for a new agency dealing with safety and health at work would be 'broadly on the lines of the Manpower Services Commission . . . an essential feature of the organisation would be that the interests of management, workers and others would be reflected in its composition'.[34] Although different in some respects from the body proposed by the Conservatives, the Health and Safety Commission established by the Labour government retained the Commission's membership structure, three members being nominated by the CBI and three by the TUC, together with three other members and an independent chairman.

The 1974 Labour government also established a Conciliation and Arbitration Service which is supervised by a ten-man council with three nominees from the CBI and three from the TUC. Will these agencies in the general area of employment policy be the forerunners of similar tripartite agencies in other areas of government activity? At present, this seems unlikely. Although the Conciliation and Arbitration Service operates in a sensitive political area, job placement, training services and industrial safety are hardly in the forefront of ongoing debates about economic policy. Certainly there is debate among employers, unions and government about the issues involved, but it is not as intense as disputes about prices and incomes policy and industrial relations. There are other areas of industrial policy too which are not subject to political debate. However, most of these areas – for example, the problem of the disposal of industrial waste – involve other influential interest groups as well as the TUC and the CBI. It is not out of the question that agencies with executive powers might be established in such areas, but they would be more likely to be multipartite than tripartite.

About training and safety there has traditionally been considerable contact and discussion, and some measure of agreement, between unions and employers' associations. Indeed throughout the 1950s, when relations between the unions and industry were somewhat desultory, meetings of the safety committee of the National Joint Advisory Council continued productively. After the Carr Report on the Recruitment and Training of Young Workers in Industry, the Industrial Training Council was established in 1958 largely as a result of the desire of both employers and unions to restrict the activities of government in this field. Subsequently, in the early 1960s, a series of informal meetings took place between officials of the BEC and TUC. These meetings were frank and often productive but once again they concentrated on industrial safety and training. Of course contact in these areas did not always bring agreement, and indeed as far as safety was concerned the employers always favoured a voluntary approach while the unions wanted firmer enforcement of statutory controls. However, the two sides generally agreed that contact was useful in these areas and that government intervention was likely to be counter-productive.

The two areas in which these agencies have been established are characterised by a considerable measure of agreement between the parties concerned both about the need for such agencies and about their long-term aims: more effective administration and cooperation between both sides of industry. Such agreement does not exist more generally in the field of industrial relations or on prices and incomes issues. The wider political climate will have to change considerably before meaningful tripartite agencies can be established in these fields. This does not seem likely. In addition, even if it did change, it is unlikely that government, the CBI and TUC would wish to increase the number of such agencies until they can see how successfully the present ones operate. The Conciliation and Arbitration Service has encountered some difficulties, but insufficient time has elapsed to pass judgement on this particular innovation.

As far as the CBI and the TUC are concerned, the new agencies will have to prove their usefulness. After all, their existence means that the interest groups have assumed a new responsibility for decision-making. This is a very important point. If agencies make a decision they can no longer blame government if their members object to that decision. They themselves will be responsible. Also, if an agency takes a decision which is not to the liking of the TUC or the CBI it can no longer appeal directly to the minister concerned. Responsibility brings problems as well as advantages and both organisations will want evidence that the advantages outweigh the problems before they support other developments. What has to be tested is the extent to which the CBI and TUC can commit their members by direct involvement in these bodies.

The development of tripartite public agencies might lend support to the view that the traditional constitutional trinity of monarch, Lords and Commons is being supplanted by a new trinity of Whitehall, CBI and TUC. However, 'even if this is acceptable . . . further questions remain – like whether one can only look at this threefold power as a balance (if so, as a factual or ideal one?)'.[35] The stock phrase – 'consultations are taking place with the CBI and the TUC' – is one that is now often heard in Parliament. However, it must not be assumed that the two organisations are equal partners with government or that they have an effective veto on government policy. As Castles has pointed out, 'a rightful emphasis on group politics can be carried too far if one fails to consider the constraints on their activity'.[36]

Perhaps the most important constraint on the CBI and the TUC is that the government is the government, that it alone is ultimately accountable to the electorate, and that in any confrontation with an interest group it can always argue that it is defending the national interest against a narrow, sectional interest. Secondly, one has to remember that the organisational resources of the CBI and TUC are extremely limited compared with those of government. The CBI employs approximately four hundred people, and over half of these are clerical and supporting staff. The TUC, which has only forty senior staff, is in a worse position. There are some 2,800 employees in the administrative grade of the civil service alone, and in addition many members of the executive grades and specialist classes carry out duties that impinge on the interests of the CBI and the TUC. The result is that one CBI staff member finds himself responsible for a number of policy areas dealt with by several high-ranking staff in government. For example, one member of the CBI's Overseas Directorate is listed as being responsible for 'Non-Communist Asia east of Afghanistan including Japan'; two members of staff are specifically responsible for mergers and monopolies; and the member of staff responsible for postal and tele-communications matters also has responsibilities in relation to the Smaller Firms Council. Obviously, both the CBI and TUC concentrate on certain aspects of government policy, but there are relatively few policy areas in which they do not have some interest.

A further problem is that both organisations are loose confederations rather than well-disciplined hierarchies. The leadership of the CBI has been more assertive than that of the FBI and less worried about advocating policies which might be opposed by some members. Nevertheless, as we have pointed out, there are limits to the leadership's freedom of manoeuvre. The CBI works by consensus, which inhibits the voluntary development of policies or standards and in particular reduces the CBI's influence in seeking their adoption by members. This may, therefore, open the door to government intervention by default.

These problems have been even more acute for the TUC, although there has been a gradual trend towards centralisation within the organisation. As May and Moran have pointed out: 'When unions relied on the Labour Party, their attempts to act as a pressure group were necessarily loosely coordinated, since each union sponsors its own MPs. Direct contact with Whitehall is, however, largely confined to the TUC.'[37] A recent indication of the move towards centralisation within the TUC structure has been the formulation of a plan for nine new regional organisations with full-time officials appointed by and responsible to the TUC General Secretary. The FBI set up an effective regional organisation in 1946. Moreover, the centralisation of the TUC's organisation must be set against the very substantial increase in workplace bargaining. Changes in the structure may reflect apparent rather than real changes in the balance of power within the trade union movement.

Nevertheless, it cannot be denied that both the CBI and the TUC have become involved in more intensive consultations with government over a wider range of issues and often at a higher level than was previously the case. However, because the prominence of the two organisations in British politics has increased, new strains have been imposed on them. In particular, there has been an increase in external pressure on the CBI and TUC from other organisations. One CBI regional secretary complained to us: 'The CBI tries to avoid getting involved in things unless they are really relevant to industrial interests, but as the CBI gets better known, it attracts all sorts of good causes it's difficult to be rude to, but which one doesn't wish to get involved in, for example, people trying to do something about deaf aids. Apart from that there are cranks wanting to put a British man on the moon and other madcap schemes.' Cranks can be dealt with, but, more importantly, as the CBI has become a more prominent organisation in public life a range of bodies have considered it necessary to attack CBI policy. For example, the Select Committee on Science and Technology attacked the CBI's attitude towards the work of the industrial research establishments as 'uncooperative and unconstructive'.[38] In 1972 the General Secretary of the Association of Professional, Executive, Clerical and Computer Staff complained that efforts by the CBI to amend a clause of the government's bill on prices and incomes represented 'a new element of interference specifically with the contractual arrangements between white collar workers and their employers'.[39] At best, the CBI has to devote some of its scarce organisational resources to countering these attacks; at worst, they may undermine its credibility with government.

There is no doubt that contacts between the government and the TUC have much improved since 1974. In addition, relations between the CBI and the government have improved steadily since October 1974, so that by the spring of 1976 some commentators suggested that the government had gone as far as it could in meeting the demands of the CBI. However, there is no sign of a genuine consensus developing between the three parties which could provide the basis for meaningful tripartite economic planning. The whole notion of tripartism assumes rather more consensus between the parties involved than is to be found at present. There seems little chance that tripartism will become a reality in the current political climate. Indeed, at no time since the establishment of the CBI, except perhaps in the first few months of the organisation's existence, has there been a relationship between the three parties which would allow for productive discussions between them on key political and economic issues. The position of the government is strengthened by the fact that it can to some extent 'play off' the CBI against the TUC. It is our view that the government must be seen as being at the apex of any new constitutional trinity.

During the Labour government between 1966 and 1970 relationships between both the government and the CBI and the government and the TUC deteriorated. The government's relations with the CBI had been reasonably good initially and, as we have pointed out, the government, and George Brown in particular, had pressed hard for the organisation's formation. However, when the government introduced its statutory prices and wages freeze relations quickly worsened. CBI members found the provisions of the 1968 Industrial Expansion Act so objectionable that they refused to talk about it to the government. The CBI was even more disturbed by proposals announced by the government in 1969 for the creation of a Commission for Industry and Manpower which would take over the functions of the Monopolies Commission and the National Board for Prices and Incomes. The Commission would have been given powers to investigate situations of market dominance as well as of monopoly and would have been able to enquire into mergers retrospectively. The CBI felt that the proposals would lay the basis for an intolerable increase in government intervention in industry.

At the same time, relations between the Labour government and the TUC reached one of their lowest ebbs after the introduction of the government's proposals for the reform of industrial relations in January 1969. The proposals were subsequently withdrawn as a result of a combination of trade union pressure and opposition from within the parliamentary party which eventually led to a Cabinet split. This particular proposal severely damaged relations between the TUC and the Labour government for the rest of its term of office and beyond. The notion of tripartism was hardly likely to be either popular or practical while such conflicts existed.

There is little doubt that relations between government and the CBI improved considerably after the return of the Conservative administration in 1970. The CBI welcomed the government's initial commitment to 'disengagement' from the affairs of industry, and it reluctantly cooperated with the interventionist policies subsequently followed by the government. Nevertheless, relations between the government and the CBI were not without their troubles. So, although new CBI members saw their former chief assume responsibility in 1970 for the key Department of Trade and Industry, they were faced two years later with the 1972 Industry Act in which he proposed the most sweeping extension of intervention into industry which had been up to that time enacted. What is perhaps more significant is that they were unaware of the full range of these proposals until the Bill itself was published in May 1972. One of the most significant pieces of legislation proposed since the formation of the CBI came as a very unpleasant surprise to the organisation. This was hardly a situation likely to deepen trust and understanding between the CBI and the government.

The CBI is in some difficulty in that it is less powerful as a corporate body industrially than the TUC and individual trade unions, who can impose their views more effectively and without losing as much as an individual employer who has his capital and/or profits at risk. The 1964–70 Labour government consulted the CBI as a logical corollary of consulting the TUC, with whom it had strong historical and emotional links. By 1974, Labour's relationship with the TUC had become stronger and, realising its power was greater than the CBI's, it attached more importance to consulting the TUC than the CBI. There had also been a considerable degree of pre-election policy planning which reduced the room for meaningful consultations with the CBI.

To some extent the Conservative party, when it was in office, considered that it represented business adequately and therefore knew better than the CBI, which it expected to be generally uncritical of its policies. During the 1970–74 Conservative government, relations tended to deteriorate partly because of this presumption and partly because of the attitude of both front-bench and back-bench Conservative MPs that accepting advice led automatically to weak government.

However, there can be little doubt that the real bodyblow to hopes of meaningful tripartism during the life of the 1970–74 Heath government came with the passage of the 1971 Industrial Relations Act. Indeed, the Act came close to marking an all-time low in government–trade union relations. The government may not have set out to have a confrontation with the trade unions, but there is no doubt at all that the unions, and the TUC, viewed the legislation in this way. This meant that those who had taken a conciliatory line in the TUC, in the style of George Woodcock, were completely outflanked. It also ensured that for two years there was little, if any, meaningful contact between the TUC and the government at any level. The abortive talks on a voluntary prices and incomes policy which took place in 1972, and subsequent discussions, were undermined by 'the atmosphere' which existed between the TUC and the government. It was very difficult to conduct meaningful tripartite talks on key political and economic issues against such a background. One should perhaps add that while the Industrial Relations Act did not improve the atmosphere, the TUC appeared acutely aware of the dangers of inflation and was anxious to play a part in correcting them. Indeed, in some respects the TUC appeared to act as if this were even more important than its increasingly successful resistance to the industrial relations legislation. On the other hand, the TUC leadership always had to look over its shoulder at the member unions, some of whom were responding to the increasingly militant mood of their own membership.

In addition, a successful tripartite system of arriving at key economic decisions requires good relations, and considerable agreement, between the CBI and the TUC. However, relations between the two organisations have not always been harmonious. There were a number of contacts between employers' organisations and unions before the formation of the CBI, but apart from wage negotiations they were usually in the fields of safety and training, as already mentioned. High-level contacts began to increase and improve at the beginning of the 1960s with a series of informal talks between the BEC and the TUC, and there is little doubt that the formation of the NEDC hastened this cooperation. The formation of the NEDC meant that for the first time the leaders of the employers' organisations and the unions met regularly to talk about key economic issues. Although the National Joint Advisory Council, set up as a system of tripartite consultation in 1939, considered some significant issues in the general field of industrial relations, it did not have the range of interest of the NEDC.

The formation of the CBI simplified relations with the trade unions. One of the most important reasons for establishing a single employers' body was that it would be 'the right medium to enable employers to get closer to the TUC'.[40] There is no doubt that at this time relationships did improve. One indication of this was the establishment in 1966 of a joint committee to investigate certain strikes. At the same time a TUC observer was invited to attend meetings of the CBI steering committee set up to examine the likely effects of EEC membership, and the TUC began to discuss its annual Economic Report with the CBI before its publication. This cooperation culminated in the formation of a Joint Committee of the CBI and TUC in January 1967. As the TUC commented in its Annual Report: 'The General Council recognised that consultation already took place between the two organisations on an *ad hoc* basis and that a regular exchange of views on such a standing committee would be valuable to both sides.'[41]

The formation of the Joint Committee owed much to the efforts of John Davies, then Director General of the CBI, and George Woodcock, then General Secretary of the TUC. Both believed in the possibility of cooperation between the two sides of industry and in the desirability of some form of tripartite arrangement. Initially, there were monthly meetings of the Joint Committee, and one of the regular features was a consideration of papers on the agenda of the relevant NEDC meetings. The meetings had a certain novelty at first and were attended by the individuals who represented the two organisations on NEDC. Some positive steps forward were made as a result of this cooperation, notably in the field of racial discrimination within industry, but attendance gradually fell away. This trend was accelerated by conflict over the Labour government's industrial relations proposals, which strained relations between the two groups. However, the withdrawal of the proposed legislation led to a slight easing of relations, and before the election in 1970 the CBI and TUC held a number of fairly cordial weekend sessions to discuss matters of mutual interest. The TUC believed that it had made some ground at these meetings, and relations seemed set to improve again. However, the report of the Neal working party (set up to review the CBI's industrial relations policy), approved by the CBI Council in July 1970, argued that while 'the essentially voluntary nature of the industrial relations system should be maintained . . . [it] needed to be supplemented by a legislative framework'.[42]

Once again the bodyblow to CBI–TUC relations came from proposals for new legislation on industrial relations, this time from the Conservatives. The TUC, believing that it had reached some kind of informal understanding with the CBI, hoped that the employers would support at least some substantial modifications of the government's proposals. Despite the misgivings held by many of its staff, the CBI gave general support to the Bill. This emphasised some of the difficulties within the CBI. The Social Affairs Directorate is advised through its Employment

Policy Committee and its employers' organisations' representative committees by industrial relations practitioners rather than general managers who have learnt to lead the life of 'sordid compromises' that their craft requires. It may be argued that the CBI's assessment of the Act as a 'balanced package' represented a victory of the general managers, who dominated the Council, over the practitioners in the relevant specialist committees, who influenced the staff concerned. If the CBI had a major reservation it was that it favoured a phased introduction of the legislation. The government opposed this as politically impractical.

After the passage of the Industrial Relations Act, the regular and formal dialogue between the CBI and the TUC ceased. However, even when relations were at their worst, CBI and TUC staff continued to meet informally to discuss less controversial matters such as industrial training and safety.[43] In addition, in 1972 a series of joint discussions led to the formation of a CBI/TUC Conciliation and Arbitration Service. Talks took place in the spring of 1974 about the development of conciliation and arbitration procedures. Despite the resumption of formal contacts, relations between the CBI and TUC have not completely recovered from the Industrial Relations Act.

The whole notion of tripartism as a method of making economic policy decisions presupposes the existence of consensus and a willingness to compromise on the part of the people involved. It is obviously crucially important that the negotiating parties should trust one another. The pattern of relationships we have sketched does not encourage one to believe that much trust exists, and even if agreements are reached by the leadership they run the risk of being subsequently repudiated or rendered ineffective by the membership. Tripartism seems to us to be a notion which will continue to have restricted application in British politics, given a continuation of the current political climate. It will be restricted to those areas such as industrial training and safety in which there is a ready basis for agreement and a history of cooperation between the parties involved.

Notes and References

1 N. Harris, *Competition and the Corporate Society* (London: Methuen, 1972), p. 46.
2 ibid., p. 65.
3 F. Oules, *Economic Planning and Democracy* (Harmondsworth: Penguin, 1966), p. 93.

4 National Union of Conservative and Unionist Associations, *91st Annual Conference, Verbatim Report*, p. 134.
5 D. Coates, *Teachers' Unions and Interest Group Politics* (London: Cambridge University Press, 1972), p. 120.
6 S. Beer, 'Pressure groups and parties in Britain', *A.P.S.R.*, **I** (1956), pp. 1–23.
7 S. Blank, *Government and Industry in Britain* (Farnborough: Saxon House, 1972), p. 100.
8 See Blank, op. cit., Chapter 6; J. B. Christoph, 'The Birth of Neddy' in *Cases in Comparative Politics* (Boston: Little Brown, 1965), pp. 44–89; R. Bailey, *Managing the British Economy* (London: Hutchinson, 1968), Chapter 2; S. F. T. White, *Great Britain: Quiet Revolution in Planning* (Syracuse: University Press, 1966), Chapters 1–4.
9 D. F. Berry, J. L. Metcalfe, W. McQuillan, *Neddy: an Organizational Metamorphosis*, London Graduate School of Business Studies working paper (undated), p. 9.
10 For an account of their work see G. D. Vaughan, 'Economic Development Committees', *Public Administration*, **49** (1971), pp. 363–83.
11 See H. Macmillan, *At the End of the Day* (London: Macmillan, 1973), p. 49.
12 H. Phelps Brown, 'The National Economic Development Organization', *Public Administration*, **41** (1963), pp. 239–46.
13 Blank, op. cit., p. 174.
14 Lord George-Brown, *In My Way* (London: Gollancz, 1971), p. 104.
15 *CBI Annual Report*, 1966, p. 20.
16 *CBI Annual Report*, 1970, p. 17.
17 *The Times*, 1 December 1972.
18 Vaughan, op. cit., p. 382.
19 Vaughan, op. cit., p. 383.
20 *The Times*, 1 December 1972.
21 Although, strictly speaking, it is not exclusively tripartite.
22 *H.C. Debs.*, vol. 852, c. 1144.
23 Its budget was expanded as part of the Labour governments' efforts to combat unemployment in 1975–6.
24 *H.C. Debs.*, vol. 852 c. 1144.
25 ibid.
26 ibid., c. 1144–5.
27 ibid., c. 1145.
28 ibid., c. 1145–6.
29 *H.C. Debs.*, vol. 846, c. 1298.
30 *H.C. Debs.*, vol. 857, c. 498–9.
31 *H.C. Debs.*, vol. 846, c. 1294.
32 *Safety and Health at Work* (Robens Report), Cmnd. *5034*, p. 36.
33 ibid., p. 37.
34 ibid.
35 R. Finnegan in *Patterns of Decision Making, Decision Making in Britain, Block 8, Parts 1–4* (Milton Keynes: Open University Press, 1973), p. 51.
36 F. G. Castles, *Decision Making Activity as Pressure Group Politics in Patterns of Decision Making, Decision Making in Britain, Block 8*, op. cit., p. 67.
37 T. May and M. Moran, 'Trade Unions as pressure groups', *New Society*, 6 September 1973, pp. 570–3, p. 571.

38 Third Report from the Select Committee on Science and Technology, 1973, *The Industrial Research Establishments of the Department of Trade and Industry*.

39 *The Times*, 21 November 1972.

40 *The Times*, 15 September 1965.

41 *TUC Annual Report*, 1967, p. 334.

42 *CBI Annual Report*, 1970, p. 33.

43 The CBI and TUC made a joint recommendation to the government in 1972 urging speedy implementation of the Robens Report.

8

On influence: case studies

IN THE PRECEDING CHAPTERS WE HAVE EXAMINED THE VARIOUS constraints which limit the CBI's ability to exert influence on government. Having drawn attention to the importance of these constraints, we shall now attempt to analyse the influence exerted on the decision-making process by the CBI. Here we present four case-studies of the CBI's involvement in particular pieces of legislation in Britain as well as one of its involvement with the EEC Commission. In the next chapter we shall embark on a more general consideration of the CBI's impact on key government policies since its formation in 1965.

We have already stressed the many conceptual and methodological difficulties involved in assessing an interest group's influence. Certainly we do not claim that it is possible to make conclusive statements about the CBI's influence on the basis of the case-studies presented in this chapter. Indeed, as we point out elsewhere, the 1975 Industry Act presents an interesting contrast with the 1972 Industry Act which we have studied here in detail. However, we have chosen our British studies carefully to provide a selection of various types of legislation. We decided to study two pieces of legislation passed by the Labour government of 1966–70 and two pieces passed by the Conservative government of 1970–74. Second, for each government we studied one major piece of legislation in the field of economic policy and one of a more technical character. Moreover, two of the case-studies are concerned with issues on which the CBI held a substantially different view from that of the TUC, two involved the CBI in a situation of competition with two smaller interest groups. The European case-study was chosen to illustrate the way in which the CBI approaches the Commission, a channel which it is increasingly likely to have to use.

The Industry Act 1972

No piece of legislation is typical, and of course one cannot measure the influence of an interest group in terms of one piece of legislation. However, the 1972 Industry Act was one of the most important pieces of legislation affecting industry that had been proposed since the formation of the CBI.

The Conservative government came to power in 1970 promising to 'disengage' the state from industry and pledged to a new approach to industrial policy which had little in common with that favoured by British governments since the Second World War. As Dell points out, 'no one could really explain what disengagement meant', although it involved such policies as less government aid for private industry, supposedly more freedom of action for the nationalised industries, accompanied by 'symbolic sacrifices of lame ducks'.[1] The CBI welcomed what it saw as 'a greater degree of realism in our economic and industrial thinking and action',[2] but the government quickly found the political costs of its new approach too high. Confronted with both rising inflation and rising unemployment, it reverted to interventionism and passed an Industry Act, which despite the subsequent denials by Conservatives cannot be seen as anything but a significant reversal of policy.

Much of the interventionist effort of successive British governments has been directed towards a successful regional policy. The scope of the problem was clearly presented in the White Paper entitled 'Industrial and Regional Development' published by the government in 1972:

> The problem of the older industrial areas is deep-seated and long-term. Its most serious symptom is the high level of unemployment, but there are others – net outward migration, slow economic growth, derelict land, old and obsolete factory buildings and often a relatively low level of amenity. Symptoms such as these only too often turn into causes of further decline.
>
> The ending of regional imbalances has been an objective of successive Governments in the United Kingdom for nearly four decades. Much has been achieved but no solution is yet in sight. A faster rate of national growth is a necessary precondition for effective regional effort as are the growing resources now being applied to modernising the infrastructure and improving the environment. Even so, however, it is clear that the accumulated measures of the years are not enough. New

measures to stimulate industrial growth and create fresh confidence are needed.[3]

The Conservative government made it clear when it assumed power in 1970 that one of its first tasks would be to initiate a review of regional policy. Consequently, since the interested parties knew that within two years a White Paper and subsequently a Bill would be forthcoming they all undertook their own reviews of regional policy. The relevant CBI committee – the Regional Development Committee – established a study group to review the organisation's position early in 1971. The group was mandated to consider in some depth whether there should be a regional policy at all before suggesting the form such a policy should take.

Obviously within the CBI's large and diverse membership there were firms with very different opinions on regional policy. Indeed some firms, notably although not exclusively larger firms, were inclined to believe that money spent on encouraging investment in the regions might be better spent on other forms of investment incentive. However, the study group, accepting the need for regional policy, was mainly concerned with how government investment could best stimulate industry in the regions. Two questions in particular were crucial: should government investment go directly to firms (via grants for capital equipment or through tax allowances), or should it be diverted to improve the infrastructure within which industry in the regions operated? Second, in administering direct investments should there be a system of grants for capital equipment or of tax allowances?

The CBI had been suspicious of all direct government assistance and particularly of the system of capital grants and had opposed their introduction in 1966. This suspicion was shared by a great many industrialists,[4] though by 1971 the organisation had come more to terms with the system, not least indeed because many members benefited from the grants. Thus, in 1970, the CBI opposed the Conservative government's move to abolish investment grants. Nevertheless the suspicion remained, fuelled by fears that such grants might be linked to more direct government involvement in the actual running of assisted companies.

Such fears had been confirmed by the Labour government's Industrial Expansion Bill in 1968. This proposed legislation not only allowed the gvoernment to issue grants on a wide scale but also to take equity holdings in the firms so assisted. The CBI and the Conservative opposition saw this as an attempt by the Labour government to achieve back-door nationalisation. The CBI's response was dramatic. John Davies, then Director General of the CBI, reacted with high ideological fury and refused to discuss with government any of the details of the proposed Bill. The CBI thus abdicated its right to consultation. This tacit opposition plus the active opposition of the Conservative party achieved no results and the Industrial Expansion Bill became law. Thus, although the CBI was beginning to accept the necessity, if not the principle, of investment grants under pressure from some of their Regional Councils and Officers, it was strongly opposed to any special government grants to industries or companies being conditional on the government's acquiring equity holdings in the firms so assisted. It is against this background that the 1972 Industry Act must be viewed.

The CBI's study group reported early in 1972, and its proposals were published on 24 February after discussion within the Regional Development Committee. They had previously been submitted to, and discussed with, the DTI. The CBI wanted the government to create a powerful commission for regional development with wide advisory and executive functions. The commission, the CBI argued, should have funds of its own to fund projects in development areas and should be directly responsible to the Chancellor of the Exchequer for its spending. The Commission should be particularly concerned with giving financial assistance to the planning and implementation of key infrastructure projects. There was no suggestion of direct assistance to firms and industries, only an acceptance of the existing structure of assistance under the Local Employment Acts. However, although the CBI did not specifically recommend a new system of capital grants, it did not come out against them. Nevertheless, the main emphasis of the CBI's document 'Reshaping Regional Policy' was on the importance of the infrastructure and on the need to establish and carry out clear priorities.

In contrast, the TUC was more concerned to stress the importance of direct grants and was particularly anxious that grants should be related to employment. Thus while the CBI's document had accepted as a premise the government's stated policy of ending Regional Employment Premium in September 1974, the TUC's document questioned this premise. There was a danger, the TUC argued, that the abolition of the Regional Employment Premium and the introduction of extensive investment grants related to capital investment would encourage capital-intensive rather than labour-intensive firms to move to the development areas. Understandably, the TUC was also anxious that grants should be extended to service firms, which were larger employers in relation to turnover, as well as to manufacturing firms. On the whole, however, the representations of the TUC and the CBI were not dissimilar, as the meeting of NECD on 1 March confirmed.[5] Both organisations stressed the need to improve the infrastructure of the development areas, to encourage the service industries in these areas and, in particular, to maintain continuity in regional policy.

Both organisations then had a number of discussions with DTI officials before the publication of the White Paper in March 1972. The White Paper itself was far from startling. Neither the TUC nor the CBI was totally satisfied, but although both gave the Paper guarded support the CBI was happier than the TUC. An Industrial Development Executive was to be established within the DTI and the new Minister for Industrial Development would be advised by an Industrial Development Board to be composed of industrialists and financiers. Although no powerful independent commission was proposed, the extent and seriousness of regional problems had been recognised by the establishment of a powerful team within government. CBI members were fairly satisfied, although they would have preferred to see more emphasis given to the problems of improving the infrastructure. Their main criticism was that the new capital investment grants would not be extended to service industries. The TUC was also disturbed about this but was more concerned that the government seemed set to continue its plans to abolish the Regional Employment Premium from September 1974.

After the publication of the White Paper, both the TUC and the CBI had bipartite talks with DTI officials. They put forward their major and minor objections and asked for clarification on various points. It seemed then that the normal process of consultation was in progress. At no time was the idea of special grants to ailing or high-technology industries discussed, and indeed only one paragraph in the whole White Paper referred to them. With hindsight, Paragraph 36 can be fully appreciated:

> On occasion, particularly in view of our entry into Europe, it may be necessary to consider the wider structure of an industry or a major project beyond the boundaries of the assisted areas. The Government will seek new powers also to provide selective assistance more widely in such cases. This would not be intended in any way to replace existing private sources of industrial finance.[6]

Neither the TUC nor the CBI appreciated the full implications of this paragraph, nor were they enlightened by DTI officials. The whole of the White Paper seemed concerned with regional policy and it was these problems which were discussed. The CBI was mainly concerned to argue with DTI officials about the detailed implications of some of the White Paper's proposals. At the time they were content with the answers they received.

Indeed no one seemed to foresee the final shape of the Bill. It is interesting that after the publication of the White Paper *The Times* leader welcomed its proposals before continuing: 'Some disappointment will be expressed over one omission. The Government have not yet plucked up courage to create a full-blooded body . . . which would be empowered . . . to provide funds at risk to encourage new ventures in areas of high unemployment.'[7] Perhaps the only comment upon Paragraph 36 which reached the press came in a letter to *The Times* from J. Bruce Gardyne, then Conservative MP for South Angus. He pointed out that: 'The only real innovation is the establishment of a Government institution to offer "selective financial assistance" to certain firms but not to their competitors. It is no doubt just as well that we are to have ministers answerable to the House of Commons for the operation of this scheme. They look like having plenty of answering to do.'[8]

With the benefit of hindsight, Paragraph 36 in the White Paper might have forewarned the CBI and the TUC to expect Part II, and particularly Clause 8, of the 1972 Industry Bill. However, when the Bill was published on 11 May both organisations were very surprised. The Bill allowed the newly established commission, with the consent of the Treasury, to provide financial assistance to firms outside development areas and also to take equity holdings in assisted firms. The CBI and a sizable number of Conservative back-benchers were alarmed. The TUC and the Labour party were pleasantly surprised. When the Bill was introduced in Parliament Mr Thorpe, the Liberal leader, accused Mr Davies of being a better socialist than his Labour Party predecessors. Indeed there was a good deal of irony in the fact that it was Mr Davies, as Secretary of State for Trade and Industry, who introduced a Bill which created powers for the selective acquisition of equity which went far beyond anything in the Labour government's Industrial Expansion Act of 1968.

There was not much immediate press reaction to the Bill's publication. The major newspapers all carried leading articles on it but none mentioned the issue of equity holdings. The key issues discussed were the future of the Regional Employment Premium and the position of the service industries. The question of equity holdings only emerged more fully during the second reading debate in the House of Commons on 22 May when John Davies was closely questioned on the provisions under Clause 8.

The CBI's own response was predictable. There were discussions between CBI officials and Christopher Chataway, the new Minister for Industrial Development, about the implications of the Bill. In particular the CBI wanted information about how the powers outlined in Clause 8 would be used. Despite assurances, the CBI wanted statutory controls which would limit the ministers' discretion.

Normally, once a Bill is published, the CBI switches its attention to the details of the proposed legislation. CBI officials may visit ministers to clarify certain aspects of policy, but at this stage their major contacts are with civil servants. CBI officials accept that once a Bill is published a government is unlikely to make major changes to its policy and therefore attempt to influence as much as possible the detail and administration of that policy. However, before the publication of a Bill, the CBI has usually already had a chance to make representations about the policy itself. In this case, there had not been any discussions with ministers about Clause 8 before publication of the Bill. Thus, while the CBI continued to discuss with civil servants the details of the provisions involved with reintroducing capital grants to development areas and in particular to push for their extension to service industries, it turned its major attention towards more political channels.

CBI officials used three main tactics in trying to extract major changes in Clause 8: they talked to ministers, they talked to the press, and they talked to Conservative back-benchers. During the passage of the Bill. CBI leaders had talks with Chataway and his colleagues on three occasions. These proved to be of little use however. The government was publicly committed to its policy and unwilling to make concessions. The second tactic used by the CBI was a more unusual one. On 15 June, over a month after the publication of the Bill, and after talks with ministers had failed, Michael Clapham, then President of the CBI, launched a spirited attack upon Clause 8 of the Bill in a speech in Bristol. Mr Clapham stated that the provisions involved in Clause 8 were 'pernicious' and in urgent need of parliamentary attention. They give the Secretary of State 'power such as we in this country are not accustomed to in time of peace'. He claimed that 'without some amendment the bill will confer a degree of political patroncy undreamed of since the Reform Bill of 1832'.[9] The CBI's aim was obviously to get wide press exposure for its arguments in order to make informed public opinion aware of the sweeping nature of the provisions. It was partly successful in this, but it was a desperate measure which did not strengthen the CBI's chances of influencing the Bill. Mr Clapham's speech was widely reported, although not always in the way the CBI would have liked. Indeed the *Financial Times* managed to do so without even mentioning his comments on the Industry Bill.[10] John Davies' reaction was more predictable. In public he contented himself with observing: 'I confess to being somewhat disappointed that my old organisation should through its President have questioned these provisions in terms which I found immoderate and unrealistic.' In private he was less restrained. Subsequent contacts between the CBI and the government on the Bill were hardly helped by this interchange.

In this case, it seemed to the CBI that Parliament was potentially the most productive channel it might use. CBI officials had already circularised both Labour and Conservative back-benchers after the publication of the White Paper, as indeed had the TUC, to try to win support for an extension of grants to service industries. Now, however, the situation was totally changed. Labour MPs were unlikely to prove receptive, but the CBI knew that a number of Conservative back-benchers were strongly opposed on ideological grounds to Clause 8. The CBI invited the most prominent of these men to Tothill Street for discussions. In particular, the CBI pressed for three major changes in the Bill:

1 It wanted stringent criteria which would limit the Secretary of State's powers to give assistance under Clause 8 to be written into the Bill. With this in mind the CBI developed and published its own criteria.

2 It wanted provisions to be included in the Bill for the 'continuing accountability' of the Secretary of State for actions taken under Clause 8. It also urged that the government should have to obtain an affirmative resolution enabling it to grant aid in circumstances which fell outside the proposed guidelines.

3 The CBI also wanted the Industrial Development Board to be given a statutory role with real powers. Indeed it suggested a provision to ensure that assistance could only be given by the minister after a recommendation from the Board.

These were the points that the CBI put both to government and, in particular, to the Conservative back-benchers. However, some back-benchers, among them Tom Normanton, Adam Butler and Harry Legge-Burke, were already informed critics of the proposed Clause. The most the CBI did in this case was to provide these men with some extra information and arguments.

Nevertheless the CBI's objections and suggested amendments were widely circulated among Conservative back-benchers and also received fairly wide coverage in the newspapers. Despite this, the CBI quickly became aware during its attempts to 'court' Conservative back-benchers of the limitations of its knowledge of, and contacts with, these back-benchers. This failing stemmed partly from lack of resources but also from the fact that the CBI rarely uses back-benchers as important channels of access. They did have contacts with certain Conservative back-bench committees (especially the Finance Committee) but these were inadequate in this unusual situation. Indeed, the CBI had most contact with those Conservative back-benchers who would have supported its position anyway. The majority of Conservative back-benchers who might have supported the CBI were only circularised, a rather ineffective way of trying to exert pressure. In the end CBI leaders concentrated, sensibly but with limited success, on the Conservative back-benchers on the Standing Committee which took the committee stage of the Bill.

Despite this, the CBI was considerably helped in this case by the fact that a number of highly articulate Conservative back-benchers opposed Clause 8, independent of any pressure from the CBI. In addition the Labour party, while generally welcoming the Bill, was anxious to give Parliament more say over the allocation of special grants. Thus an unholy alliance of the CBI, certain Conservative back-benchers and the Labour party favoured the introduction of a provision making the minister more accountable to Parliament.

As we can see, the Industry Bill presented an unusual situation for the CBI. They had not been consulted on a major provision of the Bill before its drafting; they used Parliament as a major channel in attempts to influence the legislation; and they found themselves, at least on one issue, in agreement with the Labour party in addition to certain Conservative back-benchers.

Although the CBI tried very hard during the passage of the Bill to get Clause 8 radically changed it was unsuccessful. The only major concession the government made was on the issue of parliamentary accountability, where they introduced an amendment as a result of back-bench pressure. Mr Chataway's new clause disclosed during the committee stage of the Bill put the proposed Industrial Development Advisory Board on a statutory basis and charged it with giving the minister advice on special grants.[11] If the minister disagreed with the Board then the Board members would have the right to ask for a statement to this effect to be put before MPs in Parliament. This was hardly a major concession and gave neither the Board nor Parliament significantly extended powers. In addition, it is fair to say that the concessions that were made were not solely the result of CBI pressure. The main reason for the government's change of mind seems to have been the pressure applied by a prominent section of articulate Conservative back-benchers. The government was afraid of a minor back-bench revolt. The concession which was made was hardly fundamental to Clause 8. It did provide some sort of check on a minister's patronage and discretion, but not a substantial one. The amendment the government accepted served as a concession to back-bench opinion and to CBI pressure without materially affecting the Bill. At best, the CBI had had indirect influence on some minor detail of the Bill. As Dell says:

> The CBI allowed itself to be satisfied by some fairly nominal amendments to the original Bill. These increased parliamentary control and introduced some safeguards against too enthusiastic a conversion by the Conservatives to the merits of equity participation. . . . The CBI then gave its presidential blessing urbi et orbi (to the City of London and to the world).[12]

In addition, despite its continual pressure and talks with the civil service the CBI failed to get capital grants extended to service industries. The TUC's representations on this issue also proved unsuccessful, as did their attempts to obtain concessions on the role of the Regional Employment Premium. Indeed, the Industry Bill, both in the Section concerned with capital investment grants in development areas and in that concerned with selective grants accompanied by equity holdings, escaped virtually unscathed despite continuing representations from both sides of industry.

It is understandable that once a government is committed to a policy, and that policy is enshrined in a Bill, it should be reluctant to make serious changes to that policy. But why was Clause 8 in the Bill in the first place? It was at odds with the policies on which the Conservatives had been elected, and it was opposed by large sections of their own party both inside and outside Parliament. Its inclusion is not difficult to understand, however, given the political and economic circumstances in 1970–71. One of the biggest problems the government faced was that of rising unemployment. This, together with the antagonism caused by the Industrial Relations Act, seemed to dispel any hopes which might still have existed for a voluntary prices and incomes policy. In addition, the collapse of the shipbuilding industry on Clydeside and of Rolls-Royce, together with the precarious state of the textile industry and the motor cycle industry, indicated the need for drastic solutions to drastic problems. What is more, ample evidence from areas such as the computer industry and the aeronautical industry showed that the huge sums needed for development in high-technology industries would not be available from private investment and would have to be provided by government.[13] All the presures tended towards selective assistance to various firms involved in high-technology industries or to firms employing large labour forces, both inside and outside development areas. Although this probably explains adequately why the government felt forced to make provision for selective assistance both inside and outside development areas, it does not explain why it became committed to equity holdings.

It must be remembered that the Conservative Government had come under a great deal of criticism when it had given assistance both to Upper Clyde Shipbuilders and to Rolls-Royce. The question widely asked was whether the government should invest money in industries or firms with bad performance records and/or uncertain futures without having a large say in how that money was spent. In the case of Upper Clyde Shipbuilders it had provided an open purse, giving money to a firm with a poor management record and a bad history of labour troubles. The formation of this group was understood at the time to be highly risky and could be justified only on the grounds that the alternative was to allow the firms on the Upper Clyde to collapse individually. Any hope of the group's survival depended on constant supervision and pressure from above, neither of which was forthcoming. The Shipbuilding Industry Board, established as a result of the Geddes Report, had proved inadequate for this difficult task. Could such supervision be undertaken without the government assuming direct responsibility associated with a partial equity holding? The Labour opposition and a wide section of the press severely attacked the government for not being more involved with the operation of the Upper Clyde. It was essential, it was argued, that the government should have a stake in any firm assisted on this scale. The government, remembering this criticism and the failure of the Shipbuilding Industry Board, probably suspected that such criticism would be reiterated and extended if no provision for equity holding were allowed for in the Bill. Past failures and political pressure seemed to the government to make a provision for equity holdings necessary. There were enough precedents,

BP and ICL for instance, and after all the proposal was that equity holdings should only be taken out for short periods, and then only with the consent of the firm concerned.

Thus it seems possible that the decision to take equity holdings was a response to prior criticisms and failures and an attempt to pre-empt similar future criticism. In trying to oppose and restrict equity holdings, the CBI was fighting an essentially political decision. It was not surprising that it failed.

What lessons can be drawn from this case study? A key point is surely that, despite the fact that the measure was crucially important to the CBI and that the ex-Director General was responsible for it, the CBI knew nothing about one of its key provisions until the Bill was published. This is very unusual. Why did it happen? It seems likely that Clause 8 was to some extent an afterthought – a response to immediate problems which were related to, but in important ways different from, the normal problems of regional policy. It was a rather hurried reaction to contemporary political problems and resurrected and extended provisions in the Industrial Expansion Act which the government had previously repealed. There was therefore a limited amount of time available for discussions with the CBI and other interested groups, although this was not a major problem. Though it would have taken little time to inform the CBI of the proposal it was taken completely unawares. In fact the major reason why the CBI was not consulted was probably that the government did not want the proposal leaked to the press or to Conservative back-benchers. The party, when faced with a *fait accompli*, would accept proposals which were ideologically unpalatable, but if Conservative back-benchers knew of them before the Bill was published stern opposition might be expected. The government was also anxious to distinguish its policies from those of the previous Labour government. This would obviously be more difficult if press and opposition knew of the proposals before they were published. In addition, relations between the CBI and the DTI were none too good at this time. There appears to have been a considerable amount of unease between John Davies and the CBI after he took over at the DTI. The CBI felt that Davies did not consult them sufficiently, partly because, after his experience in industry and within the CBI, he thought he knew what industry wanted. Nevertheless it seems likely that the government kept the CBI ill-informed about the true nature of the Industry Bill mainly because of the way it perceived the political situation.

Another significant point to be drawn from this case study is that, although CBI officials disagreed fundamentally with the Conservative government, they continued to hold talks with it. In contrast, when they had disagreed with the Labour government on the Industrial Expansion Act, which was less interventionist, they had broken off discussions. In 1972 the CBI at least felt that the government might be willing to listen, because it had better relations with the Conservative government than it had had with the Labour one in 1968. The CBI trusted the government more and felt that breaking off relations would be misguided when some amendments, albeit small, might be forthcoming. As Dell says: 'It is not a surprising characteristic of the CBI that whatever difficulties business-men have in understanding the ideologies of politicians, even Conservative politicians, it does feel more trust in a Conservative Government than in a Labour Government.'[14]

It is also worth noting that during the passage of the Industry Bill the CBI used Parliament as a channel of access more than normally. This made the CBI realise the inadequacy of its contacts in this sphere. Limited resources meant that there was little CBI leaders could do to improve the situation substantially, but they did respond to requests from Conservative back-benchers to examine their links with Conservative back-bench committees and parliamentarians. In fact in March 1973 Michael Clapham met a group of some forty Conservative back-bench MPs to discuss this problem. However, as we have already seen, the CBI was and is very anxious not to ally itself too closely with any party. It wanted to achieve a difficult compromise: more information about Conservative back-benchers without increased identification with them.

Despite all this, what finally emerges overwhelmingly from this case study is that once again the CBI was more successful over details than over policy. It welcomed minor changes in the regional provisions but could not get capital investment grants extended to service industries. It could not make the government change its mind on the main provisions of Clause 8 and had to be satisfied with fairly minor amendments to the original Bill. Indeed even then the CBI accepted substantially less parliamentary control than had been provided by the Industrial Expansion Act. However, it must be added that the CBI's opposition may have influenced the way this Section of the Bill was administered by the Conservative government. This would not be unusual, as the CBI often exerts its influence most successfully after a piece of legislation is passed. In this case, most, if not all, of the instances in which the powers of Section 8 of the Act were used by Heath's government met the criteria proposed by the CBI but not accepted by the government.[15] The restricted use the Conservative government made of the Section may partly have resulted from the reverberations of the row made by the CBI and certain Conservative back-benchers.

Overall, it cannot be said that the CBI had great influence on the final shape of the Industry Act in general or on Section 8 in particular. However, there is no evidence that the TUC or other groups had much influence either. The decisions were political ones. In introducing Section 8, the government seems to have been most influenced by the past record of governments generally, and by its own in particular, in this field and by the immediate demands of the economic and political situation.

The Iron and Steel Act, 1967

The Iron and Steel Act of 1967 must be viewed in the context of the historical development of legislation in this field. Indeed, the saga of the nationalisation, denationalisation and renationalisation of steel is probably the prime symbol of the ideological divide in British politics since 1945.[16] The initial nationalisation in 1951 and, to a slightly lesser extent, renationalisation in 1967 were forced through against quite bitter and well organised resistance, and compromises were consistently rejected.

The government was first closely involved in attempts to control steel production in the 1930s through the Import Duties Advisory Committee, and subsequently during the Second World War the industry was placed under the auspices of the Iron and Steel Control. Under both these arrangements the employers exerted the dominant influence. However the new Labour government of 1945 was committed to iron and steel nationalisation and after considerable delays, during which it had extensive discussions with the leaders of the steel industry,[17] the government introduced its Iron and Steel Nationalisation Bill in October 1948. The legislation had a stormy passage through the Commons, but because of opposition from the Lords it was not until after the general election of 1950 that the Bill was passed, and in February 1951 the steel industry passed into public ownership.

The majority of the Conservative party had always been fundamentally opposed to the whole notion of nationalisation. Radical mavericks such as Harold Macmillan had been advocating nationalisation of basic industries since before the war, but the opposition generated by the relatively innocuous proposal to create a Central Electricity Board in 1926 and by the transfer of coal royalties to a Public Coal Commission in 1938 indicated that most Conservative back-benchers were reluctant to accept any move towards public ownership.[18] During the passage of the Labour government's bill, the Conservatives were in fact more concerned to oppose the whole notion of nationalisation than to cite the economic benefits of private ownership.[19] Indeed, as Harris points out, many Conservatives 'saw steel as the Rubicon of British society – beyond it lay full socialism'.[20] Thus they opposed the Bill at every stage, unsuccessfully moving amendments to limit the scope of the Bill, to limit the power of the ministers and to protect consumers.

The attitude of industry to the bill was very similar. As Blank says: 'To the FBI there was a world of difference between the nationalisation of iron and steel, and of an industry such as coal which was "sick", or gas and electricity, which were public utilities already under a considerable degree of state control.'[21]

Nevertheless, despite its indignation, the FBI realised it would still have to talk to government after the legislation had been passed. So, as in most other cases of nationalisation, the FBI and other employers' organisations fought a defensive battle, accepting gradually and reluctantly the fact of nationalisation but trying to get the details of legislation amended. All this meant that the FBI in particular was less vociferous and direct in its opposition to the Bill than much of industry, including many of its members, would have liked. Indeed the publicity of the Economic League and of Aims of Industry was a better reflection of the strength of the views of industry than were the more considered representations of the FBI. However, despite the internal opposition, the FBI, and Kipping in particular, fought successfully to keep contacts with government open and to continue the policy of not engaging in direct propaganda or entering into formal ties with the propaganda organisations.[22] In addition the FBI increasingly attempted to 'educate' its membership. As Kipping has commented:

Many people were just plain frightened, for they could not see where nationalisation would end. The concept of a mixed economy that has since become a reality was not at that time within the imagination of most industrial people; they thought there would turn out to be no halfway house between complete socialism and complete private enterprise. . . . (Eventually) we begin to study our problems rationally and to get away from the atmosphere of near panic that had for a short time prevailed.[23]

Despite this effort, however, the existing management boycotted the new structure, no leading industrialist with experience in the steel industry being found to serve on the new Iron and Steel Board.

Given the ideological stance of the Conservative party and of industry, it was not surprising that when the Conservative government came to power in 1951 the first Queen's speech gave notice of its intention to denationalise steel. The process was not swift, and it was eighteen months before Parliament passed the Iron and Steel Act, which provided for the full denationalisation of the industry.[24] The Labour opposition fought the legislation throughout its passage through Parliament and was well supported by the trade union movement. However the battle lines were by now so well defined that all their efforts were unproductive.

This is the context within which the Iron and Steel Act of 1967 must be viewed. The positions of the main participants had long been laid down. Throughout its period of office from 1951 to 1964 the Conservative party came to accept, if not necessarily to favour, more government involvement in the economy, though the notion of nationalisation still evoked fears which seemed to bear little relationship to the Labour party's stated intentions. Industry also came reluctantly to accept the inevitability of government involvement in its affairs, though nationalisation still provoked fears of full socialism. In defence of the 'free-enterprise' system, the Economic League and Aims of Industry, supported financially by the FBI and other industrial organisations, made active propaganda against nationalisation particularly during the 1959 and 1964 election campaigns. The Labour party, while viewing nationalisation as its Achilles heel, especially under Hugh Gaitskell, was still committed to the renationalisation of steel, if only as a concession to its left wing. The battle lines were still unchanged and firmly drawn. The stage was set for a rerun of the 1948–51 situation if a Labour government came to power.

The Labour party returned to power in 1964 with a small majority on a manifesto committed to steel nationalisation. The mention of steel nationalisation in the Queen's Speech of November 1964 led to the formation of an *ad hoc* committee of the FBI, the NABM and BEC. This committee met regularly and continued after the CBI was formed. Its members talked to government ministers but with little hope of success and to no avail. The government's White Paper, 'Steel Nationalisation' (Cmnd 2651), was published in April 1965 and proposed that fourteen large companies should be taken into public ownership. These companies in practice dominated the industry, being responsible for over 90 per cent of its major products. The government narrowly survived a hectic debate on its proposals and decided to shelve the necessary legislation until it had a larger majority. Consequently there was no mention of steel nationalisation in the Queen's Speech of November 1965. However the industrial organisations were not deceived by this omission. Their talks with government had convinced them that the proposal would be resurrected if another election gave Labour a larger majority.

What the CBI had feared took place. A Labour government was elected in 1966 with an increased majority and, predictably enough, steel nationalisation appeared in the new government's legislative programme. The CBI renewed its representations to government, talking to Richard Marsh (Minister of Fuel and Power) and his colleagues on a number of occasions. Despite this access, the CBI was forced into the type of defensive action in which most interest groups[25] have to engage if they are opposed to a policy proposal which the government thinks is of major importance. Indeed it followed the same type of strategy that had been used by the FBI in its campaigns against the nationalisation policy of the first post-war Labour government. Representations on the policy of nationalisation were of very little use though, as the CBI Annual Report of 1966 admitted: 'In these circumstances the C.B.I. while continuing to affirm its unequivocal opposition to the principle of nationalisation necessarily concentrated its efforts on seeking amendments to the more objectionable features of the bill.'[26] The CBI talked on a number of occasions to the department about the details of the legislation. Its main aims were: (1) to reduce the power of the minister to intervene in the running of the industry; (2) to protect the consumer in relation to pricing policy by strengthening the powers of the Consumers Council; (3) to protect the position of that section of the industry which remained in private hands; and (4) to hive off to private industry the non-steel interests of the firms to be nationalised. All these points were raised at the ministerial and senior civil servant level.

At the same time, the CBI had talks with a number of Conservative MPs. They were preaching to the converted. This briefing may have provided some information and arguments for these MPs to use in Parliament, but there was never any doubt that the Conservative party would oppose the bill through all its stages. However, despite the combined opposition of the Conservative party and industry, the legislation was successfully steered through Parliament and very few concessions were made. The only amendments the government were willing to accept were very minor ones which went some way to safeguarding the interests of that section of the steel industry which was not nationalised. In detail, amendments were accepted which ensured that: the new Corporation would have to publish price lists for all its products and figures relevant to the turnover, capital employed and profit and loss of its non iron and steel activities; private iron and steel producers would have the right to appeal to the minister against any unfair trading practices on the part of the Corporation. These, however, were minor successes in what was essentially an unproductive campaign for the CBI.

What general lessons can we draw from this case study? The CBI could rely on the overwhelming support of its members in its stand against steel nationalisation, as well as the continuing strong opposition of the Conservative party. At the same time the press generally supported the CBI's position, and the efforts of Aims of Industry and the Economic League ensured that the anti-nationalisation case dominated the media. It was faced, however, with a Government committed to this legislation and determined to overcome all opposition, and once the Labour party had increased its majority in 1966 the CBI was fighting a losing battle.

Despite this, the CBI leadership persevered, although many members would have preferred them to break off relations with the government. They had little hope of real success, and indeed the amendments which they obtained on the details of the Bill were of minimal importance. However, breaking off relations would have affected their influence in other spheres of industrial and economic policy. They wanted to continue talking to government on other matters. So the CBI accepted the reality of the situation as had the FBI before it. In addition it continued to educate its members about these realities. As Sir Stephen Brown said in the 1967 CBI Report: 'Whilst our first responsibility is to represent the views of our members as forcefully and effectively as we can, and use our influence to the benefit of industry as a whole, we must also be prepared to give advice and guidance to our members as to the right policies for industry itself to pursue, based on our experience and all the information available to us.'[27]

In fact, the CBI was more successful in this respect than the FBI had been, largely because industrialists had had experience of the workings of a mixed economy and no longer feared nationalisation to such an extent. This meant that industrialists were now more willing to cooperate than they had been with the old Iron and Steel Board. The attitudes of industry had changed significantly. Industrialists still did not like nationalisation, but they no longer feared it. The CBI had played an educative role in bringing about this change. However, despite all this, the main conclusion must be that the CBI fought an almost entirely unsuccessful defensive action.

The Deposit of Poisonous Wastes Act, 1972

Until recently there has been relatively little legislation in Britain covering the discharge of solid, as distinct from liquid, wastes. In 1964 the then Ministry of Housing and Local Government appointed a committee to consider methods of disposal of solid and semi-solid toxic wastes, an example of the cautious and considered approach to environmental pollution problems of which the CBI approves. The CBI conducted a survey through certain trade associations which provided the committee with valuable information on quantities and categories of toxic solid wastes and when the committee's report (the Key Report) appeared in 1970, 'the summary, conclusions and recommendations showed that the Committee had taken into account written and oral representations made by the CBI.'[28] The CBI was consulted by the complementary Working Party on Refuse Disposal which published its report (the Summer Report) shortly afterwards.

The CBI's policy on environmental pollution has been to accept that some changes in the statutory framework are both inevitable and desirable but also to ensure that such changes as do take place occur at a pace and in a fashion that does not impose an excessive financial burden on industry. The CBI has argued that modernisation of industrial operations and increased investment in new processes and plant will in any case lead to a significant reduction in pollution from industrial sources. Conditions imposed on discharges of industrial effluent must be 'technically and financially capable of achievement' and 'conditions must be related to the circumstances of each discharge and of the receiving source'.[29] The CBI believes that its activities educate industrialists to the importance of a positive approach to pollution problems, but it is admitted that 'British industry is still coming to terms with the revolution of rising environmental expectations that has engulfed society'.[30] There is concern that 'much present criticism is in essence a disguised attack on the profit system'.[31]

The new public interest in 'the environment' had led to the formation of a number of new pressure groups, and one of these, the newly-formed Warwickshire branch of the Conservation Society, received disturbing information from a lorry driver about the unauthorised tipping of dangerous substances on a number of sites in Warwickshire. In January 1972 the story 'broke' in the national press and a few trial borings were made at one of the sites. No dangerous substances were discovered, and for a time it seemed as if the conservationists had been discredited. Then in February thirty-six drums of cyanide were found dumped in a brick-yard at Nuneaton. This discovery attracted considerable publicity for, as the then Secretary of State for the Environment, Peter Walker, later put it: 'Children's lives have been put at risk by irresponsible dumping.'[32] On 3 March, Walker announced that the Government was to rush through Parliament a Bill designed to provide new controls over the deposit of toxic wastes. The Deposit of Poisonous Wastes Act, which passed through Parliament in three weeks, created a new offence, that of depositing wastes on land, where the waste is of a kind that is poisonous or polluting and its presence on land is liable to give rise to an environmental hazard. It required anyone depositing wastes to notify in advance the local authorities and river authorities of the nature and quantity of the deposit proposed.

The speed at which events moved provided the CBI with fewer opportunities than usual to exert influence through the normal processes of consultation. However, the CBI claims that its Industrial Solid Wastes Panel was consulted over the Bill and some detailed changes were negotiated. The CBI persuaded the government to restrict the period of notification specified in the Bill to three days, although some MPs would have preferred a longer period. Mr Dalyell (Labour MP for West Lothian) complained in the House of Commons that the inclusion of a penalty in the Bill for local officials who disclose trade secrets revealed that 'once again Whitehall has bowed to CBI pressure and agreed that polluters should be spared public embarrassment'.[33] Thus the CBI was able to obtain some concessions before the Bill left the House of Commons.

As we have pointed out, the CBI often finds the House of Lords more useful than the House of Commons when it is trying to change details of a Bill. Sometimes amendments are tabled by friendly peers, not in the hope that they will be adopted but as a means of obtaining further assurances from the government. This is what happened in the case of the Deposit of Poisonous Wastes Bill. Viscount Simon, briefed by the CBI, moved a number of amendments to the Bill. Lord Greenwood remarked of one of these amendments that 'it would seriously weaken the bill'.[34] and if they had been pressed home the result might have been to provoke a 'backlash' which would have harmed rather than helped CBI members. However, the CBI was well aware of this danger. It was not anticipated that it would be possible to amend the Bill significantly, and the amendments were withdrawn after ministers had given assurances during the debate about the defences that would be available to a manufacturer prosecuted under the Act, a point that had worried the CBI. The CBI's brief for its members on the Act contains extensive references to the Lords debate and to the assurances obtained by Viscount Simon.

Although concessions of this kind were obtained, the CBI admits that the speed of events made it difficult to exert any really substantial influence on the contents of the Bill. Once the measure was enacted, however, the normal processes of consultation reasserted themselves. The CBI was involved in the drafting of the Department of the Environment's circular on the Act, particularly the two forms published as appendices. Even more important, the CBI was able to exert some influence over the draft regulations made under the Act. In particular, the CBI was able to persuade the government to extend the range of industrial wastes exempted from the notification procedures established under the Act.

The Deposit of Poisonous Wastes Act was intended to be an interim measure and has been repealed by the new Control of Pollution Act. Part 1 of the Act deals with the disposal of solid wastes and the CBI particularly welcomes the proposal that waste disposal authorities should have a statutory responsibility for drawing up comprehensive plans to ensure that adequate and appropriate provision is made for the disposal of all wastes in their areas, including those of industry. The CBI considers that the Deposit of Poisonous Wastes Act made the disposal of solid wastes by industry much more difficult and costly because it did nothing positive to ensure provision of adequate disposal facilities and because, in effect, the enforcing authorities operated an informal assent procedure against which it was not possible to appeal. Because Part 1 of the Control of Pollution Bill contained a number of novel features, such as the introduction of site licensing, the CBI has been closely consulted by government about its proposals in a way that was not possible when the Deposit of Poisonous Wastes Act was rushed through Parliament. Indeed, the fact that the Control of Pollution Act's predecessor, the Protection of the Environment Bill, lapsed when Parliament was dissolved in February 1974 made the process of consultation more prolonged than usual.

What general lessons can be drawn from this case study? The Chairman of the Warwickshire Conservation Society claimed that the passage of the

Deposit of Poisonous Wastes Act 'has demonstrated what can be achieved in the way of social reform, against powerful vested interests and official inertia, by public opinion aroused by a triple alliance of an individual citizen with conscience and determination, a small but dedicated group of fellow-citizens, and the information media well briefed'.[35] It would seem then, that, a new interest group with hardly any permanent staff can exert as much influence over a specific issue as the CBI. However, one must remember the special circumstances of the case. In particular, there was a minister who was anxious to demonstrate that his concern for the environment was genuine and who wished to 'attain the most comprehensive system of control of dangerous materials on land, on water and in the air'.[36] The combination of emotive media publicity and a sympathetic minister is an unusual one. Moreover, as the Key Report stressed: 'We would emphasise that legislation and regulation cannot provide the whole answer. It is also important to foster a spirit of mutual cooperation and helpfulness.'[37] Because the Bill was rushed through as a panic measure, considerable administrative difficulties resulted. All the appropriate forms were not available and in the Coventry area alone 174 requests for advice were received from industrialists during the first five months of the Act's operation.

It would be easy, however, to dismiss the Deposit of Poisonous Wastes Act as a legislative aberration of no lasting significance. It had the important indirect effect of leading industry (particularly large firms) to give waste disposal problems even more serious thought than hitherto. However, it was an aberration in the sense that it represented a temporary disruption of the normal processes of consultation between government and CBI on environmental pollution problems. The long-standing 'tradition of consultation and cooperation'[38] between government and industry has since reasserted itself. This relationship has often been criticised as 'excessively cosy', but it is not insulated from popular opinion as this case study shows.

There is now, of course, more popular concern about 'the environment' than was once the case, and, more importantly, a number of active conservationist groups transmit this concern to government. Groups such as the Conservation Society present environmental problems in such a way as to excite considerable attention from the mass media. The government's willingness to consider urgent legislation on the disposal of solid wastes seems to have increased as the revelations in the press and on television became more dramatic. 'Toxic solid wastes' is a subject unlikely to arouse much public interest, but the dumping of cyanide in a place accessible to children evokes an immediate and emotive public response. However, this public concern would probably not have led to new legislation if the Conservation Society had not exerted effective pressure upon a receptive minister. The dialogue between the CBI and government on environmental pollution has been affected by changes in the state of public opinion and particularly by the existence of new and more effective environmental pressure groups. It is, of course, difficult to maintain public interest and concern about these issues, and once the Deposit of Poisonous Wastes Act was enacted the close working relationship between government and industry on environmental matters established over the decades came into operation once again. Nevertheless, new environmental legislation is being introduced at a more rapid pace than was once the case. The CBI can obtain detailed (often important) concessions for its members, as it was able to on the Deposit of Poisonous Wastes Act, but it cannot significantly alter the general trend of events. Even on relatively technical legislation, the influence of the CBI is limited by the state of public opinion, the determination of ministers to build a legislative reputation and the activities of other interest groups.

The Clean Air Act, 1968

The Clean Air Act of 1968 extended the provisions for abating air pollution contained in the Clean Air Act of 1956. Although 'not simply a bit of administrative tidying up',[39] it built on the legislative base established by the earlier Act. The main objects of the 1968 Act industrially were to empower the minister to prescribe limits on the level of grit, dust, and fumes to be emitted from furnaces and to extend to a wider range of furnaces the obligation to install plant to arrest grit, dust and fumes. On the domestic side, the minister was given power to direct local authorities to submit programmes of smoke control and to require them to carry such programmes out, thus enabling him to deal with councils that had not been exercising their powers of smoke control where a local need for them existed.

The sponsors of the Bill were at pains to stress that 'it is not a harassing Bill. Least of all it is not meant to be a harassing Bill for industry'.[40] In the Lords it was claimed that 'all the measures in the Bill have been agreed . . . by the CBI and the latter body has been extremely helpful in drawing them up'.[41] Certainly, the CBI felt able to claim that it was 'conspicuously successful in getting the Clean Air Act 1968 satisfactorily amended during the Bill's progress in Parliament'.[42] The CBI agreed not to object to the Second Reading of the Bill provided that the government was prepared to make amendments to meet the CBI's objections. Such a strategy was feasible because, although it had government backing, the Bill was a private member's measure sponsored by Robert Maxwell MP. As Lord Kennet, then Joint Parliamentary Secretary, Ministry of Housing and Local Government, frankly admitted: 'Mr Robert Maxwell's place in the ballot is a marginal one – thirteenth – and the Bill was and is, therefore, somewhat vulnerable to attack and sinking by a well-directed shot from objectors to this or that provision. It cannot therefore be a very radical or controversial measure.'[43]

Although there was some criticism of the Bill as inadequate and insufficiently radical, it did not come from the principal organisation concerned with pollution of the air, the National Society for Clean Air. As the Society pointed out, 'It may not contain everything that everyone would like, but it does include as much as is wise and practicable for a private member's measure.'[44] The Society was particularly concerned with the clauses concerned with domestic smoke which they considered helped to remedy some of the defects of the 1956 Clean Air Act. They believed that the most important parts of the Bill were those which gave the minister or secretary of state power to make a default order directing a local authority to make orders for smoke control and which made it an offence to buy and use unauthorised fuel in a smoke control area.

Government speakers in the various debates lavished praise on the CBI for the way in which it had 'assisted in the preparation and drafting of this Bill'.[45] Mr Maxwell was at pains to stress that 'no one is forced to take or leave the Bill as it stands on Second Reading. Reasoned amendments to improve it in any respect will be welcomed.'[46] One amendment was moved to a clause which gave the local authority power to exempt an individual furnace from the requirement on the owner of the furnace to have a grit and dust arrester. The CBI thought that industry should be safeguarded against local authority severity, and a right of appeal to the Minister was incorporated in the appropriate clause.

The government also emphasised that considerable parts of the Bill would be brought into force by subsequent regulations and that it would be possible 'to be flexible'.[47] For example, it was agreed that Clauses 2 and 3 should not apply generally to the emission of fumes. The Minister was given power to apply these clauses to fumes by regulation, but it was stressed that he would 'consult the interested bodies in the usual way before proceeding to make regulations'.[48] The CBI was consulted over the drafting of exemption orders made under the Act in 1968 'to ensure that industry's problems under the new Act were taken fully into account'.[49] It was also consulted over the preparation of explanatory memoranda published by the Ministry.

The CBI would seem to be justified in claiming a considerable measure of success in achieving substantial modifications in the drafting and implementation of the 1968 Clean Air Act. Why was the CBI so successful in relation to this particular Act? It should be stressed that the CBI set itself reasonable objectives. The government stressed that the CBI's approach had been 'extremely responsible'.[50] If the CBI had attempted to defeat the Bill completely, it might have succeeded in the short run, but the government would have been pressurised to introduce a measure of its own which would have certainly taken much less account of industry's objections. The CBI was successful in attaining the objectives it set itself, but this does not mean it would have been equally successful if it had pursued alternative strategies. The CBI may be able to delay and modify air pollution legislation, but it cannot completely prevent legislation on the subject; indeed, the CBI would claim that it would not wish to do so.

Clearly it was important that the Bill was a private member's measure. Even though the government supported the Bill, it indicated that there were limits to the amount of legislative time and effort it was prepared to devote to ensuring its passage. The main group supporting the Bill, the National Society for Clean Air, was more concerned with its domestic than with its industrial clauses. Any criticism on its part of industry's approach to air pollution legislation might have had the effect of jeopardising the entire Bill. However, now that an effective legislative framework for the control of domestic smoke has been established, the Society is becoming more interested in the problem of industrial air pollution. In his presidential address to the Society in 1970, Sir Kenneth Hutchinson stated: 'We must avoid becoming too involved with the problem of domestic smoke. . . . During the next few years our attention will inevitably become directed towards the problems of industry. . . . The Society must be well informed and not make the mistake of pressing for the impossible, but they should also be able to judge what is possible and not hesitate to remind industry of its responsibilities to the community.'[51]

What is clear from our studies of the Deposit of Poisonous Wastes Act and the Clean Air Act is that the CBI has been able to exert substantial influence on legislation concerned with pollution. What is also clear is that the ability of the CBI to exert influence is affected by the existence and strength of other interest groups with different concerns. The new public interest in pollution problems and the growth of a new breed of interest groups dealing with environmental problems has affected the CBI's ability to modify legislation in this area. Moreover, as government acquires new sources of information of its own, the expertise of the CBI may become less crucially important. This is not to say that the CBI will be unable to protect the interests of its members, but it may find it more difficult to influence the pace of legislative change. The more general lesson to be drawn from these case studies is that the influence of an interest group changes over time in response to changes in the political environment.

The CBI and the EEC: the case of Economic and Monetary Union
As we have pointed out, British membership of the European Community means that the CBI must devote some of its resources and efforts to attempting to influence the development of Community policy. One problem which engaged a great deal of the organisation's attention in 1973 was the future development of Economic and Monetary Union (EMU). The final objective of EMU was described in the 1969 Werner Report as 'making it possible to realise an area within which goods and services, people and capital will circulate freely and without competitive distortion, without thereby giving rise to structural or regional dis-equilibrium'.[52] EMU was planned for realisation in three stages, the last of which would end on 31 December 1980.

In fact, by 1973 the only clearly visible step that had been taken towards achievement of the policy was the so-called 'snake' which limited fluctuations among member countries' currencies to narrower margins than those relating to the dollar. Britain, Ireland and Italy had opted out of 'the snake', but in the spring of 1973 it retained an importance which was perhaps as much symbolic as substantive.

While endorsing the objective of EMU, the CBI had been a consistent critic of the route by which the Community sought to reach it. The CBI considered that the Community had failed to uphold its own principle of parallel progress in the field of economic and monetary integration, as set out in the decision of the Council of Ministers of March 1971. The CBI argued that the Community had all but adopted a policy of pushing ahead with forms of monetary integration in the hope that this would force progress towards the coordination of government economic policies and aid industrial and economic integration generally. To put monetary objectives before general economic and industrial objectives in this way was at odds with the fundamental view of the CBI that governments should first decide their economic and industrial objectives and then ensure that their monetary objectives are compatible.

The CBI, then, was dissatisfied with the Community's increasing concentration on certain monetary aspects of EMU. In April 1973, the Commission produced proposals for the second stage of EMU (sometimes called the Haferkamp Report)[53] which did little to allay the CBI's disquiet. In the CBI's view, the report placed too great an emphasis upon monetary integration centred on the currency 'snake'. The CBI did not want a blueprint for the future which essentially offered 'more of the same'. Looking at the problem from industry's point of view, the CBI argued that increased trade and investment would best be sustained if governments kept up the momentum towards the creation of a common competitive climate within the Community. The CBI considered that member states had not devoted enough effort to the construction of a community of economic interests which would underpin EMU. For example, while earlier agreements to reduce tariff barriers had improved access to a wider market, there had been little progress in the CBI's view in removing technical and other non-tariff barriers to trade. The organisation maintained that an effective regional policy should be a precondition of further progress towards limiting the freedom of member states in economic and monetary matters. Above all, monetary union should follow as a natural development from economic and industrial union.

However, although the CBI was firmly convinced that the degree of integration among the economies of the member countries was far less than was required to make monetary union possible, they realised that their approach could be portrayed as involving only destructive criticism. They therefore set up an 'in-house' working party to undertake a reassessment of EMU with a view to putting forward constructive proposals. Because they saw other policies with different labels (e.g. Common Industrial Policy) as interrelated with EMU, representatives of five directorates were involved in this working party (Company Affairs; Social Affairs; Overseas; Education, Training and Technology, and the Economic Directorate). The broad lines of the working party's mandate were approved by the appropriate committees and by Council, and a draft report went to the

Financial Policy Committee, the Europe Committee and the Economic Policy Committee at the beginning of October 1973.[54] It was also shown at this stage to chairmen of Regional Councils and a final version was approved by the CBI Council in November.[55]

In Brussels the CBI had been debating its views with its sister federations in UNICE. The initial position of most of the other federations was clearly distinct from that of the CBI, especially on the question of 'the snake'. The differences of opinion on 'the snake' in particular featured prominently in reports of the meetings of UNICE working parties.[56]

Nevertheless, the industrial federations of the 'old Six' appeared anxious for new ideas which would help to reinvigorate arrangements that were becoming increasingly unworkable. The CBI found the atmosphere at the September meeting of what was later to be called the Economic and Monetary Problems Working Party more receptive to its point of view. A request was made for a preview of the CBI's reassessment of EMU. Nevertheless, the report of the meeting makes it clear that the priorities of the other delegations still differed from those of the CBI.[57] The CBI played down monetary integration in the form of 'the snake', although they suggested that the European Monetary Cooperation Fund should be given some resources of its own by pooling some parts of member states' reserves, as the Commission had already proposed.

What followed was a complex process of negotiation and drafting in which the other members of UNICE were gradually won round to a position more sympathetic to the CBI's point of view. It is not possible to give here a detailed account of the process that eventually led to the production of an agreed UNICE paper on EMU. However, one difficulty that was encountered was the order in which certain topics should be dealt with in the final version. The CBI wanted priority to be given to the creation of a common competitive climate, convergence of economic policies coming second and monetary integration last. Some federations would have preferred to place 'convergence' first, and others would have given first place to monetary integration.

The final version placed 'convergence' first but left monetary integration to the end, placing what was now termed 'the creation of a common industrial base' second. These considerations may seem rather technical, bu the ordering of a paper can indicate the emphasis which is attached to different parts of it. The process of reaching agreement among the member federations of UNICE often involved detailed discussions about the drafting and ordering of a paper, discussions which were frequently complicated by the fact that words and phrases in one language do not have precise counterparts in other languages.

In this particular case, the greater part of the CBI's effort was directed towards UNICE as it was felt that if the CBI's view could be accepted as that of European industry the organisation would be speaking with a much stronger voice. The British government had always had reservations about the snake and there was therefore less need for the CBI to exert influence in that direction. However, the Treasury was kept informed about the development of the CBI's thinking and the organisation did apparently have some influence on the government's ideas about reserve pooling. The CBI also kept in touch on an informal basis with Commission officials in Brussels. Before UNICE produced the final version of its report on EMU, the Commission produced in November a revision of its proposals for the transition to the second stage of Economic and Monetary Union.[58] The new report was much more in line with the CBI's thinking. It recognised that care must be taken to see 'that the shortcomings of the first stage are left behind'[59] and stressed that it was 'not the purpose in the second stage to secure like policies on the part of Member States, but to see that their policies are compatible'.[60] The elimination of exchange rate fluctuations was seen as a long-term aim and there was more emphasis on the background elements and the interrelationships of EMU with other Community policies.

Clearly, the CBI's efforts in relation to EMU in 1973 were in many ways a 'success story' for the organisation. Both the final proposals of the Commission and of UNICE were broadly acceptable to the CBI, unlike the original thinking of both bodies. How much of this was due to the efforts of the CBI and how much to fortuitous external events? As with so many other questions posed in this book, a precise answer is not possible. As the year went by, most employers' federations came to realise that the snake was increasingly difficult to sustain without action to lessen disparities in structure and performance between the member states' economies and that it was of little value even as a status symbol. The situation was ripe for a new initiative from the CBI. The CBI did not depart from its basic view that it was wrong to give the defence of exchange rates primacy over other economic and industrial objectives. The organisation considered that the lesson of British experience in the 1960s was that governments should not sacrifice growth or other economic interests for the sake of maintaining an exchange rate, and it did not want to see a similar mistake being made again in Britain or in other EEC countries. By elaborating and developing its policy on EMU through a close and detailed study of the related problems and by moderating its views when necessary, the CBI had at least a substantial impact on the thinking of the representative organ of European industry.

What more general lessons can be drawn from this case study? It would seem that the CBI has made a rapid adaptation to the rather different problems posed in any attempt to exert influence on European as distinct from British decision-making. Clearly, the mix of strategies it uses in any particular case will depend on whom it needs to influence. In this case, British government thinking was not greatly out of line with CBI thinking. Its main problem was to persuade UNICE, and via UNICE the Commission, that a major reappraisal of EMU was necessary. In this it was largely successful, but it was helped by the fact that external events were creating a policy vacuum which demanded a new initiative from someone. Also, events even before the energy crisis (e.g. the re-valuations of the Deutschmark and the guilder) combined to illustrate the CBI's basic case about the vulnerability of the snake and the folly of placing that first. Again, the lesson to be emphasised is that one cannot isolate considerations about the 'success' of an interest group from the political environment in which it operates.

Notes and References

1 E. Dell, *Political Responsibility and Industry* (London: Allen and Unwin, 1973), pp. 19–20.
2 *CBI Annual Report, 1970*, p. 7.
3 *Industrial and Regional Policy* (London: HMSO, 1972), p. 7.
4 Dell relates an experience which is indicative: 'The melancholy condition was illustrated by one spokesman of the Chamber of Shipping after investment grants had been abolished. The spokesman had delivered a strong speech attacking the govern-ment's decision. It had greatly weakened the shipping industry and its international competitiveness. He subsequently told me in private that the government was of course quite right in what it had done because investment grants, whatever their beneficial effect, were objectionable in principle.' Dell, op. cit., p. 151.
5 *The Times*, 2 March 1972, p. 17.
6 *Industrial and Regional Policy*, op. cit., p. 4.
7 *The Times*, 23 March 1972, p. 17.
8 *The Times*, 27 March 1972, p. 18.
9 See *The Times*, 16 June 1972, p. 18; the *Guardian*, 16 June, p. 17.
10 The *Financial Times* merely reported Clapham's remarks on the CBI price restraint initiative, 16 June 1972, p. 16.

11 See *The Times*, 12 July 1972, p. 14.

12 Dell, op. cit., p. 150.

13 ibid., pp. 161–71.

14 ibid., p. 18.

15 On the operation of the Bill, see S. Young, 'How is the Industry Act working out?', *New Society*, 30 August 1973, pp. 510–12; and *The Industry Act Annual Report* (London: HMSO, 1973).

16 For a summary of the story up to 1951, see G. W. Ross, *The Nationalisation of Steel* (London: MacGibbon and Keen, 1965). A much shorter analysis which takes the position up to the present can be found in L. Tivey, *Nationalisation in British Industry* (London: Jonathan Cape, 1973), pp. 59 ff. Also relevant is Duncan B urn, *The Steel Industry (1939–1959)* (London: Cambridge University Press, 1966).

17 There were discussions throughout the summer of 1948 between leaders of the steel industry and members of the government. These seem to have resulted in a tentative agreement between the steelmen and Herbert Morrison. However, the idea of such a compromise was anathema to a large number of Labour politicians and was rejected by the Cabinet. See Hugh Dalton, *High Tide and After* (London: Muller, 1962), Chapter 30.

18 In 1938, eighty-nine Conservative MPs refused the Whip on a Bill to nationalise the land on which the mines stood. N. Harris, *Competition and the Corporate Society* (London: Methuen, 1972), p. 44.

19 See Harris, ibid., Chapter 6, especially pp. 97–103.

20 ibid., p. 98.

21 See S. Blank, *Government and Industry in Britain* (Farnborough: Saxon House, 1972), p. 85.

22 ibid., pp. 102–3.

23 Sir N. Kipping, *Summing Up* (London: Hutchinson, 1972), p. 16.

24 The ownership of the steel industry passed to the Iron and Steel Holding and Realisation Industry Agency. This was a small independent body whose task was to sell sections of the industry back to private owners. In the first five years of its operation it sold off most of the firms. However, in 1964 it still held Richard, Thomas and Baldwin and a number of small companies.

25 The successful Trade Union action which led to the withdrawal of the Labour Government's Industrial Relations Bill in 1969 provided an unusual exception. See P. Jenkins, *The Battle of Downing Street* (London: Charles Knight, 1970).

26 *CBI Annual Report, 1966*, p. 18.

27 *CBI Annual Report, 1967*.

28 *CBI Annual Report, 1970*, p. 65.

29 *CBI Annual Report, 1970*.

30 E. Felgate, 'Industry and Pollution', *CBI Review* (September 1972), pp. 27–36, p. 36.

31 ibid., p. 36.

32 *H.C. Debs.*, vol. 833, c. 199.

33 ibid., c. 250.

34 *House of Lords Weekly Hansard*, no. 826, c. 1035.

35 N. Newsome, 'Government forced to act on toxic waste', *Conservation*, no. 40, pp. 1–5, p. 1.

36 *H.C. Debs.*, vol. 833, c. 200.
37 *The Report of the Technical Committee on the Disposal of Toxic Solid Wastes* (London: HMSO, 1970), p. 106.
38 Felgate, op. cit., p. 28.
39 *H.C. Debs.*, vol. 757, c. 1802.
40 ibid., c. 1802.
41 *H.C. Debs.*, vol. 292, c. 1025.
42 *The Policy Work of the CBI* (London: Confederation of British Industry, 1970), p. 29.
43 *Smokeless Air*, Summer 1968.
44 *Smokeless Air*, Spring 1968.
45 Baroness Serota, *H.C. Debs.*, vol. 292, c. 1024.
46 *H.C. Debs.*, vol. 757, c. 1806.
47 Mr J. McColl, then Parliamentary Secretary, Ministry of Housing and Local Government, *H.C. Debs.*, vol. 764, c. 799.
48 *H.C. Debs.*, vol. 764, c. 800.
49 *CBI Annual Report*, 1969, p. 63.
50 *H.C. Debs.*, vol. 764, c. 802.
51 *Clean Air*, 1970.
52 As quoted in 'A reassessment of Economic and Monetary Union', *CBI Committee Document E 261.73*, p. 2.
53 Commission of the European Communities, Communication from the Commission to the Council, COM(73) 570 final.
54 *E 261.73*, op. cit.
55 'A reassessment of Economic and Monetary Union', *CBI Council Document*, C 75 (11) 73.
56 See 'Opinion of the UNICE Working Party on monetary problems prior to the discussions to be held on 1 June 1973' (2 A.4, 14 May 1973, translation from German original); 'Conseil des Présidents, Réunion du 29 juin 1973, Exposé du Dr Baumann, Président du Groupe de Travail "Problèmes monétaires" ' (14 A.4/2.1 A.4, le 23 juillet 1973); 'État des travaux du Groupe de Travail "Problèmes monétaires" ' (2 A.4, le 25 septembre 1973).
57 2 A.4, le 25 septembre 1973, op. cit.
58 Commission of the European Communities, Commission Communication and Proposals to the Council on the Transition to the Second Stage of Economic and Monetary Union, SEC(73) 4200 final.
59 ibid., p. 2.
60 ibid., p. 3.

9

On influence: the crucial issues

THROUGHOUT THIS BOOK WE HAVE EMPHASISED THAT IT IS EASY TO be mesmerised by the formidable organisational capacity of the CBI and by the prominence it is given in mass media accounts of the political scene. In particular, the organisational resources of the CBI seem less impressive when one reviews the scope of the task to be undertaken. In addition, the organisation's freedom of manoeuvre is limited by its internal divisions, although these have been perhaps less of a constraint than was the case with the old FBI.

Our examination of four case studies of particular pieces of legislation has shown that the CBI's ability to influence events is limited by the government's need to retain the support of the electorate and by the activities of other interest groups. Above all, what has emerged from our study is a reaffirmation of the autonomy of the political sphere from the economic sphere. Clearly, economic considerations are of considerable importance as an influence on the actions of both the CBI and government. However, it is also clear that the range and final choice of policy options are affected by factors which may be termed 'political' – such as the state of public opinion and the emergence of new interest groups – rather than 'economic'.

In our analysis we have so far referred only tangentially to the two issues which have dominated the British political scene since the formation of the CBI – prices and incomes and industrial relations. In this chapter we will be examining the activities of the CBI in relation to these two policy areas, both because of their substantive importance and in order to develop further the analysis of the earlier chapters. Thus we will be employing the second of the decision-making approaches outlined in the introduction, the general approach which considers a policy area over a period of time. As we pointed out, Bachrach and Baratz have criticised the decision-making approach on the grounds that, by concentrating on decisions actually made, it often fails to analyse the influence which a group can exercise by limiting the scope of decision-making to 'safe' issues. In the final section of this chapter we shall analyse the role of the CBI in British politics in the light of the perspective offered by Bachrach and Baratz.

Prices and incomes policy

The CBI has been conspicuously unsuccessful in the area of prices and incomes policy in so far as it has consistently expressed a general preference for a voluntary rather than a compulsory policy. Its acceptance of statutory controls has always been reluctant. For the greater part of the period we are concerned with here (up to the general election of February 1974), successive governments have come to pursue statutorily based prices and incomes policies. The CBI has been able to persuade government to change some detailed aspects of its policies, and some of these changes have been of considerable benefit to sections of the CBI's membership. However, the general pattern has been of the CBI reluctantly accepting the unpalatable economic medicine handed out by government. The one exception to this general pattern was the CBI's voluntary prices initiative of 1971–72. For a time it seemed as if the initiative in the management of the economy had passed to the CBI and that the organisation might emerge as the body which had set the economy on a new road. However, although the CBI initiative was an act of considerable enterprise which had a substantial effect on inflation in the short run, it failed to offer a basis for a long term solution to the intractable problems of the British economy. Perhaps it was too much to expect that it would, and although the initiative enhanced the CBI's image as an organisation pursuing the national interest rather than its own sectional objectives it also revealed some of the CBI's inherent limitations. However, before returning to analyse the prices initiative in greater depth, we must trace the way in which the CBI's attitude towards prices and incomes policy developed up to 1971.

The initial involvement of the newly formed CBI in prices and incomes policy must be set against the background of the good relationships it enjoyed at first with the Labour government. The Statement of Intent, signed in December 1964 by the CBI's predecessors, reflected genuine hopes that it might be possible for the employers, trade unions and government to devise an effective voluntary prices and incomes policy. However, it quickly became apparent that increases in wage rates and average earnings were substantially in excess of the agreed 3 to 3½ per cent norm. In September 1965, the government announced that it intended to obtain powers for a statutory system of notification of proposed increases in prices and wages. In the meantime, the employers and trade unions were asked to act as if a statutory 'early warning' system were already in operation. The CBI did not like this development, which it saw as the first breach of the voluntary principle. Nevertheless, its general relationships with the government were still good and 'against the background of a serious foreign exchange situation and in an effort to restore overseas confidence'[1] it decided to cooperate in the operation of an 'early warning' system, although it refused to act as a channel of communication between its members and the government.

These arrangements worked satisfactorily, but in the summer of 1966 a deterioration in the balance of payments and an associated sterling crisis led the government to introduce an emergency package of deflationary measures. The government also announced that it proposed to introduce a prices and incomes standstill for six months. A number of aspects of the standstill White Paper[2] offended the CBI, particularly the requirement that almost all manufacturers contemplating a price increase would have to notify government. However, the CBI reluctantly decided that 'against a background of acute national crisis the Government's call for a standstill on prices and incomes should be supported'.[3]

These events and growing doubts among industrialists about the wisdom of the government's policies had placed an increasing strain on the hitherto satisfactory relationship which had existed between the government and the CBI. In October 1966 the government made an Order freezing laundry and dry-cleaning charges which enraged the CBI and placed its entire relationship with the government in jeopardy. The CBI felt that the government had broken an understanding about the way in which powers would be used and that consultations which had been promised had not taken place. The CBI's President, Sir Stephen Brown, complained that the Order had been issued in a 'precipitate and arbitrary manner'.[4] The CBI called a special meeting in November to review its relations with the government. Faced with the possibility of a complete withdrawal of CBI cooperation, the Prime Minister admitted that there had been too little time allowed for consultation in the laundry and dry-cleaning case and assured the CBI that its views would be given proper consideration in future. Although this assurance prevented a complete breakdown in the relationship between the CBI and the government, the CBI's confidence in the Labour government's willingness to take full account of its views was badly shaken and the old atmosphere of mutual trust and cooperation was never completely restored. Indeed, by 1969 relationships had deteriorated so badly that the Director General, John Davies, and the Prime Minister were exchanging public insults with each other.[5]

Meanwhile, the CBI continued to press for modifications of the government's prices and incomes policy and had a number of minor successes over such matters as the relaxation of conditions relating to the introduction of new incentive schemes during the 'period of severe restraint' in the first six months of 1967. After 1967 there was a greater reliance on voluntary restraint and the CBI considered that 'the provisions of the 1967 Prices and Incomes Act generally corresponded with the views expressed by the CBI in April'.[6] However, this should not be taken as an indication of substantial CBI influence on the development of the policy, as the CBI had 'reluctantly'[7] accepted that the government would retain some powers after July 1967.

Nevertheless, although the CBI continued to have substantial reservations about the general trend of the government's economic policy and about its prices and incomes policy in particular, there were some signs of change in the CBI's attitude about the desirability of such a policy. It was perhaps more willing to recognise that some form of price restraint on the part of the employers was necessary to induce employees to accept restraint of their wage demands. In a major policy review published in February 1968, *Industrial Management and the Next Two Years*, it accepted that 'workers and unions could not be expected to accept incomes restraint while prices rose unchecked'.[8] The CBI was also prepared to admit that the government's policy had had 'a significant effect on negotiating attitudes and objectives',[9] particularly in persuading the unions of the importance of the relationship between pay and productivity. Finally, and perhaps most importantly, the general condition of the economy remained poor. An important factor in the CBI's support of the prices and incomes policy 'arose from its recognition that the country faced a most difficult economic situation'.[10] In what the CBI's President saw as a year of 'dour struggle'[11] the CBI felt that it was particularly necessary to be fundamentally constructive in its criticisms of government policies.

Throughout 1968, the CBI continued to press for modifications in the government's prices and incomes policy. It was particularly opposed to the government taking powers to require reductions in existing prices. It was unable to prevent the government from pressing ahead with this particular proposal, but it did obtain assurances about the ways in which the powers would be used. The CBI was rather more successful in persuading the government not to proceed with, or at least to modify the terms of, certain references about both prices and incomes to the National Board for Prices and Incomes. However, although the government kept in close touch with the CBI about the implementation of this aspect of its policy, the CBI did not enjoy an absolute veto over references and it was unable to prevent a reference of claims under negotiation in the building and civil engineering industries.

The CBI was generally unhappy about the proposals for a further relaxation of its prices and incomes policy made by the government in December 1969.[12] It was felt that the proposals would tend to encourage substantial wage claims and the CBI was particularly critical of the new emphasis on the lower-paid worker. However, by this time the CBI was rather more concerned with the government's proposals to establish a Commission for Industry and Manpower, which was seen as laying the basis for substantial further government intervention in the affairs of private industry, than it was with the future development of prices and incomes policy. In any case, a general election and a possible change of government could not be far off and the CBI started to consider the kind of voluntary incomes policy it would like to see emerge in the 1970s.

Prices, and more particularly incomes, dominated the discussions between the CBI and the new Conservative government returned in June 1970. The government was anxious to persuade employers to try to 'damp down' the level of wage increases. Eager to play its part, the CBI attempted to foster employer solidarity by facilitating discussions among negotiators from those large firms which were seen as 'wage leaders'. At the same time, of course, the government was endeavouring to exercise wage restraint in the public sector.

It quickly became apparent, however, that the government's policies were not working. By the early months of 1971 retail prices were running at an annual rate of increase of 10 per cent. It was evident that if this trend continued union leaders would start to put in higher claims. The CBI believed that this could lead to a self-perpetuating inflation which would have very serious effects on profits and investment. Moreover, what perhaps worried them more than anything else was the fact that the old bogeyman of a statutory prices and incomes freeze was being seriously discussed in informed and influential quarters. The CBI felt at the time that such a statutory policy would hit profits without effectively restraining growth in incomes.

The government had been elected on a pledge to curb inflation and was unlikely to stand idly by for ever, despite its expressed distaste for a statutory policy. The CBI decided to act in a way which was audacious in its conception and skilled in its execution. The organisation secretly consulted its leading members, along with financial and retail interests, about the possibility of their undertaking to limit their price increases over a twelve month period. As a *quid pro quo*, the government would reflate the economy. It was also hoped that the example of employers moderating their prices would lead the unions to moderate their wage claims. This aspect was of crucial importance in securing the support of industry for the initiative. The initiative was not undertaken for purely altruistic motives or to enhance the prestige of the CBI as an organisation, although that was a welcome by-product. Companies were worried about the imminent prospect of a situation in which they would be in the front line, holding down costs and inflation, and yet they would have no opportunities for growth. The initiative was thus a fairly smart and calculated move to avoid that situation, and it enabled the employers to get off the defensive and 'put the finger' on the unions.

The government was naturally grateful that the CBI had offered them a way out of the increasingly tight political corner in which they found themselves. On 19 July the Chancellor of the Exchequer announced cuts in purchase tax, the abolition of hire purchase restrictions and more favourable capital allowances. He also announced that the nationalised industries would operate within the terms of the CBI initiative. The arrangement of this part of the package was not easy, as many of the industries (particularly British Rail) felt that acceptance of the CBI package would pose special financial problems for them. Clearly, however, if the basic goods and services produced by the nationalised industries had not been subjected to the same price restraint as the products of private industry the scheme would never have got off the ground. However, these difficulties were overcome and the CBI announced that the Chancellor's statement, coupled with the measures already announced to assist the development areas, fully justified the implementation of their initiative.[13]

The essence of the scheme was its simplicity. No fewer than 179 of the 200 largest private sector members of the CBI agreed to sign a document in which they undertook not to raise their prices, unless they were forced to make an unavoidable increase, in which case it would be limited to 5 per cent. Signatories agreed that if circumstances made it difficult for them to adhere to the undertaking they would notify the Director General and discuss their difficulties with him or his officials before taking action. In addition to the 179 large firms who signed the agreement, 700 smaller firms also signed the undertaking and a number of industry associations indicated their support. It should also be remembered that many small and medium-sized firms, both inside and outside the CBI, were obliged to keep price rises down to 5 per cent as they were suppliers to large firms who were hardly likely to pay large increases when they themselves were holding their prices.

In the first five months of the agreement's operation, two major companies broke the agreement. A further twenty-seven companies were given permission to breach the 5 per cent norm because of special circumstances, but fifteen signatories who wanted to introduce increases of over 5 per cent were persuaded to keep them within the limit. From time to time, accounts appeared in the press of ways in which it was possible to break the spirit but not the letter of the CBI agreement.[14] For example, it was pointed out that in a large company, the manufacturing side could keep to the agreement while subsidiaries – for example, engaged in service work – which had not signed the agreement could substantially increase their charges. However, whilst the CBI initiative is open to criticisms of this kind, the fact that it was circumvented by a few firms could not obscure its general success. In the first year of the CBI initiative, the wholesale prices of manufactured products rose by only $4\frac{3}{4}$ per cent, although retail prices rose by $5\frac{3}{4}$ per cent. It may be argued that inflation was beginning to slow down anyway, but undoubtedly the CBI initiative affected the rate of decrease. Perhaps a more serious defect of the initiative, particularly as regards its impact on trade unionists, was that it only directly affected industrial goods. Whereas the all-items index of retail prices rose from 153.4 in 1971 to 164.3 in 1972 (twelve-month averages) the food price index rose from 155.6 to 169.4 and that of housing from 172.6 to 190.7. Private house prices rose by about 40 per cent over the two years to the second quarter of 1972. Moreover, from June 1972 the all-items retail prices index began to rise sharply upwards once again. By September the annual rate of increase had risen to 7 per cent and a $1\frac{1}{2}$ per cent increase in the retail price index was registered in October.

Certainly, the initiative did not have the impact on industrial relations that was hoped for. A damaging miners' dispute which began in January 1972 ended with a substantial pay settlement and increases in coal prices which breached the CBI norm. When the CBI met to consider the future of its initiative in April, against the background of a major railways dispute which eventually ended with a substantial wages' settlement, it was clear that the initiative was already under strain. It was agreed to postpone a decision until July, and the Chancellor of the Exchequer, referring to the fact that he would not have been able to make tax cuts in the Budget if it had not been for the CBI initiative, seemed confident that a further extension would be possible.[15] However, the decision in April to give British Leyland a special dispensation to increase its prices in view of the losses which it had incurred as a result of power cuts during the miners' strike only served to underline the fundamental difficulties which the initiative faced.

When the future of the initiative was discussed again in the summer, a number of the CBI's leading members expressed serious reservations about the desirability of continuing it. The oil and chemical industries were particularly reluctant to exercise continuing restraint, many of the nationalised industries were worried about their financial position, and Lord Stokes of British Leyland 'expressed forceful opposition to the extension'[16] of the initiative. However, the government had decided that its strategy of non-interventionism was no longer tenable. Tripartite talks between the government, the CBI and the TUC on the problems facing the economy were started under the auspices of the National Economic Development Council in July. The ground for these talks had been laid in a series of informal meetings which had been going on in the National Economic Development Council's offices at Millbank Tower since September 1971 between 'the group of four' – Sir Frank Figgures, Director General of the National Economic Development Council; Sir Douglas Allen, Permanent Secretary of the Treasury; Victor Feather of the TUC; and Campbell Adamson of the CBI. In July they were joined by Sir William Armstrong, head of the home Civil Service, as the Prime Minister's unofficial representative and were thereafter referred to as 'the five wise men'.

These discussions initially focused on regional policy and were seen by some CBI officials primarily as a means of facing the TUC with 'the realities of the economic situation'. The group became involved in some detailed discussions about wage differentials and the problems of the lower paid, and, in the view of one CBI official, 'it very nearly worked.

In my view it failed because the miners' strikes and the rail and dock strikes put the union leaders in an untenable position. . . . Because (they realised) that they might be to blame if inflation was stoked up again, the leaders were edging towards compromise. But they were restricted by the pressure for high claims building up because of these earlier settlements and by the deadline of the expiry of the CBI's extended initiative in October.'

At any rate, these meetings helped to promote better understanding between the government, the CBI and the TUC at the highest level, though the CBI recognised that something more was necessary if the tripartite talks were going to succeed. The CBI's anxiety that the talks 'should be conducted in as helpful an atmosphere as possible'[17] was undoubtedly the major factor in persuading the CBI Council to recommend that the prices initiative be extended for another three months from 31 July 1972. British Leyland, Courtaulds, Marley and the building materials giant, Redland Holdings, refused to extend their pledges along with twenty other major companies, but 155 companies did re-sign and five who had not signed in 1971 decided that they would in 1972. However, the continuation of the initiative failed to have the impact for which the CBI had hoped. Ten top-level tripartite meetings were held. The CBI found itself in broad agreement with the proposals put forward by the government on 26 September for a £2 a week limit on pay increases plus threshold payments of 20 pence for every point over 6 per cent, but the TUC found them far from acceptable. By the middle of October, it was apparent that there were serious disagreements between the CBI and TUC over the control of retail prices, the CBI favouring a system of voluntary control operated in conjunction with a monitoring body and the TUC demanding at least a partial system of statutory control over retail outlets. The CBI was eventually persuaded to accept a system of voluntary control of prices with statutory backing. In a sense, of course, the CBI's reluctance was a negotiating tactic. In many ways it was the difference between statutory and voluntary control rather than control or no control that was significant because it was thought that voluntary control by the CBI would be more flexible and less onerous than a statutory policy. The compromise formula envisaged retailers and manufacturers who broke the agreed limits being summoned to appear before a monitoring board which would then adjudicate and pronounce on their cases. Although it later seemed that the TUC might be prepared to accept the limitation of stringent controls to a list of key foods, another fundamental stumbling-block to agreement remained. The TUC wanted concessions on such policy matters as the Housing Finance Act and, above all, the Industrial Relations Act. The government did not regard matters such as these as being negotiable within the context of tripartite talks. The government was prepared to take the effect of these policies into account, but it regarded them ultimately as matters for its own decision, subject to the approval of Parliament.

The talks collapsed on 2 November and on 6 November the Prime Minister announced a standstill on prices, pay and dividends. This was a bitter pill for the CBI, which had fought valiantly for a voluntary policy. Its own voluntary policy had, of course, lapsed at the end of October. Throughout the tripartite talks, the emphasis had been on devising concessions that would persuade the TUC to accept a voluntary policy, and the CBI found itself in the unwelcome position of appearing to be firmly aligned with a Conservative government in serious dispute with the trade union movement, although in fact the cosiness of the CBI's relationship with the government had been somewhat soured by disagreements over the Industry Act throughout the summer. Certainly, however, the introduction of a statutory policy was far from what the CBI had aimed for when it launched its voluntary prices initiative in the summer of 1971.

In the short run, the initiative had been a great success. It contributed substantially to a reduction in the rate of inflation for the fifteen months it was in operation, thus helping the government out of an awkward political corner – and nothing enhances an interest group's status more than its ability to deliver something the government wants badly. Moreover, the initiative helped the CBI's public image by demonstrating that the organisation could act effectively to promote what appeared to be in the national interest rather than in its own sectional interest. However, there is no doubt that, in the long run, the prices initiative left a nasty taste in many industrialists' mouths. Not every firm adhered to the CBI's price restraint policy, and those that did were subsequently caught by the government's compulsory policy. Admittedly, in its Phase 2 arrangements, the government allowed the Prices Commission to make exceptions for companies which could prove that adherence to the initiative 'significantly' reduced their profit margins. However, many industrialists felt that this concession was inadequate. When we started our interviews with industrialists in the spring of 1972, the comments we heard about the CBI's prices initiative were generally favourable. By the summer of 1973 we were hearing comments like: 'The voluntary prices initiative was a bloody nuisance in the end, it caused resentment in the end.'

The difficulties caused by the voluntary prices initiative may have made CBI members more wary of the organisation's leadership, thus reducing its room for manoeuvre. Certainly there were signs that the CBI leadership was responding in the early months of 1973 to the increasingly restive mood of its membership. As 1973 began, considerable increases in the prices of raw materials caused a mood of widespread concern among manufacturing industrialists. While Campbell Adamson was away on a four-week tour of Australia and New Zealand, the CBI began to develop a much more belligerent attitude towards the government. In a particularly tough speech in February, sprinkled with references to 'last ditches' and 'battlefields', the CBI President, Sir Michael Clapham, warned the government that it would be unwise to antagonise industry. Collaboration by companies was essential to the working of Phase Two. The policy involved thousands of firms and would be difficult to police. It was dependent on goodwill and adherence to the spirit, as well as to the letter. It is difficult to assess what effect this veiled threat of non-cooperation had on the government. Certainly, the White Paper published in March 1973 contained a number of concessions to the CBI's position which had not been included in the Green Paper a month earlier. The revised terms allowed companies to pass on rises in the cost of bought-in services such as transport, and introduced modifications to the general rule that companies must absorb 50 per cent of wage increases in a way designed to make things easier for labour-intensive companies.

These concessions did not impress one cynical industrialist we inter-viewed who commented, 'You can never tell how influential the CBI is. Industry was outraged by certain things in the Green Paper. I think that points were built in so that they could be given away.' The stern and uncompromising line taken by the CBI when the shape of Stage Three was being discussed showed that it was responsive to the disillusion with the government felt by many of its members. Apart from rebuking the Prime Minister for some criticisms of top management, the CBI emphasised its implacable opposition to the continuance of rigorous profit controls and took a sideswipe at the TUC for 'misrepresenting the relationship between prices and incomes this year'.[18]

The CBI was able to win some concessions from the government on the details of the Stage Three policy. In particular, there was help for industries, such as construction, which operate with long-term contracts, and for capital-intensive industries (such as chemicals), which had been facing problems as a result of the under-utilisation of capacity. The CBI also persuaded the government to modify restrictions on companies which sub-divide themselves and to provide additional relief for companies emerging from a period of low profit. The CBI's involvement in the subsequent history of Stage Three will be analysed in the next section of this chapter when we turn to examining the organisation's role in industrial relations.

What has emerged from our analysis of the CBI's role in prices and incomes policy since 1965 confirms what we have already pointed out in case studies in earlier chapters. The CBI has a good record of extracting detailed concessions from government which, although they do not represent a substantial change in overall government policy, may be of considerable benefit to its members. However, when it comes to influencing the broad shape of economic policy, the CBI is limited by the way in which the state of the economy narrows the range of possible policy options, by the government's determination to pursue whatever happens to be its economic strategy at the time, and by the government's need to secure the cooperation of the trade unions. The unions can withdraw the labour of their members, the City can induce a wave of selling in sterling,[19] but the CBI can only criticise the government's policies or perhaps tell its members not to cooperate in their implementation. The former tactic is limited in its usefulness by the fact that, while the CBI is listened to seriously in what are often termed 'informed circles', it is difficult for the 'bosses' trade union' to mobilise public opinion on its side. Use of the latter tactic could well damage the CBI's public image and leaves the organisation open to the charge of trying to frustrate the policies of an elected government. Moreover, if the CBI antagonises the government it runs the risk of being unable to negotiate the detailed concessions which can confer substantial benefits on its members.

Industrial Relations
Unlike Confindustria in Italy or the Swedish Employers' Confederation (Svenska Arbetsgivareföreningen, SAF) the CBI is not a central negotiating organisation; it does not negotiate and conclude pacts on the general shape of wage settlements with the TUC. However, as the Devlin Report forecast, 'We foresee the possibility of an even larger role for the CBI in industrial relations at national level with the possibility of a number of questions being settled in broad principle between the CBI and the TUC.'[20]

To what extent has the CBI increased its role in industrial relations in recent years?

When the CBI was formed, the original Labour and Social Affairs Directorate, largely composed of former BEC staff, took over where the BEC had left off, although it had the advantage of dealing with companies direct instead of through their employers' organisations. As the old hands have retired and new men have been brought in (a particularly significant appointment was that of Alan Swinden as Deputy Director General, Industrial Relations, in 1970), old frictions between the FBI and the BEC have been forgotten, and the Directorate (now called Social Affairs) has been effectively integrated into the work of the CBI. The increased political interest in industrial relations, and the burden of work imposed on the CBI by major pieces of legislation such as the Industrial Relations Act, have tended to enhance the importance of industrial relations within the work of the organisation.

What is the CBI's role in industrial relations and how does it perceive its role? The CBI emphasised in its evidence to the Donovan Commission that it was not a central negotiating organisation, and the Commission accepted that 'any attempt by the CBI to imitate the Swedish organisation would be irrelevant to the central need of British industrial relations'.[21] However, the Commission stressed that the CBI had 'a most important role to play in the reconstruction of British industrial relations',[22] and the CBI itself pointed out in its evidence that in recent years it had 'paid more attention to the identification of areas in which changes in policy may be needed and to the initiation of studies and action rather than confining its role to the passive one of commenting on Government proposals or responding to trade union pressure'.[23]

Clearly, the long-drawn-out sequence of events leading to the eventual passage of the Industrial Relations Act – Donovan, *In Place of Strife*, the Conservatives' proposals set out in *Fair Deal at Work* and elaborated in the consultative document of October 1971 – occupied a great deal of the CBI's time and energy, as did the subsequent monitoring of the Act's operation. The CBI put forward a number of suggestions for changes in the government's proposals, but only one of any significance was accepted, making it possible for an agency shop agreement to be made on behalf of more than one employer. Some twenty-five amendments were also tabled on behalf of the CBI by Members of Parliament, but because of the operation of the 'guillotine' only two of these were debated and neither was accepted. The CBI was subsequently involved in identifying problems arising from the implementation of the Act and in providing advice to members. Explanatory memoranda were published on matters which might cause difficulty for employers and summaries were issued of the major cases arising from the Act. However, although the volume of work was considerable and the substantive importance of the legislation very great, the CBI's activities in relation to the Industrial Relations Act were well within the bounds of its traditional role. In attempting to shape a piece of legislation in accordance with its views, the CBI was acting in a way in which interest groups are conventionally expected to act.

However, more recently there have been indications that the CBI's role in industrial relations is changing, that, almost accidentally and unintentionally, it is becoming involved in major industrial disputes as a negotiator. It should be stressed that this does not mean that the CBI is evolving into a central negotiating organisation on the Swedish model. What has happened is that major industrial disputes have come more and more to occupy the centre of the political arena. As the organisation representing employers, it would be difficult for the CBI to avoid becoming involved in disputes which are politicised in this way. This point may be illustrated by a consideration of the miners' dispute of the winter of 1973–74, although similar points could be made about earlier disputes: for example, the 1972 miners' dispute with Campbell Adamson's evidence to the Wilberforce enquiry and before that the dock strikes in 1970 and 1972 when the CBI was in close and continuous contact with the National Association of Port Employers.

In the initial stage of the dispute, the CBI confined itself to attacking the miners for acting illegally and 'striking at just every single member of the public'.[24] Admittedly, evidence submitted by the CBI to the Pay Board at the end of November proposing special arrangements to allow selected groups of workers to receive wage rises in excess of the government's Stage Three limits was seen by some commentators as 'a call for Ministers to "buy off" difficult cases'.[25] However, the CBI's emphasis at this stage of the dispute was on attacking the miners and other workers engaged in industrial disputes and on urging the government to display firmer leadership and abandon its plans for expansion, the latter demand eventually being satisfied. A proposal by the TUC on 21 December to postpone the implementation of the three-day week received a cold reception from the CBI.

The CBI maintained this hard line in the new year. The CBI gave an unenthusiastic reception to the initiative launched by the TUC at the meeting of the National Economic Development Council on 9 January. The TUC proposed that if the government gave an assurance that it would make a settlement between the miners and the National Coal Board possible, other unions would not use such a settlement as an argument in negotiations for their own settlements. The CBI was unimpressed by the TUC's offer. Campbell Adamson stated that it was not enough for the TUC to tell unions not to take any notice of a miners' deal. The question was whether Stage Three limits could be afforded in the energy crisis, not whether Stage Three could be exceeded by the miners. Some commentators felt that the CBI's attitude towards the initiative helped to make its implementation impossible. Whether or not this was the case, the CBI's President, Sir Michael Clapham, reaffirmed the organisation's view after a meeting with the Prime Minister on 11 January when he stated, 'We are not really interested in settlements outside Stage 3, which is more generous than the country can afford.'[26] Undoubtedly, the CBI's attitude at this stage was influenced by its optimistic forecasts of the prospects for industry. On 16 January it stated that its members believed that output would not fall by more than 3 or 4 per cent in February unless the energy situation changed drastically.

The energy situation did change drastically when the executive of the National Union of Mineworkers decided on 24 January to hold a strike ballot of its members. On 28 January, after a meeting with the Prime Minister, the CBI made it clear that it felt that the Government was right to insist that any settlement of the miners' dispute should be within the terms of Stage 3. The next day, however, Mr Derek Ezra, the chairman of the National Coal Board and a CBI activist, told a meeting of senior industrialists at Tothill Street of 'the high cost both of the miners' strike and of the settlement which miners would insist on to end a national shutdown'.[27] On 4 February, against the background of an overwhelming vote by the miners in favour of strike action announced that morning and reports that some companies were encountering serious financial difficulties, the CBI Council agreed that the organisation should support the pay relativities body proposed by the Prime Minister. The CBI Council also accepted that the miners' claim would be the first to be examined under the new machinery and that this would almost inevitably mean more money for the miners. The CBI thus abandoned its earlier argument that it would be wrong to use the Pay Board relativities report as a means of ending the dispute and that it would be wrong for the miners to receive payments outside the Stage Three limits.

Having decided to take a more conciliatory line, the CBI attempted to launch a joint peace initiative with the TUC. The talks were very much a 'last ditch' effort and were overtaken by the announcement on 7 February of an election. What is interesting is that they took place at all. In the absence of direct CBI–TUC contact in the preceding few weeks, much of the time was taken up with each side establishing the other's position on the dispute and the various formulas which might have been used to reach a settlement. However, what was in effect taking place was negotiations between the CBI and the TUC. Any agreement reached by them would, of course, have been far from conclusive. It would have had to be accepted by the government and by the mineworkers. Many trade unionists would, of course, argue that meaningful negotiations can only take place between the employer and the union concerned. Nevertheless, it is clear that on this occasion the CBI and the TUC did consider the shape of a possible settlement to a specific industrial dispute and it is at least conceivable that, given sufficient time and understanding between the two organisations, they might have come up with a package which would have provided a basis for a settlement.

Whether the CBI's role in the miners' dispute will be seen in the long run as an isolated and untypical incident or the beginning of a new role for the CBI in industrial relations as, in effect, a negotiating body remains to be seen. In large part, this will depend on how the climate in industrial relations develops, whether there is a statutory incomes policy and what the political significance attached to industrial disputes will be. However, if a dispute similar to that involving the miners occurs in the future, the CBI may try at an earlier stage to explore the possibilities of providing a framework for a settlement with the TUC. If this becomes the established pattern in major disputes, it will represent an important development in the CBI's role in industrial relations. It is most likely to occur in disputes arising in the nationalised industries, where there are no powerful employers' organisations likely to resent any usurpation of their role by the CBI.

Whether or not the CBI does play a more active part in the settlement of industrial disputes in future, it is clear that the CBI was unable to exert any influence on the course of the miners' dispute. The CBI is not in a position to persuade men on strike to go back to work; it is just possible that the TUC might be able to mediate between the union involved in a dispute and the government. Much of the focus of attention was therefore on the TUC rather than the CBI. Though the government consulted extensively with the CBI and was anxious to obtain its approval of such initiatives as the utilisation of the relativities procedure, one cannot escape the conclusion that the CBI had little influence on the course of events.

The other face of power

It could be argued that our method of study has influenced our conclusions and that in concentrating on the analysis of decisions we have neglected the fact that 'power may be, and often is, exercised by confining the scope of decision-making to relatively safe issues'.[28] As Bachrach and Baratz have pointed out: 'Of course power is exercised when A participates in the making of decisions that affect B. But power is also exercised when A devotes his energies to creating or reinforcing social and political values and institutional practices that limit the scope of the political process to public consideration of only those issues which are comparatively innocuous to A.'[29]

Bachrach and Baratz have made an important contribution to the study of the decision-making process in society, but their approach is not without its limitations. In an important critique of Bachrach and Baratz, Parry and Morriss succeed in exposing some of the absurdities of the non-decision-making approach. In particular, they point out: 'One apparent meaning of "non-decision" is any political activity which is not a decision – i.e. that "non-decision" stands to "decision" as *non-p* to *p*. The wider the term non-decision is the more it approaches this clearly useless notion.'[30] However, whilst one can agree with their recommendation that 'it is better to replace blanket terms like non-decision with a more precise analysis of the many different patterns decision-making can take',[31] this does not preclude an examination of the part that the CBI plays in what Bachrach and Baratz term 'the mobilisation of bias' in society. While we accept that a comprehensive analysis of British politics on the lines suggested by Bachrach and Baratz would be a substantial undertaking, we need to examine the part the CBI plays in restraining pressure for fundamental change in society and thus preserving the parameters within which decisions are taken.

One of the difficulties in assessing the role played by the CBI (or any other group or organisation) in the perpetuation of the *status quo* is the difficulty of deciding what represents fundamental change. Researchers tend to avoid this question. In particular, Marxists such as Poulantzas fail to specify the criteria that render an issue 'fundamental', although their implicit assumption is that only a basic change of ownership and control counts. Other change is dismissed as unimportant and of only peripheral interest to the capitalist class. Thus if that ruling class appears to accede against its own interests to working class demands, such change as results is categorised as a mere tactical concession.[32] In this vein Marxists would argue that what nationalisation there has been in Britain has not changed the real nature of ownership and control and indeed has only occurred in those areas of the economy where state intervention has benefited the capitalist class by keeping down the price of various basic inputs. The absence of more extensive nationalisation is seen as resulting from the false consciousness of the working class. The fact that the majority of the public does not appear to favour further extensive nationalisation or at least is apathetic about the whole issue simply shows how successful big business has been in winning a general acceptance of its definition of the situation.

Such an analysis presents grave problems. In particular, the supposedly less fundamental changes are crucial to any understanding of the continuing operation of the political system and indeed are the only ones amenable to behavioural evidence. In addition, as Miliband himself points out, different capitalist systems have different political and economic structures and such differences should be of considerable interest, especially to the Marxist who is concerned with analysing the possibility of further fundamental change.[33] In this way a Marxist such as Poulantzas is dismissing as unimportant a type of change which might have great significance in the development of any given capitalist system.

Such criticisms are important, but we do accept that the ability to mobilise bias gives an individual or group considerable potential influence. In this section we will examine two related questions. First, how far do business in general and the CBI in particular depoliticise the issue of nationalisation? Secondly, in what other ways do they attempt to influence which issues appear on the political agenda? These are difficult questions to answer because of the methodological problems involved. If we look first at the direct attempts to proselytise against nationalisation most of them come from organisations such as Aims of Industry and the Economic League. These organisations have mounted advertising campaigns during each election since 1950, although they were particularly active in 1959 and 1964. It is difficult to measure the effectiveness of such campaigns. However, Rose's analysis of the 1964 campaign suggests that few electors remembered seeing anti-nationalisation advertisements. Indeed he argues strongly that such advertisements tend to reinforce existing attitudes rather than to establish new ones.[34]

It would seem, then, that the campaigns had little direct effect on the general electorate. This is not surprising. After all, politics have never been important for most of the population and nationalisation was not a topic of key concern to them. However, despite this, the majority of electors were and continue to be antipathetic to nationalisation. Why should this be so? One of the most important reasons was that no significant organisation was strongly proselytising in favour of extensive national-isation.[35] The Labour party's commitment to nationalisation was at no stage very strong, and it can be argued that the anti-nationalisation campaign did play an important role in convincing Labour party leaders that nationalisation was an issue which could lose them votes.[36] This had the effect of countering pressure for nationalisation within the Labour party.[37]

So it might be said that business, acting through its ideological arms, has had some influence in restricting extensions of nationalisation. However, the CBI itself played little part. It has tried to avoid becoming too closely involved in party political arguments about nationalisation, leaving organisations such as Aims of Industry to make the ideological running. In fact it has tended to concentrate its efforts in relation to national-isation on scrutinising and attempting to modify detailed proposals for changes in the manufacturing powers of the nationalised industries. The committee on State Intervention in Private Industry has tended to main-tain a low profile within the organisation, partly because of the need to avoid embarrassing the CBI's nationalised industry members. The kind of detailed patrolling of the boundary between state and private enterprise carried out by the CBI may prevent 'nationalisation by encroachment', but it has little to do with fundamental debates about the respective roles of public and private enterprise, although since 1974 the CBI has been more outspoken in this respect. It remains to be seen whether this repre-sents a permanent change of strategy. Certainly, it seems to us that what-ever contribution Aims of Industry may make to public antipathy towards nationalisation its activities do not offer a complete explanation of the existence of such antipathy. Other factors, such as the performance of the existing nationalised industries, are of considerable importance.

The fact remains that in many areas of policy the CBI's influence may be subtle and indirect, contributing to a climate of opinion over a period of time until its views are accepted by other experts in the field. This form of influence is particularly apparent in higher education policy. It takes every opportunity of putting its views to those concerned in a professional or other expert capacity with higher education – the list of bodies to whom representations are directed occupies eight lines of the CBI publication, *The Policy Work of the CBI*. An example of the influence which the CBI may exert on informed opinion is provided by the 1973 report of a sub-committee of the House of Commons Expenditure Committee on the subject of postgraduate education.[38] The report drew heavily on the evidence (and recommendations) of the CBI. Parliamentary select com-mittees are not very influential bodies. However, by contributing to a climate of informed opinion they can help shape the way in which policy choices are presented and made. Much of the CBI's work must be in the nature of a long-term effort to shape the climate of expert opinion; the results of this effort may be undramatic and difficult to trace.

Although this example may suggest that the CBI does influence the parameters of debate in specific policy areas it is necessary to stress one important point. The CBI itself does not see the mobilisation of bias in British society operating in a way which serves the goals and underpins the values of its members, but rather it feels itself to be operating in an environment which is increasingly hostile. For example, Lucien Wigdor wrote before joining the CBI as its Deputy Director General, 'There can have been few greater follies than the willingness of the British people to denigrate the role of industrial profit in the advancement of the whole nation.'[39] The CBI President's Policy Coordinator, Martin Wassell, has written: 'It is a major indictment of our educational system and of all who are in a position to shape social attitudes that the distinctive features and very considerable merits of the market economy are so little understood in our society.'[40] Both these comments were made in a personal capacity, but they are probably not greatly out of line with the thinking of many members of the CBI. Moreover, the CBI has commented officially on what it sees as the harmful effects of the decline in company profitability.

It would be difficult to demonstrate that the CBI has been able to confine political debate to what it would regard as safe issues. For example, the distribution of wealth has increasingly become the subject of public debate in Britain in recent years, and the CBI has not been able to stand aside from this debate. Sometimes, of course, it may attempt to steer the debate into what it sees as safer channels. For example, in discussing the interim report of the CBI's Company Affairs Committee on the role of the public company, the committee's chairman, Lord Watkinson, explained: 'We were very conscious that if private enterprise was to continue to prosper, it had to show itself capable of a continuous process of self-reform and change. . . . We felt that our main task was to try to suggest ways of improving Britain's long established company system and encourage the maximum degree of self-reform rather than to impose revolutionary innovation.'[41]

Certainly, the CBI has no difficulty in gaining access to the mass media to air its views. Sir Michael Clapham, a former CBI President, has commented on 'the close attention paid by the information media to (the CBI's) activities and utterances'.[42] However, while the CBI is listened to with respect, its pronouncements do not always reach a sympathetic audience. Our interviews with CBI members revealed more disquiet about the CBI's handling of its 'public relations' than any other issue. In fact, on a professional level, the CBI's handling of its information services is competent, even if they are operated on a relatively small budget; the real problem is a more fundamental one of a general lack of public sympathy towards the 'bosses' trade union'. Nevertheless, it is not always *public* opinion which is politically significant and undoubtedly the CBI's reputation with, and impact on, informed or expert opinion assist it considerably in the pursuit of its goals.

This chapter has shown that the CBI has had relatively limited impact on the major issues which have dominated British politics since its formation. As in other policy areas, it has been able to extract detailed concessions which are of benefit to its members. However, the CBI faces the fundamental difficulty that it is operating in a political environment which is increasingly unsympathetic to its aims and aspirations. One does not have to accept the right-wing view of a left-wing media conspiracy to see that, with its limited resources, it is difficult for the CBI to win the support of public opinion for its policies.

Notes and References

1 *CBI Annual Report, 1965*, p. 10.
2 *Cmnd.* 3073.
3 *CBI Annual Report, 1966*, p. 12.
4 *CBI Annual Report, 1966*, p. 5.
5 S. Blank, op. cit., p. 233.
6 *CBI Annual Report, 1967*, pp. 17–18.
7 ibid, p. 17.
8 *CBI Annual Report, 1968*, p. 23.

9 ibid., p. 25.

10 ibid., p. 25.

11 ibid., p. 5.

12 *Cmnd.* 4237.

13 Letter from the President of the CBI, Sir John Partridge, to members, dated 26 July 1971.

14 See, for example, the *Daily Telegraph*, 27 March 1972.

15 The *Daily Telegraph*, 21 April 1972.

16 The *Observer*, 30 July 1972.

17 *CBI Annual Report, 1972*, p. 8.

18 *The Times*, 16 June 1973.

19 For an example of the impact of such a move on policy, see G. A. Dorfman, *Wage Politics in Britain* (Ames, Iowa: Iowa State University Press, 1972), p. 123.

20 Devlin Report, op. cit., p. 58.

21 *Royal Commission on Trade Unions and Employers' Associations* (London: HMSO, 1968), p. 202.

22 ibid.

23 *Royal Commission on Trade Unions and Employers' Associations, Selected Written Evidence* (London: HMSO, 1968), p. 250.

24 Speech by Campbell Adamson, 21 November 1973.

25 The *Financial Times*, 30 November 1973.

26 The *Financial Times*, 12 January 1974.

27 The *Financial Times*, 30 January 1974.

28 P. Bachrach and M. Baratz, 'Two faces of power', *American Political Science Review*, **56** (1962), pp. 947–52, p. 948.

29 ibid., p. 948.

30 G. Parry and P. Morriss, 'When is a decision not a decision?' in I. Crewe (ed.), *British Political Sociology Yearbook*, volume 1, *Elites in Western Democracy* (London: Croom Helm, 1974), pp. 317–36, p. 323.

31 ibid., p. 325.

32 See our discussion of nationalisation, below pp. 204–5.

33 See R. Miliband, 'Poulantzas and the capitalist state', *New Left Review*, **82** (1973), pp. 83–92.

34 R. Rose, 'Pre-election public relations and advertising' in D. Butler and A. King, *The British General Election of 1964* (London: Macmillan, 1965), pp. 369–80, p. 379.

35 There is, of course, the Public Enterprise Group, but this concentrates on 'informed publics' such as the Select Committee on Nationalised Industries and on providing ideas, information and analysis for those already committed to the extension of nationalisation.

36 Although, clearly, not all Labour leaders hold this view.

37 R. Rose, *Influencing Voters* (London: Faber and Faber, 1967), p. 186.

38 Third Report from the Expenditure Committee (1973–74), *Postgraduate Education*.

39 *CBI Review*, No. 1, p. 21.

40 *CBI Review*, No. 9, p. 4.

41 *CBI Review*, No. 8, p. 6.

42 *CBI Annual Report, 1972*, p. 5.

10

In conclusion

WE HAVE DEALT AT LENGTH WITH THE HISTORY, ORGANISATIONAL structure and influence of the CBI. In the process it has been possible to identify factors which strengthen and factors which weaken the CBI's position as an interest group.

The CBI's strengths

A key factor which strengthens the CBI is the size and quality of its membership. It has in membership almost all large manufacturing companies. The decisions taken by these firms, particularly on investment policy, have a crucial effect on the performance of the economy and are therefore likely to have a direct influence on the success of any given government and, hence, on its chance of re-election. The crucial role which many of the CBI's member firms play in the economy ensures that the CBI has a level of access to the government decision-making process which few interest groups can equal. The most important interest groups usually have close contacts with their 'sponsoring ministry', but the CBI's contacts are wider. It has continuing access at Cabinet level. Such access was particularly stimulated by government intervention in the field of prices and incomes policy and seems likely to remain as successive governments strive for a voluntary policy. In addition, the CBI's contacts with ministers and civil servants are also aided by the fact that senior CBI officials and committee chairmen share social and educational backgrounds with these politicians and administrators. This is an advantage which the TUC does not enjoy. On the other hand, it should be pointed out that in the spring of 1974 the new minority Labour government made a special effort to develop 'relationships with the TUC to the same degree as now exist with the CBI',[1] and subsequently the TUC has enjoyed much improved access at Cabinet level.

There is, however, no doubt that the CBI is viewed by government as a peak organisation which can speak for manufacturing industry. The government is aware not only of the strength of the CBI's membership among large firms but also that the broadly democratic appearance of the decision-making process in the CBI allows most views to be expressed and to be seen to be expressed. This means that once the government has talked to the CBI it is able to claim that it has talked to manufacturing industry, thus cutting down time-consuming contacts with other bodies. In addition the CBI's initiative on prices, which received the overwhelming support of its membership, considerably impressed both politicians and civil servants. At the same time some of the CBI's publications, notably its *Industrial Trends Survey*, are increasingly accepted as authoritative contributions to ongoing debates on economic policy. The CBI has thus earned considerable respect in government circles; this respect ensures access to key decision-makers and a willingness on their part to listen to what the CBI has to say.

The CBI's weaknesses

In contrast, several factors weaken the CBI's position. Although it has a wide membership, it has been extremely unsuccessful in attempts to extend membership beyond the manufacturing sector. Thus when political pressures ensured that the key item of concern to the Heath government was retail prices, the Government turned to the newly established Retail Consortium, admitting it to talks with the Cabinet on prices policy. Even within the manufacturing sector the CBI is stronger in some spheres than in others. It is strongest among larger firms and, despite the establishment of the Smaller Firms Council, the continued existence of the Smaller Businesses Association indicates that many small firms see the CBI as an organisation dominated by large firms. Thus although the organisation's membership is large it is limited in a number of ways. However, even if the membership were successfully widened, the resultant strains might impair its ability to operate effectively. Increased membership would not necessarily bring more influence if it led to increased dissension within the organisation.

Moreover, doubts have recently been raised about whether the CBI does really represent the views of its member firms. As we have pointed out, there is always potential tension in the CBI between those members who would prefer to see the organisation follow a 'strategy of responsibility', cooperating with government in the implementation of its policies in the hope of securing concessions, and those who would like the CBI to engage in more frequent and more outspoken criticisms of government policy even if this impairs the organisation's ability to negotiate concessions from government. Despite intermittent outbursts of criticism from some members, the CBI leadership has tended to follow a strategy of responsibility. However, recently the internal strains in the organisation have become more pronounced and a number of firms have actually resigned. Clearly, if the CBI were to lose many more big firms from its membership its credibility as a spokesman for manufacturing industry would be undermined. This may not happen, but in engaging in more vigorous criticism of the government to appease its membership the CBI may impair its ability to secure detailed concessions which benefit industry. It could, of course, be argued that the government needs the CBI's cooperation and advice and would be prepared to put up with denunciations of its policies from the CBI leadership. Certainly, when the CBI threatened to withdraw its cooperation in 1967, the Labour government was quick to give the assurances it required. Similarly, under the presidency of Ralph Bateman (1974–76) the CBI was often outspoken in its criticisms of government policy, but this did not prevent the government from making a number of significant concessions in response to CBI pressure: for example, the tax relief on stock appreciation given in 1974 was worth several hundred million pounds. Nevertheless, the CBI's room for manoeuvre is limited by the need to reconcile the divergent views of its membership and by the problem of taking at one and the same time a stance which satisfies its membership and yet does not place in jeopardy its relationship with government.

The CBI is also short of resources in relation to the tasks it attempts to undertake. Its income, despite a recent increase in membership fees, is small compared with its European equivalents. Despite this, it offers a wide range of services and indeed must continue to do so if it is to attract and retain its members. At the same time it is involved in constant contacts and negotiations with government which themselves demand ever increasing resources as government intervenes more in economic and industrial life. There is no doubt that the CBI's resources are inadequate for the role it attempts to play and that this does not strengthen its position with government. The inadequacy of resources is reflected in inadequate staffing, particularly at the lower levels, and a lack of in-house information in certain areas.

The standard of the CBI's staff is often surprisingly high considering that it cannot offer salaries, except at the top, which are likely to attract top quality recruits from industry or government service. Nevertheless, each CBI staff member deals with a wide range of concerns and in his discussions with civil servants will be faced with a number of civil servants who specialise in much narrower areas. As Desmond Keeling, a senior civil servant, has commented: 'Increasingly in recent years analytical methods have come to be used to limit effects of pressure except when it is itself supported by research or analysis.'[2] The CBI official, with inadequate information and limited research facilities, is at a considerable disadvantage. The shortage of staff also means that in certain areas the regional organisation is small and is unable to spend sufficient time recruiting and retaining members. Many non-active firms in hard-pressed areas are fortunate if they receive one visit a year from a member of staff.

The shortage of funds can cause other kinds of problems. Our case study of the 1972 Industry Act presented ample evidence of this fact. The CBI was considerably hampered in its actions within Parliament on that occasion by its lack of in-house information about back-bench Members of Parliament. The CBI did not have extensive contacts with Conservative back-benchers and could really only approach prominent back-benchers who were already known to support its stand. With more resources such problems might be avoided.

The resource problem is an important restriction on the activity of the CBI, but despite this weakness it has good contacts with government. Many of its most important weaknesses stem from the fact that it is not a tight, cohesive body. We may say the CBI represents manufacturing industry, but in reality it represents many different manufacturing industries. As such the CBI is a collection of various interests rather than one cohesive interest group. This presented a greater problem to the FBI than it seems to do to the CBI. Indeed, the FBI tended to sit on the fence of indecision. The CBI has been more decisive, but nevertheless if a section of its membership opposes its position (as did the footwear industry over VAT, for example) it feels obliged to make this clear to government. In addition, the fact that the larger industry associations, such as the Engineering Employers Federation, often consider it necessary to make their own representation to government on major issues cannot strengthen the CBI's position. However, what is more important, at least to the government, is that the CBI, like the TUC, cannot bind its members to a decision. Suppose the CBI and the TUC make an agreement with government accepting a voluntary prices and incomes policy, there is no way in which the CBI could compel its members to accept its decision. It might expel offending firms, but that is unlikely and hardly a viable sanction. The CBI has a democratic structure and is a loose confederation of individual firms and employers' organisations. The strength of its position with its membership results from its ability to influence, not to compel. The price restraint initiative was a conspicuous if short-term success, but in many ways, as we have shown, it rebounded upon the CBI. It is difficult to imagine the CBI achieving a similar initiative again and this fact is not lost on government.

The CBI not only has no meaningful sanction to impose on its members, it also has no very effective sanction on government. It can, of course, conduct a campaign against government policies but, as we pointed out in the last chapter, this is a hazardous course to follow. As an alternative strategy it could refuse to cooperate in the administration of any particular piece of legislation, but again such a sanction depends on the cooperation of the industrial firms directly involved. Such firms are likely to be reluctant to damage their own position with government by with-drawing cooperation. The CBI might also recommend that its members attempt to influence the economy by withholding investment as a threat to government. This is even less likely to be successful. Indeed, although throughout 1972 and 1973 the CBI was issuing glowing commentaries on the economy and urging industrialists to invest and expand, its exhortations had little direct effect on investment patterns. Investment decisions by companies are not taken at the behest of the CBI. The CBI's influence on the economy and the administration of legislation is thus indirect and hardly crucial. This is perhaps the most important point. Neither the CBI nor individual manufacturing firms have a direct sanction equivalent to the political strike or to the City's ability to move vast amounts of capital out of the country.

The CBI thus has strengths and weaknesses as an interest group. How much influence does it have on policy? Does the picture we have described fit better with a Marxist or a pluralist description of the distribution of power in capitalist society? We believe a fairly clear picture emerges. The general conclusion must be that the CBI has little consistent direct influence over the policies pursued by government. This is not to say that

the CBI is not able to influence considerably a particular piece of legislation, for example the 1975 Industry Act. However, we are concerned
with the general picture over the period of our study. The CBI's influence
is greatest over the details of legislation rather than over policy itself,
although it must be stressed that in influencing the details of legislation
the CBI can save industry a great deal of money.

Our evidence thus seems to confirm the autonomy of politics and to
indicate that government acts largely independently of business interests.
This might therefore seem to support the pluralist model. Does it in
fact do so?

Miliband, in his analysis of the role of the state in capitalist society,
concentrated upon the subjective relationships between industrialists,
politicians and administrators and on the interaction between them, their
shared attitudes and policy objectives. His work indicated most strongly
that the two groups shared common social and educational backgrounds,
and our research tends to confirm this impression. However one must not
assume common attitudes and policy objectives from common backgrounds. This is a weakness of Miliband's work, for he presents more
evidence of shared backgrounds than of shared policy objectives. Our
work suggests that on many occasions the CBI and industrialists generally
have different policy objectives from those held by government. The 1967
Iron and Steel Act and the 1972 Industry Act provide ample evidence that
such differences can exist no matter which party is in government. There
are obviously other occasions on which government and wide sections of
industry share policy objectives. The decisions taken by the Conservative
government to enter the Common Market and to introduce one fixed rate
of VAT are examples of such occasions. Nevertheless there is sufficient
evidence to say both that the CBI is not a tightly-knit organisation with
one common aim and that the decisions taken by government cannot be
consistently identified with the interests of manufacturing industry and
the CBI.

All this seems to fit happily with a pluralist analysis. We have shown
that the CBI competes with other interest groups, notably the TUC,
for influence and that the government does not seem consistently to be
furthering the interests of one group. Above all it seems that the political
sphere is largely autonomous, the government most often making decisions
on the basis of political criteria. An excellent example of this can be
found in our case-study of the 1972 Industry Act. Despite all this,
however, it is impossible to say that our evidence is in any way decisive,

and we must return to two crucial problems. We have used almost exclusively behavioural evidence, and we have concentrated upon the positive face of power.

There is much force in Bachrach and Baratz's argument that power has another face. Indeed, a Marxist such as Poulantzas would be most concerned with power which is 'exercised by confining the scope of decision-making to safe issues'. The most important feature of British society to Poulantzas and Marxists would be that, despite the existence of various groups which seem to have different interests, the basic nature of the capitalist system persists. The persistence of this system is ensured by the interest and efforts both of the state and of other fractions of the ruling class such as manufacturing industry. In support of Poulantzas' position, it is true that despite an extension of public ownership and government control over industry many inequalities of ownership and wealth remain. In addition, employers' organisations such as the CBI have fought hard to defend free enterprise. Indeed they have tacitly supported, and many of their member firms have financially supported, organisations such as the Economic League and Aims of Industry which have consistently, and at considerable expense, opposed the extension of nationalisation. At the same time, it has been argued that even when government has intervened it has in fact been helping the capitalist class, even if industry did not always think so at the time, by nationalising sources of power and means of transport, so keeping down industrialists' costs, and by giving government aid to ailing firms.

Although these arguments have some validity they are not totally convincing. In the first place government has often intervened in industry in a manner which does not benefit it. In its continued attempts to decrease pollution caused by industrial waste, for example, government has introduced a great number of regulations which have cost industry a great deal to bring into effect. Industry may have slowed down the government's attempts to control such pollution, but it has had no success in preventing it, as we pointed out when we considered the 1972 Deposit of Poisonous Wastes Act. Industry has also consistently attempted to prevent, restrict and reduce government intervention, the 1972 Industry Act is a good example of such action. Perhaps more important, it must be realised that in refusing to extend public ownership and thus to change significantly the mode of production successive governments have been responding as much to political considerations as to economic interests. After all, there has been consistent opposition to nationalisation among public opinion, whether as a result of the false consciousness of large sectors of the working class or of other reasons. Thus the Labour party, by placing less emphasis upon its commitment to public ownership during the 1960s, was responding at least as much to electoral considerations as to pressure from industrialists.

We are faced here with a related and crucial problem. Can the type of behavioural evidence we have considered answer some of the problems that have been raised? Many, indeed most, Marxists would deny, or at least severely question, the utility of our analysis. Poulantzas, for example, would argue, and Miliband himself would agree, that the basic nature of the relationship between the state and the economic class is an objective one which must result from the very nature of the capitalist mode of production. Subjective relationships may more or less reflect this objective relationship but need not necessarily do so. So different capitalist societies will be characterised by subjective relationships which reflect to a different degree the basic objective relationships. In this case what we have shown is that in British society the subjective relationship is a far from perfect reflection of the objective relationship. Ultimately the state apparatus may be an agent of the ruling class, but the members of that apparatus (politicians and administrators) and the industrialists who must be key members of any ruling class do not seem in many cases to share policy objectives. Although other case studies of policy decisions and policy areas might find a closer connection between the subjective and objective relationships, the fact that there is not a close one in the key areas we have studied is very important. In addition, a crucial point must be made. If the subjective relationships are not always and do not need to be a close reflection of the objective relationships at all stages of the development of capitalist society, then the political sphere at such times can have a considerable autonomy. This means that in many important respects the Marxist description of the relationship between the state and the economic sphere can at such times be similar to that of the pluralists. In fact our evidence, which might seem to confirm the pluralist model, cannot deny such a conceptualisation of the Marxist model.

The dilemma is obvious. If the Marxist model is to be tested, then in effect only historical and comparative evidence is appropriate. If one could find a developed state which had totally changed the capitalist mode of production to a socialist one then that could cast doubt on the utility of the model. Our evidence is not of this type. We can merely show that, as far as our evidence is valid, the subjective relationship between state and industry does not appear to be very close.

The CBI appears, to some extent at least, to have escaped the emasculation by the British consensus seen by Nettl as the fate of business interest groups. Perhaps the major problem it faces is the growing hostility of many organised workers, if not the electorate in general, to many of its central values and objectives. It may be that the CBI will be more ready in the future publicly to assert and defend those values and objectives, especially in the areas of EEC membership and government intervention in industry, although in 1976 a senior Conservative politician, Geoffrey Rippon, criticised the CBI and its members for failing to speak out against the Labour government.

In its first decade, the CBI has established itself as an important element in the British political system; in its second decade, it may have to make some difficult choices about the price it is prepared to pay for cooperation and concessions from the government and the trade union movement. For although the CBI can influence the direction and content of political debate it must also adjust to changing political realities. It may find some changes so unacceptable that it may have to clash more openly with the government, the trade union movement or even with the prevailing mood of public opinion than in the past. What Presthus has termed 'the rough consensus among the political elite about the nature, utility and propriety of the politico-economic system'[3] may be placed under increasing strain. Any real and persistent breakdown of this consensus would, of course, affect the political role of the CBI.

Leaving aside speculation about future developments, it is clear that the CBI is sufficiently democratic internally, well organised and well informed to be accepted at present as the authoritative and legitimate voice of manufacturing industry. British business, however, does not speak with a unified voice, and although the CBI is always prominent and sometimes influential it is in no sense politically dominant. No analysis of the British political system can ignore the CBI, but it is only one of many centres of power.

References

1 D. Keeling, *Management in Government* (London: Allen and Unwin, 1972), pp. 61–2.
2 Tony Benn, *H.C. Debs.*, vol. 958, c. 199.
3 R. Presthus, op. cit., p. 283.

Index